Best w:
Susie Merrill

Police, Ponies & Husbands in-between

By

Susie Merrill

Published by New Generation Publishing in 2022

Copyright © Susie Merrill 2022

First Edition

The author asserts the moral right under the Copyright, Designs and Patents Act 1988 to be identified as the author of this work.

All Rights reserved. No part of this publication may be reproduced, stored in a retrieval system or transmitted, in any form or by any means without the prior consent of the author, nor be otherwise circulated in any form of binding or cover other than that which it is published and without a similar condition being imposed on the subsequent purchaser.

ISBN   978-1-80369-542-6

www.newgeneration-publishing.com

New Generation Publishing

To Ruth & Phillip

For making life worthwhile

HOMAGE TO THE HORSES

This is the list of the many horses I have bumped into along the way. Including those who have bitten me, kicked me, and trampled on me, driving me insane with frustration, as they farted about distracting me from other troubles.

Gemma, my constant companion, more a sister than a pet.

Solitaire, Gemma's mother - purchased for £10 circa 1972.

Sykes, Gemma's father, diminutive ex racehorse described by his jockey as useless. He went on to get the championship at the annual Ponies of Britain in the late 70s.

Norman, the grey I was riding in 1979 when we were hit by a brand new Mini Cooper S on trade plates - Norman was shot. I might have been too if the ambulance hadn't arrived in time.

Stoker, Irish Draught colt, one of Gemma's friends.

Maybe, Ronni's lovely upstanding young horse.

Spice, a pony only 12 hands high who lashed out in the field and broke my arm.

Molly, Solitaire's friend and companion on their last journey.

Magpie, a memory held dear and a talented gymkhana pony.

Fudge, stolen and recovered by me, returning him to his owner.

Beau and **Highwayman**, Erika's ponies and friends of Gemma's,

Squire, Gemma's friend in Surrey.

Brown Trix, he lived next door and won the Grand National in 1987. This would have been quite something if his jockey had been on him.

Mars, One of the Queen's stallions. Mo invited me to join her on a ride over the South Downs, he was a true gentleman.

Richard and **Thomas**, my first encounter with the Suffolk breed.

Clive or **Thornset Major**, Cleveland Bay and sire of Gemma's foal.

Police, Ponies & Husbands in-between

Koh-i-Noor, Gemma's daughter, known as Koko.

Ruby of Virginia House, my first Suffolk Punch.

Noble and **Samba**, Percherons who worked the farm in Stoke by Nayland.

Orchid and **Punch**, these were the Suffolks on loan to Otley College from HMP Hollesley Bay Colony.

Mounted Branch school horses

Flame, a sweet little chestnut too narrow to balance safely if you ever got the urge to stand on her rump.

Cranwell, a big handsome bay with a white face.

Falcon, he was a complicated horse who would sooner kick you than befriend you.

Galleon, my all-time favourite as balanced on two legs as he was on four.

Frederick, guaranteed to have every new recruit bite the dust.

Arabella, she was a hyper thoroughbred, waking each morning with an air of 'Oh my God I'm still alive.'

Dresden, Strawberry roan, he was a good copper but with feet not strong enough to stand the hard London roads.

Mounted Branch patrol horses at West Hampstead and Great Scotland Yard (GSY)

Condor, I astounded the skipper by spending my own money to buy him a girth that actually fitted correctly.

Ultra, she didn't like to walk near the gutter because her feet couldn't cope with the camber of the road.

Eve, Like a steam train in a cavalry charge, you couldn't hold one side of her.

Lydia, the sergeant's horse, I saved her life and went on to escort the Irish State Coach on its maiden road test after renovation.

Ivor, my reason for the visit to the London stables in the small hours.

Eileen, my second horse, sweet enough.

Dragoon, 17hh plus, not the best horse for shopping.

Inca, rotund little grey, it was a challenge to get his girth tight enough.

Debbie, my last, and by far the best police horse.

I would like to raise a glass to all those I have mentioned in the book.

Plus my string of proof readers, Elke Jury, Lu Bryant, and Gill Onslow

Police, Ponies & Husbands in-between

Chapter One: Under Starter's Orders

"We are gathered here today to put right a relationship that has been going on for over a year," the Baptist Minister began his address to the congregation. His words droned tunelessly inside my sleeping head, "God looks not at the wrong we have done, but at how we put right those wrongs...."

Coming out of my dreams I blinked into the waking world remembering the recent ceremony uniting me to my new husband.

"This is not a celebration" ... the Minister announced, and the memory of these words jolted my eyes open in much the same way that they had done at the time, just two months earlier.

Not a celebration!? Christ alone knows what a monumental achievement this was for me. Never in my wildest dreams did I think this would happen, as I considered that I must be a pretty optimistic person to marry for the second time.

This man of God had been difficult from day one. His opinion labelled me sullied in the eyes of the Lord and he would only permit us to have 20 guests, no flowers, and no white frock. Clearly he considered me far from pure, though I did bend the rules slightly with a soft magnolia creation.

I continued to stare into the darkness from my bed, musing with satisfaction how happy I was to be married to Hugh, and as my waking thoughts led me on to the reality of what was happening in my world, right at that moment, I knew with all certainty, I had to get up. It was four o'clock in the morning!

I was not surprised that I had woken up so early, my brain began spinning with the activity of the here and now, and those thoughts were with my horse, Solitaire, out there in her field, giving birth to her umpteenth foal. She was on loan to Maggie as a brood mare and it had been agreed between us that I would have the next foal and Maggie would keep my mare. This foal was going to be mine and I wanted to be a part of every step in our journey together.

Hugh was stirring from his slumbers under the duvet, "Where are you off to at this hour?" he asked.

"Solitaire was really uneasy yesterday I can't rest; I must go out to Pages Farm and see if she is OK. Are you coming?" I finished pulling on some clothes.

"Are you joking? At this hour! What time is it anyway?"

"Quarter past four. I'll be back as soon as," and I scooted out of the door and down the stairs. The cat, Sylvester, dead spit of his cartoon counterpart, wound his way round my legs nearly tripping me over. "Breakfast!" he demanded, and being exceptionally large and persuasive, it was difficult to ignore him. I slopped some cat food into his dish before disappearing out of the front door.

***

Climbing over the locked gate I could see Solitaire alone in the corner of her field. Through the low-lying morning mist, I could just make out something on the ground. Was there something? I strained my eyes to see. Oh my goodness yes, there was, I raced towards her at a kind of speed walking that said 'I'd like to run but stay calm…....just STAY CALM!'

I reached her side breathless and panting and there on the ground was the most delightful little foal - still wet and fresh from the warm confines of Solitaire's belly, blinking at the world, taking in everything it could see in the vastness. It was a really lovely little chestnut foal.

Chestnut! I didn't expect that, Solitaire was bay, and so was Sykes, there must be a chestnut gene in there somewhere.

"What's occurring here Solly?" I asked her. She ignored me as usual. "You've been busy girl. What have you got here?" I persisted to get her attention.

"What does it look like, dummy," Solitaire replied, she always talked to me as though I was an idiot.

The foal was beautiful and looked healthy, bright, very pretty, with a star! I watched in awe, waiting until it got up. Had it already stood up and sucked? No, I doubted it, this baby was new-born and I just drank in the scene.

At that moment there was an ungainly struggle and the spindle legs scrabbled about in all directions trying to get a foothold on the dew-soaked pasture. It must have taken a while but I didn't notice time, I was completely captivated and felt at one with this little miracle. It raised itself up, standing awkwardly and a bit spread-eagled, I could see then that it was a filly. A filly, I've got a filly! I bit my knuckles and the excitement welled up inside me, I had never dared dream anything so wonderful would happen. I now owned a chestnut filly foal, and she was superb.

Solitaire greeted her baby and made an encouraging little nicker that said, "Don't be afraid, this is the buffoon who comes to feed us." I stretched my hand out towards the soft muzzle and as her head stretched towards me she offered a young throaty greeting that made her nostrils quiver and tingle against the tips of my fingers.

"Hello Gemma," I said.

Hugh was up when I got home, usefully employed in the kitchen preparing some breakfast. "Well?" he asked.

"She's had it," I blurted. "A filly, a lovely chestnut filly. Isn't that fantastic? She's beautiful, she's absolutely beautiful."

What are you going to call her?"

"I'm calling her Gemma."

"Gemma? That's nice." He nodded approval and when the hour was more respectable I returned to Pages Farm with Hugh. Maggie was ready waiting to give me the good news when we got there and was surprised to find that I had already been to visit. We walked across the paddock to see them, "What are you going to call her?" Maggie asked.

"Gemma." I replied and Maggie pulled a face without adding any further comment.

We could not dally long at the farm as Hugh and I were both on late turn. We were both Officers in the Metropolitan Police Force. My career was looking good, I could actually afford to keep a horse for the first time having muddled along on a wing and a prayer previously.

Hugh was the area car driver at Wealdstone, driving the big flashy Rover, all singing and dancing with blue lights and a two-tone siren. I was on a relief at Mill Hill. Our respective patches were joined by the boundary of the Edgware Road, historically Watling Street, the old Roman Road to North Wales and Anglesey.

We had both served our probationary period of two years at Willesden Green, with Hugh having a couple more years' service than I did. After a stormy beginning, our relationship blossomed, and grew with the inevitable outcome. Rather than wait to be transferred, I applied for a posting to 'S' District and they sent me to Mill Hill which was was very close to where we lived.

As it turned out, Hugh was moved from Willesden Green anyway

Police, Ponies & Husbands in-between

and sent to Wealdstone. This had been the result of disciplinary action following a punch up one night duty. It all happened in the police canteen between policemen who were actually on duty and another officer who was not. The off-duty officer had come into the station during the small hours rather the worse for drink, bringing with him two young ladies he had picked up in a nightclub on the Edgware Road. His expectations being one of providing gratis hospitality for them on police premises. This did not meet favourably with our boys, and Hugh was not shy about voicing his opinion on this behaviour. He was known by some as 'G.B.H', a re-arrangement of his initials, and this verbal interchange led to a heated exchange of views and a right royal affray followed, sending the tables and chairs, plus coffee cups and contents in all directions. Biddy Mulligans in the Kilburn High Road could not have boasted a more enthusiastic brawl.

The Chief Superintendent had said to Hugh and the other officers during the investigative interview, "There will be no disciplinary action against any of you obviously. We do understand that Police Constable blah-de-blah-de-blah was well out of order, and it is commendable that all of you were prepared to step in. So? Where do you want to be transferred to on the Monday of next week?" Hugh was posted to Wealdstone, squealing like a stuck pig all the way up to the Chief Super's office and the welcoming address.

***

Life at Mill Hill police station was quieter than Willesden Green. Far from the formal 'parades' I had been used to, at Mill Hill the first officer to report for duty got the pick of the police vehicles. I liked to book out the Sherpa van which was fitted with a main-set. This is a direct radio communication with New Scotland Yard where all the exciting calls come from. Not for me the local boring stuff like burglaries two days earlier or shop lifters seen running away last Wednesday, I wanted action!

I was out one Friday evening, patrolling in the Sherpa with our garage man, Tom. He could drive the police vehicles for maintenance in his day job, but in his role as Special Constable he could not drive any of them. So he was my passenger when we had an 'all cars' call come over the main set to a punch-up at The Honey

Pot, a public house on Wealdstone's patch. I love a punch-up, me, so I put my foot down and activated the old fashioned 'gong' that was fitted to the van and crossed the Edgware Road.

We were the first to arrive and lo and behold it was our old friend Frank, drunk as a skunk and ready to take on the world, well! Tom and me anyway. We knew without doubt that his removal would solve the problem, so both of us attempted to take an arm each and frog march him to the van. He was like an enraged stick insect flailing his arms and legs about while Tom and I tried to grab him, jumping away from his punches before getting straight back in there ducking around to find a bit we could hold on to! Man! He was an octopus. But we did get hold of him and we were doing well, until we got to the van and I needed a free hand to open the door.

"Come along Frank, be a good boy," I said "have you got him Tom?"

"Yes, I think so."

"I aint goin' nowhere," Frank swung his arm away from the van door pulling me with him.

"Whoa there sugar-plum" I shouted. "You're coming whether you like it or not."

"Shhhheeeres notz wantin......"

"Hurry up, Sue, for goodness sake,"

"I'm doing my best," and I grabbed the door for the third time only to be pulled away beyond its reach yet again.

"Letz go o mee."

"I'll try," said Tom, dangling about like a string puppet.

"Where are the Police when you need them," I said.

Then two members of the public got involved and tried to help us.

"It's OK," said Tom, "we can cope."

"No, we CAN'T!" I said on impulse. Then Frank got his arm from out of my grip throwing me to one side. He spun sideways to shake off Tom. The two helpers tried to get a hold on him but before they could do that Frank took a swing at Tom with his free fist, Tom ducked, the blighter, I was behind him and Frank's bunch of fives connected with my face. I got a black eye.

At that moment a big shiny white Rover pulled up from Wealdstone. "Are we having trouble, girls?" Hugh asked getting out of the driver's side, with all the confidence of a man who knows how to handle himself. He put Frank into a hammer lock and bar and bundled him into the back of the van. Tom and Hugh's operator, Taff, got in with him to keep control while I drove. "Wealdstone! And don't spare the horses." Shouted Taff from the back of the van.

Under the flood-lighting of the back yard at Wealdstone my eye was beginning to colour nicely. Hugh took one look at me and I saw the raw anger beginning to rise in him. "Now Boyo," Taff instructed Hugh, "let's not be silly."

"It's OK, Taff, I'm quite calm," he replied and looking lovingly into my eyes, Hugh asked, "Are you OK Sue?"

"Yes, I'm fine."

Opening the back door of the van Hugh took hold of Frank's arm. "Come along Sir, please mind your head as you get out." Frank minded his head. "And the steps, Sir, mind you don't trip up now." Frank managed the steps with no trouble but one of the paving stones by the door to the charge room was slightly raised. Frank tripped, he made a grab for Hugh to keep his balance, and that was the only trigger G.B.H. needed.

It took three constables and a sergeant to pull them apart.

"Now look what you've done," Taff swung on me.

"ME .... What have I done? It was all Tom's fault he shouldn't have ducked."

"Pardon me for breathing," said Tom.

I got £50 compensation from the Magistrates for the black eye. I call that a result personally. If I had received £50 for every black eye I have ever had! Well! - Let's not go there.

***

I was just so excited at the prospect of owning my own horse again, and this certainly was a new beginning for me. As soon as she was born, I wanted to shout it from the rooftops.

I told everyone about her, all my friends and family had to endure the smallest detail. I couldn't wait to introduce her to my two children, Ruth and Phillip. Everyone came to visit her. Most of the policemen at Mill Hill were dragged across the field to admire her, and I proudly informed everyone that I had only paid ten pounds for Solitaire.

Now, that is a good story, and I proceeded to bore the pants off Hugh one evening while he was preparing supper. "It only seems like yesterday when there was a knock on the front door of the cottage at Woodcock Farm." I began.

"I think I've heard this story," Hugh protested.

"It was while I was expecting Phillip, my child number two."

"Yes," sighed Hugh in resignation, "I know who Phillip is."

"Well anyway," I persisted. "I had asked John if I could buy a little pony to breed from. Ruth was three-years-old, and I thought it would be nice if she had something to play with. I knew I would have to sell my Clydesdale, Bobbysox.

"How interesting." Hugh's lips thinned with irritation.

"We didn't have any cash to spare, as you know, the cottage was tied to John's job," I explained, "and free keep for a horse too."

"Really? That's pretty jammy."

"Believe me, there were few things 'jammy' about Woodcock Farm."

"Yes, alright Sue, you're not the only one who's been through the mill."

"Can I continue?" I pulled a face.

"If you must." Hugh tutted.

"Anyway, out of the blue this lady knocks on the front door. It was the kind of front door used only for funerals and weddings, so it was a challenge to get it open. The poor woman was met by an affray of barking collies, and me heaving on the door like I was pulling the milkman off my mother." I chuckled.

Hugh laughed wantonly, "That's a good one!"

"She told me her horse had been diagnosed with a bone spavin and the prognosis was that it would be lame for at least a year, it may never come sound, and so, she asked if I knew anyone who would be willing to give the horse a good home."

"Fancy."

"Do you know? She paid over £350 for that horse! It was serious money ten years ago."

"It's serious money now, damn it!" Hugh interjected, half my monthly salary in fact."

"Umm, I suppose it is," I continued undaunted. "I had to go and have a look at her, didn't I? When I saw her, I could not believe what was in front of me. She was lovely, she was dark bay. Why am I telling you this? You know what she looks like."

"Why indeed?"

"Anyway, I saw the quality in her, who wouldn't, and I couldn't believe my luck." "She wasn't asking for any money, she just wanted a good home for her, but when I offered she said any contribution would be acceptable."

"But there was no money to spare, you said." Hugh stated the obvious.

"No, there wasn't, but I scratched together as many pennies as I could find, rummaging in the back of drawers and down into the depths of the armchairs."

"Why did you bother?"

"I thought I would have to pay something to make the deal legal and binding. Amazingly I managed to muster ten pounds, representing two weeks housekeeping. But then," I added, "I could be up early in the morning and out on the golf course where there would be rabbits a plenty to shoot."

"Did you really go out shooting rabbits, Sue?"

"Yes, of course I did, it was the only way to keep us fed. I not only shot rabbits, I shot pretty much anything that moved, if it was edible."

Hugh shook his head in disbelief. "And now you are a police officer. Unbelievable."

"Poacher, turned gamekeeper." I grinned.

Chapter Two: Wearing Different Hats

I was so excited at the prospect of owning my own horse again, and Gemma meant so much more than Bobbysox or Solitaire. This was a new beginning for me. I had everything to live for, a new job, a good job, and a new husband, he was good too. This was a new start, this was a reason to live, and Gemma was going to be part of that.

Some months earlier, I had begun having private lessons to hone my riding skills in preparation for training a young horse. My instructor, Charmian, was brilliant and I hung on her every word. I worked as hard as I could to achieve the desired seat and sensitivity required to be a good rider and ultimately a horse trainer.

When Gemma was almost three weeks old, I noticed she was a little quieter than usual, she was just a bit dull. Maggie was not about but I was so concerned that I told Gina, the daughter of Maggie's partner, Peter, also a policeman at the same station as Hugh. "Oh, thank you," Gina replied, "that means Solly is coming into season, we will get her covered. Sykes will be pleased."

I stopped worrying but not for very long. I had a riding lesson the following evening and when I told Charmian that Gemma was a bit subdued, she told me I should be careful not to let that go unattended for too long before investigating. "They are tough little nuts in some respects," she said "but life is also fragile at that age." I called in on the way home and there was no change.

The following day she was still no better. Solly was taken off to meet 'Sykes' while I stayed with Gemma in the stable. Sykes told them that she was in season so maybe there was nothing to worry about, but there was light brown liquid oozing from Gemma's bottom. She had spread it over the cheeks of her butt where she had flicked her tail back and forth, and this had burned the skin and made it sore. I bathed it in soapy water that Maggie had given me. It stank; I then rubbed in zinc and castor oil cream. I noticed Solly's udder was a bit hard. I told Maggie. "Yes, OK, I'll get the vet out," she said, "don't worry," - I worried.

The vet arrived and we had to practically carry Gemma beside her mother into a stable. All interest in life had gone. "It's not good," the vet said. "She has a temperature of 103." I was frantic inside. "She has foal enteritis," the vet continued to explain. "It's not uncommon and can be fatal. I'll give her a dose of Penicillin and that should do the trick."

My whole insides were churning; I couldn't lose her now. "Please don't let me lose her." I prayed that night, "not now, not ever, **not ever.**"

***

I didn't sleep well and the following morning I couldn't wait to get up to the farm and see how Gemma was. She was a little improved, thanks to the antibiotics and careful nursing but she was still not herself. I checked her in the evening and Maggie told me to stop fussing. I continued to fuss.

"I wouldn't be surprised if this foal gets pneumonia, and dies." Maggie offered her assessment, thinking aloud and predicting the outcome. I blew my top.

Most people who are survivors of abuse struggle to find the confidence needed to be quietly effective when attempting to fight their corner. But when the blue touch paper is lit, the desire to have your voice heard manifests itself into an explosion of verbal diarrhoea. This is exactly what happened here.

Suitably shocked, Maggie called the vet out again, and this time she came with a saline drip and some fairly serious drugs to take hold of this infection.

Once the escalating infection had been arrested, Gemma slowly recovered from her foal enteritis and probably because of that early scare I visited her daily realising to my dismay how little I knew. I was hungry for information on equine management so I asked Charmian if she would be kind enough to give me some stable management homework. She readily agreed and I soaked up every ounce of information like a sponge.

When Gemma had finally recovered the pair went back out with the other mares with their foals. There were big hunter types like Solly to tiny show ponies. I just loved to watch the foals racing around the field together, bandy-legged and looking quite ungainly until they turned on a sixpence to buck and kick out at each other in a frenzy of tangled activity.

Then the game would come to an end while they returned to their mothers for comfort and sustenance. I watched her endlessly, as she dominated her mother when she was feeding. Solly would want to graze and would walk on leaving the youngster stranded. Gemma would chase after her and cut across in front of her as if to say "Oi! stand still." Solitaire, ever patient, would stand still and Gemma would go back to feeding. Gemma's personality was developing and I enjoyed every moment.

***

Back at home, we had a pet rabbit, it was Phillip's really, to enjoy when he came to stay with us. I acquired the rabbit shortly after I had been posted to Willesden Green. I had returned to the station in the small hours during one night duty, to find several of my colleagues in a disagreement as to what to do with the rabbit that Hugh and Taff had found hopping down Dartmouth Road. There was talk of rabbit stew, and I didn't have a problem with that. Lord knows, I've shot more rabbits than I can shake a stick at. I peered into the box on one of the tea room tables and saw the most delightful little face peering back up at me. He was 'police uniform' blue with no guard hairs so his coat was like velvet. He was a Black Rex. I picked him up out of the box and gave him a cuddle. "Isn't he a sweetie," I said.

"Do you want him?" they asked me and from over the top of a pair of pricked ears I explained that he would make a good pet for my son when he came to stay with me. "He's yours then," they said, and so I took him home and gave him to Phillip. He attacked Hugh on sight and he wasn't particularly nice to Sylvester the cat who in turn merely tolerated him. He frequently wee wee'd on Sylvester

thus claiming dominance, and I watched in horror one day as he went hoppety hopping up the back of the flower bed and nine gladioli in full bloom keeled over one by one as he snapped them off at the base. The rabbit was a menace.

The last straw, which resulted in eviction to the hutch, was the day when it bit Hugh's foot as it dangled out at the end of the bed. I'll never forget that! "Did the earth move for you, my darling?"

***

Many years earlier the sight of a rabbit meant only one thing, something for supper. Back in the days of Woodcock Farm, when I was a farm hand's wife in a different hat and we were as poor as church mice. I was utterly astounded when John spent the best part of a week's wages on a single barrel shotgun, so he could go out shooting with his mates. To say that I was disappointed at the money this cost is putting it mildly, we had baby Ruth to feed as well as ourselves, to say nothing of the collies.

The pittance housekeeping hardly amounted to my having my own money and independence was just something other people had. But I am ever practical, even in unusual circumstances, so I reasoned that I could actually make the gun work for us. I expressed such an interest to our good friend, Jim, who came out from the smoke to stay with us every weekend. He obligingly offered to show me how to use it, and suggested we go out to the back field to have a practice.

"Lookie here," he began explaining the parts of the gun. "Bring the stock up to your right shoulder and you will find a purpose-built groove between your collar bone and shoulder joint."

"Like this?"

"Yeah that's right, it sits comfortably, doesn't it? especially if you pull the gun tight in, lean your weight against it, index finger on the trigger - - - - and squeeze……."

BANG!!!!!

"Jumpin' jehosafat!" I was shot off my balance.

"You'll get used to that," he laughed, "here have another go."

BANG!!!! "That was better wasn't it?"

"Umm, if you say so," I replied

"Now let's see if you can hit something" Jim set a piece of unwanted crockery on the fence.

BANG!!! And I was more surprised than anyone when I found I could hit a target, again and again! I began to see that this shotgun was not such a bad idea after all.

I planned my strategy and made plans to go out alone. I hoped I would succeed in bagging many, many meals; this could be a lifesaver. Just as it was getting light a few mornings later, 'um 4.30am ish, I crept downstairs, taking the gun and a pocket full of cartridges.

I didn't tell John my plans and I managed to slip out of the house without waking him. I crept round the edge of the rabbit damaged fields of barley and on towards Scratch Woods where my ears were filled with the dawn chorus.

I followed the fence of the M1 extension, which was still under construction, then, slowing my stride to a creep, I approached the railway embankment. I knew this to be a hotspot for rabbits because of the finely nibbled grass, little piles of droppings and scratchings in the earth. I very slowly moved towards the opening in the bushes, being careful not to give myself away by treading on twigs that might crack under my footfall. Peering through the scrub I looked up the pathway that flanked the railway. There I saw several rabbits going about their early morning routine.

I took aim,   I fired,   TOOOUFFE!!!

The crack of the gun split the morning apart with unexpected violence and the dawn chorus fell silent. The rabbit that had been in my sights keeled over kicking furiously to overcome its injuries, in a blind panic I raced over to it and taking hold of the hind legs I held it to the ground and dispatched it forcefully with the butt of the gun across the back of the neck. I had seen the boys do this many times. Then I sat down and wept. I wept and I wept, cuddling the dead rabbit as I did so.

***

Sometimes, when I was patrolling my beat at Mill Hill, I couldn't always get a panda and had to walk. It was on one of these jaunts returning to the station from Burnt Oak High Street, when a car pulled up alongside the kerb just in front of me. "Do you want a lift, Officer?" the occupant asked.

"How kind," I said and hopped in. I don't know, it comes to something when members of the public have to rescue police officers appearing to be in pain.

"I saw you limping," he said, "where are you heading? Mill Hill?"

"Yes, thank you, did you say I was limping?"

"Yes, quite badly, what have you done?"

"Nothing recent" I replied, "I broke my leg a while ago but I didn't know I was still lame, I don't feel as though I am limping, are you sure?"

"Darlin'!" he shook his head, "you're as lame as a cat."

***

The previous year I had had the most horrendous accident while exercising Norman, a friend's retired racehorse. I had been doing something I will never do again and should not have done then; I had cantered along the grass verge next to the road. The horse, 'Norman', shied suddenly at something in the hedge and jumped sideways into the road and before I could regain control we were hit by a car. The horse had a broken leg, as did I, but I was spared the outcome that awaited him. This was not something you wanted to happen to someone else's horse.

I knew Norman's leg was broken; I could see it swinging as I lay in the gutter chewing on gravel. People stopped their cars and came to try and assist. One fellow was trying to control Norman by holding the bridle, also broken. A brave man indeed to tackle a prancing beast but the uninitiated rarely know that to look at a horse directly in the face will send it backwards away from you, and this is what was happening now. Norman, frightened beyond belief was backing away from his handler towards me! His dancing hind legs were getting dangerously close and acting purely on primeval instincts I got up and ran, finally collapsing by the hedge.

I was wearing rubber top boots, this single act of survival had pushed the busted fibula bone in my leg out through the skin at the back and the larger tibia slid down alongside the corresponding broken edge. A fractured pelvis and a couple of broken ribs, which only hurt when I laughed, left me on traction in the Stanmore Orthopaedic Hospital. My parents were at my side very soon after I came out of the recovery ward, my mother admitting wistfully: "I've been waiting 30 years for something like this to happen."

***

As a result of being told about my limp, I had an X-ray at the Royal National Orthopaedic Hospital at Stanmore and it was suggested that I had a bone graft. It meant I would be on crutches again but the prognosis of a proper repair was good so come autumn I was in a hospital bed waiting my turn. I had been wiped over and made sterile with a black arrow on my leg, thankfully the correct leg, and told the operation would not be for a couple of hours. Hugh was given permission to wheel me round the grounds in the wheel chair so without fuss or discussion we put the wheelchair in the back of the car and drove off purposefully to see Gemma!

A friend, Val, brought me a set of watercolours so I was able to pass the time while I was in hospital. I painted Gemma's picture on the front of my plaster using a mirror, easier to do than you might think. The days passed quickly as I worked my way around the ward painting everyone else's plaster for them. Being off work gave me more time for the studying of all things horsey and as my knowledge and library of books grew, so did Gemma.

I was not a person to get bored easily and finding myself at home recovering from the bone graft sent me to a frenzy of creativity. I sketched, painted, crafted and wrote poetry and then when Hugh was home from work we visited Gemma, friends and family, it was a happy time.

One wet afternoon found me sprawled across the living room floor, in my full length plaster cast, cutting card with a nice sharp scalpel. Holding the card steady with my left hand, thumb and forefinger spread out close to the edge I cut down through the card steadily pulling the blade towards me and applying more than a small amount of pressure.

Suddenly, and these things always - but always happen suddenly, the scalpel slipped and sliced straight through my thumb. As a matter of instinct I grabbed the injured digit quickly with my right hand and lay there wondering what to do next. With great difficulty I managed to get to my feet, thank goodness for elbows! With my hands locked together and notwithstanding the plaster cast, I hopped, no hobbled, slowly into the kitchen leaning on the walls for support.

Still holding my left thumb I turned on the cold tap to fill the empty washing-up bowl in the sink and held both hands under the water for as long as I thought it would take to stem any blood flow. Very gingerly I released my thumb, and being just a touch scared of what I might see, I peered into the bowl to assess the damage. Oh! How the blood was now pumping into the clear water from my thumb with heart beat regularity - I passed out!

At that moment Hugh walked through the front door having decided to take a couple of hours of work. Overtime earned and chosen as 'time-off' in lieu was lost if not taken within a set period. So that's where he found me, crashed out on the kitchen floor.

"Oh, for goodness sake Sue." His voice brought me round, "what have you been up to now, I can't turn my back on you for two minutes. Come on Tatty Old Bit, let's get you on to your feet" and a much needed hug made everything OK.

Chapter Three: From Flames to Ashes

Finally, at a healthy twelve hands high Gemma was weaned. She was seven months old. The Christmas celebrations were upon us, although the 25th could have been a happier day for me because Ruth and Phillip always spent Christmas with their father. I didn't bring up my children. Their father saw fit to fight me for them threatening to disappear into the Irish Republic if I attempted to take them from him. At the time I was convinced he could do this and although I later appeared before the law courts for custody, it was not to be. Anyway, a few days later we did the whole Christmas caboodle again with them, along with a stonking good nosh up with crackers and paper hats and the exchanges of gifts. Ruth told me in adult life that having two Christmases was really rather good.

Hugh professed not to like children very much, referring to Ruth and Phillip as the cuckoos in the nest. He did, however, introduce Phillip to the noble game of rugby, enrolling him in Junior Saracens at Enfield. He also supported Ruth with her passion for horses and the lessons that she enjoyed each week at the Riding School.

Meanwhile, I threw myself into Gemma's education with enthusiasm but I had a very troublesome time teaching her how to be led on a head collar. Worrying about all this prompted me to ring a friend who knew loads more about horses than me.

"What you want to do first of all, is to get a fully adjustable head collar so that it fits snugly, then when you exert restraint, she feels resistance immediately and it will not be so easy for her to make fun of you." This I did, and the improvement was very noticeable. All I needed to do now was to win every battle and she would eventually respond.

The show scene that first year was fraught with disappointments. The expectations are always so high and the realities often quite low. I was as proud as punch of my horse, standing quietly in line waiting to trot up for the lady judge. I was pulled in third and when my time came, I walked her forward and trotted her, first away from the judge and then towards her. The judge walked all around her.

"What a pity, she has dreadful curbs," she snapped at me. I reeled in disbelief. "I simply cannot tolerate a horse with curbs," she looked directly at me with an accusing glare as if to say 'how dare you bring such a dreadful screw to this show ring.' Then she spun on her heels to look at the other entries, the pleated tweed skirt spiralled out in a swirl of dominance as she turned away. We came sixth.

"They're what is known as false curbs," Maggie explained later. "It is a sign of strength, it means she has substantial hock joints and she will grow into them. You wouldn't get a yearling with real curbs. Curbs are caused by concussion and trauma to the joint; for goodness sake, she's not old enough to have those things. The woman's mental, doesn't know what she's talking about."

I turned to my books and surfaced more confused than ever. One of my books said "False curbs are of no consequence and should be disregarded, young horses would grow into them like a small boy with big knees. But a tentative suggestion at later shows that they were only false cut no ice with the hard-nosed lady judges of the showing world.

I rang my 'go to' expert friend. She talked at me in mind blowing techno speak and as always I struggled to follow her thinking. I felt such an idiot, I always did when I spoke to her, and if I had not been confused before, then as sure as hell I was confused now.

My beloved riding instructor, Charmian, came to cast a critical eye over her and tell me what she thought. Charmian thought she was lovely, indeed what else could she say, Gemma was lovely. She added that she was the sort of horse who could turn her talents to any sort of competition. She had no firm views on curbs in youngsters and could not see what all the fuss was about.

I was looking forward to having more involvement with Gemma's winter care, but I elected to keep her at full livery so everything was done for me. I wanted to record her daily rations and learn from the people round me who clearly knew so much more. I must have been the most awful nuisance asking the most trivial of questions and making random observations on just about anything that popped up into my head. I talked incessantly to those stupid enough to stand still and listen, they must have been thoroughly fed up with me.

Then, out of the blue, I had a phone call from Mote End Farm in Mill Hill. "Are you still looking for somewhere to keep your horse?" the owner asked, "because I am expecting to have a vacancy shortly." I bit the bullet and agreed to move Gemma there as soon as a stable became vacant and I was very excited about the prospect of having her to myself. After all, I wasn't going to learn anything if it was all done for me.

I had made some good friends at Pages Farm and I was sorry to leave, but I felt I had to move on. So I said my goodbyes promising to stay in touch.

***

Life on the beat continued pretty much as it always did but occasionally things got quite exciting in my neck of the woods. I was patrolling my beat in Edgware's Station Road and proceeding, as they say, towards the tube station when I heard running steps behind me. "Officer! Officer!" The voice called to me as I turned to investigate, "I think we have a problem in the shop just up there," and he pointed to where he had come from.

"What is it"? I asked, at that point quite unconcerned.

"There's a fire, it's not much at the moment but it is dripping flames from the ceiling. Quickly! Come!" and I followed him to what must be one of the worst of the 1950s concrete monstrosities. It was a furniture shop showroom on the ground floor and above there must have been around 12 floors of private flats. Sure enough inside the display window there was indeed a fire, just like the man had told me. There were drips of flame clinging like limpets to the melting goblets of polystyrene ceiling. They were falling to the carpeted floor which was burning enthusiastically as the drops landed, each became a fast growing circle of fire spreading outward at an alarming rate. I looked up at the condominium floors, and looked back at the growing danger. "First things first," I thought.

People were beginning to gather and watch the progress; I got immediately on to the personal radio. "Sierra Whiskey! Are you receiving me, over?"

"Go ahead 529."

"We have a fire in Times Furnishings showroom in Station Road, Edgware. Can you call the Fire Brigade Urgently?"

"Doing it now, 529."

By this time there were several sofas and occasional tables being eaten by the flames. A substantial crowd of shoppers had now gathered round the window and watch, mesmerised at the action. The flames were beginning to lick the inside of the window and I suddenly realised the new danger that the increasing number of spectators were in.

"Clear the pavement everyone!" I shouted. They looked back at me, blankly it seemed.

"Get away from the window, NOW!" I shouted to them again. It became clear that to empty the pavement for the whole of the showroom length was near on an impossibility. "Quickly!" I shouted with sudden inspiration. "Get behind the bus shelter."

Realisation of the danger began to show on their faces and they began to follow my instructions. "Get away from the window, all of you! Quickly, behind the bus shelter, NOW!" They moved slowly at first but gathered speed as the window became a wall of flames.

"COME ON, ALL OF YOU!" I shouted to make myself heard, "MOVE!" Standing to one side of the shelter holding my arms out to demonstrate where they should go, I held out a hand to an elderly lady moving as fast as she could. "It's alright my darling, I've got you." and the pair of us managed to get behind the glass side of the shelter just in time, and with everyone safe - I hoped. The flames of fire, orange and red, shiny and flat against the glass window began to roar as the inferno increased in volume before the entire length of the window of the showroom blew out....

A spectacular blast of shattered glass exploded into Station Road, and the heavy shower of splinters fell all around the bus shelter. Just at that moment, the Fire Engine pulled up all blues and twos. Further police cars screeched to a halt to take charge of the highway and the whole drama was finally under control.

From being so important to proceedings I was now totally

insignificant and I faded into the background. It is a fine testament to the quick actions of the man who alerted me just in time, and lucky that there had been a humble Bobby so near at hand. Thanks to the quick professionalism of the fireman, the structural safety of the building, with all its occupants, was not weakened. Ugly as it is, it stands there today, as does the bus stop.

***

Hugh and I took my parents to Heathrow airport to start their holiday in New Zealand. For the first time I realised how vulnerable they looked as they disappeared into emigration. They were indeed vulnerable, or at least my father was, as it was not long after the holiday he was diagnosed with cancer. "I don't want this condition to be treated like a sacred cow," he told me. I wasn't sure what he meant at the time but I suppose he didn't want us to hedge around the subject of cancer but speak openly. He didn't want it to become the 'elephant in the room.' But I couldn't speak of it, the news was so dreadful.

Time marched all too quickly onward towards the inevitable with my father's health deteriorating significantly.

"I don't want those thieving undertakers to rob my body of all its value," he said one day propped up in his armchair. He made gargantuan efforts to spend some of the day sitting up as he feared the evils of congestion from lying down. "I don't have any gold teeth, so you will be spared the unenviable task of pulling them out when I'm gone. "Oh goody" I chipped in.

I do, however, have a gold ball behind my glass eye" and he tapped the glass pupil to indicate which eye. My father, David Scott Blackhall, poet, writer, BBC broadcaster, lost the use of his sight at the tender age of forty five. I was seven years old and very excited when my mother broke the news to me that my Daddy would never see me again. Finally my prayers were going to be answered and we would have to get a dog.

I digress, back to the glass eye. "When I've gone," he continued, "just get a knife from the kitchen and remove the glass eye first, it will come out easily, and he demonstrated taking the eye out, bouncing it in the palm of his hand and popping it back in again.

Didn't I know it! He used to wake me up in the mornings by

cradling the eye in between his thumb and forefinger, then putting his hand round the door of my bedroom he would say in a slow, deep and spooky voice

"I-t i-s t-i-m-e t-o g-e-t u-p S-u-s-a-n."

"So, once the glass eye is removed, just get the knife behind the ball, you might have to dig deep into the eye socket and then just pop it out. It will be covered in fat and gook but you can wash that off easily enough." We cringed at the thought of it. "Then I want Edna," (my mother) "to have it put on a chain, and I want her to wear it round her neck." What Edna was wearing, right at that moment, - was a face of disgust!

"Then," continued my Dad, "Then, when people ask her what it is, she is to say 'Oh! It's one of my husband's balls.'

***

Lying across his chest with my arms around him one morning I whispered "I love you Dad, I will do anything for you, just say what I can do, and I will do it"

"Sell your horse" he replied.

"Um, steady on," I replied, "When I said anything, I didn't mean ANYTHING."

All summer long we supported and loved my father while his health deteriorated, his life ebbed slowly into decline along with the summer. Then, in the early hours of the 14th September 1981 my father passed away.

My mother rang us at about 8.30am to tell me the sad news. She asked Hugh and me if we would be kind enough to go to the hospital and collect his belongings. As we drove over to Barnet, I remembered that far away day in the living room of number 9 Melrose Avenue, and his wish to resurrect the gold ball from behind his glass eye. Although the request was highly irregular, I refused to leave until I had my Daddy's gold ball. "I'll go into the morgue and retrieve it myself if I have to" I said determined to carry out my father's last wishes while saying nothing about that horse selling nonsense!

In the end a doctor at the hospital said he would conduct the extraction but wanted a witness with him, as this really was highly irregular. Hugh readily agreed to accompany him saving me from the distress this might cause. When we arrived at the family home, I gave it to my mother who told me that putting it on a chain was a step too far for her, so she put it in a box and kept it beside her bed.

On the 2nd October, together with my two sisters, and brother-in-law, I climbed up the Miner's Track to the top of Snowdon with my father's ashes which we scattered as we recited the words of one of his poems.

CARNEDD DAFYDD
As indiscriminately the mountain stream
Goes fiercely gallivanting to the plain,
Haphazard thoughts flow through me, twist and gleam
And surge and flicker in my restless brain.
Nor flood nor thought will halt me in my behest.
An image blurs and glows and blurs again.
The random stream lulls me to idleness,
Would have me fold my book and cheat my pen.

But halfway down the mountain there's a sign:
The waters widen to a deep, clear pool....
The secret of the patient hills is mine,
And all my inner world is stilled and cool.
The tumbling stream is quiet. Let me rest.
Hushes are the strident voices in my breast;

Police, Ponies & Husbands in-between

One of the family dilemmas we had following my father's death was what to do with his guide dog, 'Otis'. He was a fine handsome German shepherd, the last of three. My mother, restricted by arthritis, was not able to look after him. He had come to stay with us many times over the summer, much to Sylvester's disgust, but now a permanent home was needed. He was only seven years old. My father's secretary, Jean, had lived across the road from my parents' house. She was Val's mother, who had brought me the set of watercolours when I had been in hospital. Her husband, Frank,was a retired Police dog handler. They now lived in Devon and readily agreed to give him a home. Jean came up by train to collect him and when she rang to say she had arrived safely home, she reported that it had been 'love at first sight' between Frank and Otis. I just love happy endings

Chapter Four: Cops and Robbers

One of the first people I told about Gemma's birth was my very dear friend Lynette. She had kept her own horse at Woodcock Farm back in the day. We lost touch for a few years, Lynette and I, but then one day, I was patrolling the streets at Willesden Green, I was the passenger in a panda car. While we were waiting at the lights in the High Road I noticed a white van alongside us waiting to turn right. It was Lynette! "I know that girl," I said, "I haven't seen her for about three years. Beep your horn, could you please?" So the driver beeped his horn. Lynette stuck her nose in the air and looked away. "Oh for goodness sake, try again" I urged. He beeped, and there was further denial on Lynette's face. "He wound the window down," and I called to her, "LYNETTE - it's me." She didn't hear me. I waved my arms about, I bounced up and down, clenching my fists and let out a growl in frustration. Then, just as the lights changed, she swung her head round in angry defiance, throwing up two fingers at us, and on seeing it was me and did that girlie look of pleasurable recognition letting out a little scream. I gesticulated with my index finger to pull over up ahead.

"We are committed to going left," the driver said.

"We're in a police car for goodness sake," I replied. "We can go where we like!"

Having crossed the traffic, unceremoniously, we parked up the kerb and Lynette and I jumped out of our vehicles and began hugging each other, jumping round in a circle at the same time. "We mustn't lose touch again," I said and she agreed.

The resulting 'catch up' over coffee in later days revealed what we both had been up to. "Are you still in Dyne Road?" I asked her and she said she was. Among so many of the stories we exchanged, I recalled one night-duty when I, and the other members of the relief at Willesden, did some Police Dog training in Dyne Road. I related the story thus:

"It had all begun during our tea break, in the canteen," I told her. Keith, the dog handler had said how difficult it was to get a woman to run for a police dog. You know, pretend they were the criminals. I explained at this point that there were no lady dog handlers at the time and not many ladies had a mind to volunteer.

"I'll do that," I had said without hesitation. Betty, the only other woman constable on our relief, was thoroughly bemused and looked at me aghast, shaking her head.

"Really?" said Keith.

"Yeah, how hard can it be?"

"All you have to do is run," he said.

"I can't run very fast," I replied.

"All the better, Sparks won't have to work so hard."

The following night, when it was quiet, as if there is ever a quiet time in Willesden Green, the whole relief trooped down to Dyne Road where there was an alleyway, which would serve well as a dog run. "I did think about you," I told her, "I wondered at the time if you still lived there."

"Yes, I'm still there," she replied.

Keith dressed me up in dog protection gear; thick twill sleeves and a jacket that was so heavy I wondered how anyone could even break into a trot let alone keep it up. I reminded myself I had carried hundredweight sacks of corn often enough before now.

So Keith gave me the command, "when you are ready, run like stink down the alleyway and Sparks will do the rest."

"Blimey." Lynette interjected.

I cannot, and never will, believe the sheer force with which the dog hit me in the back, grabbing my arm and pulling me to the ground. I was flipped over in a wink and dragged several feet, as Keith ran towards us shouting for Sparks to "LEAVE!" I had laddered all my stockings and scuffed my navy police skirt, but it was just the best fun. I must add here that Sparks became the Metropolitian Police Dog Champion three times. No one minds being flattened by a champion. I was up for doing it all again but Keith thought once was quite enough.

"When was that again?" Lynette questioned, I told her and she laughed confiding in me that the Serious Crime Squad had been keeping an observation on her partner, later storming the flat with a warrant for his arrest. Libby was accused of armed robbery. It was quite an event, he opened a security van with a chainsaw in Leverstock Green. I would love to have been a fly on the inside of that vehicle as the detectives watched the entire night-duty strength of Quebec Lima roll up with a dog chasing a police woman at three o'clock in the morning!

Lynette and I saw a great deal of each other after that and she came visiting frequently. Hugh was unsure of the implications of me befriending a gangster's moll and there was a bit of a mock love/hate relationship going on between her and Hugh. Her husband was now serving his time and this made Hugh feel a bit uncomfortable. Every time she called round Hugh would invariably answer the door, seeing it was her, he immediately tried to prevent her from coming in shouting; "Oh no, not you, go away!"

"Let me in" Lynette would shout back.

"No, go away, we don't want any riff raff round here."

"Let me see my friend, I want to see my friend."

"You haven't got any friends" and Hugh would push the door, and Lynette would push the door, and in the end I had to intervene.

***

We were just settling down to a night curled up in front of the telly when there was a knock at the door. Hugh answered it and there stood Lynette, along with a tall handsome man who he instantly knew to be her infamous husband. He spoke with a deep cockney sandpaper of a voice. "The name's Libby," he greeted us holding out his hand in friendship. "Nice to meet you at last, I feel I know you, I've heard such a lot about you both."

"I've heard a lot about you as it happens," said Hugh, a virtual shadow of the policeman's helmet began to manifest itself where the halo should have been.

Lynette looked worried.

Hugh looked worried, damn it!

"You've been very good to my lady wife while I have been away, um on holiday, and we want to take you out for a meal."

Hugh was in a state of stunned silence.

I peered round him in the doorway, "Come in, come in," I said. "We didn't think you were going to be released until next week."

"I am out on parole," Libby replied as they stepped into the hallway and on into the living room. "They let you out for the odd day or two beforehand to um - to eh, you know ease you back into the community."

I think Hugh struggled with this situation, he was a serious 'thief taker'.

Every Friday he would wake up in the morning and rub his hands in anticipation because it was 'Armed Robbery' day. I did the same thing on Fridays but that was because the 'Horse and Hound' came out on sale.

Anyway, there we were sitting amicably in our own living room with a convicted armed robber, practically one of the family. Hugh coped remarkably well considering and Libby took us out for a meal in Edgware where we had a really good evening. I liked him enormously, he was great, although I'm not convinced about Hugh with his firm views.

***

I could be a serious copper too, though. I was beginning to develop a particular interest in Crime Prevention. Police forces across the country were promoting the permanent identification of property and in particular, the dye stamping of pedal cycles, as proof of ownership. It involved the owner's postcode followed by the house number making recovery so much more viable if it were stolen. I reasoned that this property identification scheme could be used in the same way to permanently mark saddlery as it was becoming apparent stable crime was on the increase. I was given time to visit various local stables to mark their saddlery for them on request. Being part of the local horse world through Gemma, I found it easy to put the word around and the scheme was enthusiastically embraced.

I became 'a bit of a name' within crime prevention and equestrian circles, once being described by 'The Job,' as the 'Leading Light in tack marking'. This was the fortnightly police newspaper.

Hugh made disparaging noises regarding my efforts. "What are things coming to," he remarked emphatically as he thumbed through the pages, "when a police constable, a man I remind you, is reported performing herculean bravery arresting a burglar with a knife and the write up is hidden away on the back page of The Job. Then lo and behold, a bint buggerin' about with a horse, dominates headline news on the front page. You must agree that this is not right."

"Gee, thanks, Hugh."

There were sometimes interruptions in the police routine which meant you couldn't have your day off when expected because of some impromptu demonstrations that were happening somewhere in London. Sudden unexpected bomb alerts from the IRA, had us scuttling into the capital when we would rather be doing something else. Hugh and I had watched the television news in July horrified as they reported the bombing of the Household Cavalry's Blues and Royals and The Royal Green Jackets on the bandstand. The loss of the horses and soldiers killed rocked the nation to its knees with the injustice. Notting Hill Carnival got violent again and it seemed clear all was far from well in London that year, it seemed the city was being ripped apart.

***

Gemma looked simply wonderful to me in the spring of that year and I was again getting excited about the coming show season. We managed to get to many of the local shows and true to the predictions, Gemma had grown into her joints and was becoming a really beautiful horse. It was a 'red letter' day for me at Stevenage Show winning the strong class of ten before going on to get the Championship. Yep, success is certainly sweet.

***

I hitched a ride with Maggie to Towerlands Show and we all had the jolliest time made extra satisfying with the success of coming second. This sent me skipping about with ecstasy. Maggie's two year old colt, 'Stoker' had won the class, nobody minds coming second to a good horse.

It was considered by the farm manager of Mote End Farm that Gemma was now old enough to be turned out in a lovely big pasture with all the other mares, and I was up at 5.30am one morning to bring her in away from the flies. She was with the other horses dozing under a large oak tree as the summer sun was beginning to appear. I walked down to them head collar at the ready, but as I was about to put it on, Spice, a little pony came over to investigate. Gemma put her ears back and pulled a face and with the speed of a lizard's tongue Spice spun round and lashed out. "CHRIST!!" I shouted, and swung the head collar instinctively at the pony who danced nimbly out of reach. As I staggered backwards I knew, with all certainty, my left arm was broken. I felt faint, I was going to faint....

"Don't pass out" Gemma said, "it's dangerous, this lot of hooligans will tread on you"

"Don't pass out," I said to myself, "the other horses might trample on me,"

"Don't go down, don't go down," Gemma insisted, but I was going down..... I grabbed at Gemma's mane to hold myself up and fell against her warm shoulder. She stood, rock still she stood.

"It's OK, I've got you," she whispered to me, "just hold on and don't go down." I felt the blood draining away from my head and I looked around me to assess what else was going on.

It really was the most magical sight that I saw. "I've never noticed before," I told her. All the trees and the grass had turned silver and gold, shimmering in the rising sunlight, they sparkled with the most unbelievable glistening, casting shadows of all shades of gold and copper, the leaves danced silvery pearl. "Look at that," I whispered again as I hung on to keep myself standing. I don't know how long it lasted, seconds? Minutes maybe? But as the blood began to return to my brain the green hue of nature's beauty began to pour back into the scenery; I was really quite disappointed.

Regaining my composure I could not bring myself to leave her where she was, having gone out there specially to bring her in. Anyway there were the flies to consider which looked set to be as bad as ever. Her head collar was on the floor in front of me, Goodness knows my arm hurt, but with the hand of the damaged arm, I clutched the front of my jumper on my opposite chest. I reached down for the collar. With the help of my teeth I got it fitted on to Gemma's head and we made our way forlornly back up the field. The gate was tied to the fence post rather than with hinges and my heart sank at the realisation this could prove a challenge too far. But Gemma was a star, waiting patiently whilst I lifted it one armed wide enough for us to pass and then again while I struggled to close it after me. Luckily no other horse followed us so I didn't have the task of keeping them at bay.

With everything ready in her stable I had only to pop her in there and unclip the lead rope. I was then able to set about solving the problem of the arm; I could see it was broken. Getting out a tail bandage from my box I wound it round and round my arm and my wrist. Then I wound it round my neck to form a kind of splint and sling which, once the full weight was taken off it I felt pretty chipper. It was still very early in the morning with no other liveries about so there was nothing for it but to return home. 'Thank the lord for an automatic car,' I rejoiced.

Relieved to be home I told Hugh what had happened. "I've broken my arm," I announced. "Can you take me to the Orthopaedic hospital?"

It was 7.30pm by the time I got up to Mote End to turn Gemma out again and I was sporting a nice new clean white plaster cast. She was keen to go out and thankfully Hugh was able to give me a hand. He was not at all happy about what had happened to my arm or about keeping Gemma any longer.

As the story of my accident circulated, other people at the farm rallied round to help me. There would be no more in-hand showing for the rest of the year. My arm got better with no lasting incapacities. 'Put two bones in a room and they will mend,' that's my motto anyway.

***

I lived in a council house when I met Hugh. I was given the house so I could try to get custody of my two children but the attempt failed so it meant that I had to be content with seeing them every weekend, but at least there was somewhere for them to sleep over, with the added bonus of each having their own bedroom. Shortly after we married we were able to buy it thanks to Maggie Thatcher's new policy of the right to buy. Having installed central heating and redecorated Hugh was keen to fit double-glazing.

Throughout the coming weeks there was one topic of conversation: "If we hadn't got the cost for Gemma we could afford double glazing in no time at all," he protested. He could not help himself developing a jaundiced view towards my horse when it came to discussing our finances. My mother took me to task over it all. "Well," she had said firmly, "I don't know about you but if I was Hugh I would object strongly to all that money being squandered to pay for a darned horse."

The simple fact of the matter was, she did not understand me not one little bit. She just didn't get it. "I bring home over £600 a month," I told her, "it's a poor show if I cannot spend some of it on myself."

"I'd never thought about it like that," she buckled. "I suppose when you put it like that…"

"We'll get our double glazing soon enough," I reassured her, "just not immediately."

I was not my mother's child, not in spirit anyway. "You're a changeling," my mother had wailed throughout my upbringing. "There is a nice feminine little girl somewhere in the world that belongs to me and it's not you."

Hugh was persistent, he talked to colleagues at work who were all having their houses double glazed and he got quotes in from local companies. I was slowly worn down and there seemed nothing for it but to see if I could find somebody nice to have Gemma on loan. I thought highly of this 'go-to' expert friend and I wondered if she would like to have her for eighteen months to breed a foal, so I told Hugh I was prepared to send her away, only if my 'go to' expert friend wanted her. It took me some time to come to terms with doing this and I secretly thought she might not want her. I rather hoped so, after all she had not had a good word to say about her when she last saw her. But I would do the decent wifely thing and ask the question.

Chapter Five: Climbing My Own Mountain

My 'go-to' expert friend came to scrutinise Gemma. She was picky, of course she was. She wanted her mane and tail pulled; she wanted her to be examined by a vet to ensure that she was producing two follicles. "Nevertheless," she said, "I will agree to take this mare, at the very least I should get a half decent foal in spite of everything."

I felt my back was against the wall but I was confident she knew how to look after horses because she had told me often enough. There was no micro chipping in those days and freeze marking was the only way to identify a horse and I didn't want her to go without identification. I had promoted this strongly enough to others when engaged in the crime prevention thing I had going, so I did feel I should put my money where my mouth was.

The other thing I wanted to do before Gemma left my care was to get on her and introduce her to the gentle art of being ridden. I made full use of the outdoor manège at Mote End and with Hugh's help it really was a most exciting time. She took to the job without any fuss whatsoever, quietly walking round the school with me on her, I was as proud as punch. I even let Hugh have a little 'sit', and she was just great, we did a little trotting but left the lessons at that. She was ready to turn away for 18 months and when that time was up I could bring her back to the saddle and it should not cause her any alarm.

***

I had been offered a home beat, earlier that summer, which meant I had my own area of streets to police. I was expected to get to know the people in it and to win their trust, solve their problems for them and generally make myself useful and make the right noises. I thoroughly enjoyed this responsibility and I enjoyed the freedom of working on my own initiative. It did mean however, that Hugh and I were now working different hours and this brought with it other problems. But hey! We were strong enough for this; we loved each other, didn't we? We were solid enough surely, weren't we?

Because I was frequently off my beat marking saddlery, one of the Inspectors at West Hendon got the idea into his head that I was always hiding away in the West Hendon Mounted Branch Stables and he did not approve. I can only assume that because he had heard I did so much with the horses, he put two and two together and didn't come up with four. He took it upon himself to give me quite a dressing down over being off my beat for no good reason other than to skulk away in the stables tearoom. I showed him the records I had kept, the calls I made on my beat and also the good work at stables I had been to. It cut no ice! The man was a bully.

"And," he went on to say, "if you were under my command you would be in serious danger of losing your job so I expect you to shape up." The whole thing was blown up out of all proportion.

The Sergeant of the Mounted Branch stables blew his top too. "If I was the one to catch you in here I would have something to say to you on the matter," he said adding some weight to my argument. "This accusation reflects on me as much as you," he insisted.

"If you ever caught me in here at all it would be a miracle," I ranted. "I've hardly ever stepped foot in your stables, let alone stopped for tea. Why would I? I don't aspire to join the Mounted Branch. I have my own horse, why would I want to look after anybody else's."

We were both asked to account for ourselves and the Inspector, being so sure of himself, dragged me into the office of the Chief Superintendent. I desperately needed the Mounted Branch Sergeant to come with me and back me up. Though he was not the one in trouble, he very kindly came and added his support. As it happens, the Chief Superintendent had been our next door neighbour when I was a little girl, and I had grown up with his four sons. They all came to my father's memorial service. It was quite a positive interview all in all I concluded. The Inspector left me alone after that.

***

It was a sad day for me when they came to collect Gemma in April 1983. Hugh and I visited her 10 days later, and again a week after that when Hugh was playing rugby. I dropped him off at the Police Social club and went on to see Gemma. I didn't tell them I was visiting and I don't think they were pleased to see me. As always she came to my call and I enjoyed a happy hour with my lovely horse. When I returned to collect Hugh, the rugby team was in a state of elation because they had won the cup. The air was thick with noise and testosterone, the big jug of beer was passed around the bar and we made merry with much singing of ribald songs,

"…………..Was it you, you sly woodpecker,
Had it with me girl, Rebecca,
Footprints on the windscreen upside down…………………….."
And other such fine renditions.

**

My friend Ronni, had a small livery yard in Bricket Wood. Some of the horses she had to look after also required riding and I was more than happy to pitch in and help out. As Hugh and I just had the one car between us, it took a degree of planning for us both to be in the places we wanted to be. Because Hugh had been spending some time playing golf recently, it worked out quite well. I could go and ride while he did a leisurely 18 holes before coming to collect me, or that is what he told me anyway.

On one occasion we took the M1 just one junction to Bricket Wood and the traffic was at a standstill. Hugh became really agitated, claiming to be late for goodness knows what. He was impossible in the car, while we waited, trapped in the slow lane, I finally put it to him "Listen, if I get out of the car now, I can walk across the fields to Ronni's place and you can get on with your precious golf if it means that much to you."

"Do you really mind," he said, "it would save me some time." I couldn't believe that he leapt at my offer so readily. So I got out of the car and walked. By the time I got to Ronni's I was in tears, she had already ridden, and I was just so upset about the whole episode. Hugh had been uncharacteristically difficult and I could not understand why, and what was so important about a sodding game of golf anyway.

**

I was thankful for the opportunity to escape from the atmosphere at home and I went away for a long week-end with a charity my father had started for blind mountain climbers. He called them the Milton Mountaineers as the poet John Milton had been blind and Dad was a prolific poet. I had never been away with them before but in memory of my Father I wanted to be part of their return visit to climb Ben Nevis. My mother also came along with my sister Anne and friends from America, Lillian and Al Sperber. Al was the compère for an American radio show, 'Out of Sight' which catered for the blind and similar to 'In Touch', which was Dad's magazine programme here in the UK.

We were erecting a blue commemorative plaque on the wall to the entrance of our hotel, appropriately part of the Milton Hotel chain.

I decided it might be a bit of fun to write some verses and incorporate some of the exciting things that happened during the week-end.

The wonderful boys from the RAF mountain rescue acted as guides, as you would expect they were a lively bunch and looked after us well. We had a system whereby, as we disembarked from the coach waiting for the off, if you had any visual impairments and needed assistance to climb the mountain, then you put your hand into the air and a young squaddie would come and claim you for his own.

It worked well and no one went unguided with the help from sighted group members.

Here follows an example of my scribblings.

The heat of the day made the air really thick,
They ran out of water and a guide dog was sick,
By the end of the day we'd walked seven miles long
But it would have been three if we hadn't gone wrong.
The RAF rescue saw us up The Ben,
A group of fit, healthy and nubile young men,
They were lithe, they were slim, they were quick on their toes,
And if I put my hand up, I'll get one of those.

I had the most fabulous time meeting all Dad's friends. His best friend George, had taken over leadership and I felt immensely proud to be part of such a worthwhile charity. The break had been good for my home life and I returned refreshed.

***

The phone rang one evening just as we were settling down to have supper, which Hugh had so lovingly prepared for us. It was Suzanna from Llandrillo in North Wales. "Hi Sue," she greeted me cheerfully. "We are coming down to London tomorrow for the CND rally."

"We were thinking that if we were to get arrested…."

"You won't be arrested."

"We might, anyway, we are concerned we will be kept in custody until the early hours of the morning."

"I hope not."

"We have heard that they do this deliberately so you miss the coach to take you back home."

"We wouldn't do that," I insisted. "But it might take time to complete reports and the process of interviewing."

"C'mon Sue, we all know the police do these things just to be vindictive."

"Yeah, alright, go on, I'm obviously not going to persuade you differently."

"Well, if this does happen, can Tony and I come and stay overnight with you?"

"Yes, of course you can, I'll leave a key round the back of the house in case you get home before we do."

"Are you on this rally then?"

"Yes, Hugh and I both. In different places though, I'll look out for you and give you a wave," I laughed.

"I can see that happening, do you know how many are planning to go?"

"I know there are said to be 1000 plus police going to be there,"

"I'll see you tomorrow then," she chortled, "if not in London then later in Burnt Oak"

Hugh and I had a chuckle about the conversation as we settled down to eat another one of his excellent curries. The following day we had to report to our respective stations early, Hugh boarded his operational bus and I boarded mine and we both travelled into London to do our duty. I was posted near Hyde Park and later in the afternoon I was sent to the Bayswater Road together with more policemen than I have ever seen in one place before. "Good Lord," I said, "We have a peel of policemen." We were told to form a cordon to direct the coming demonstrators across to the north side of the road away from the art stands and paintings being offered for sale along the railings to the park. This was to prevent any inclinations the demonstrators may have to committing criminal damage. We all linked arms as we heard the crowd coming from quite a distance away, and we waited.

There were three main fragments of the march occurring in London that day and we heard through radio link there had been the odd skirmish. I was neatly positioned between two burly uniforms, tall and imposing, unlike me who can only boast 5ft 5 inches. They looked down at me with amusement in their eyes.

The march approached, it was impressive to say the least, there were hundreds of them and they began to file past us 20 or 30 deep filling the remainder of the road that we allowed them to occupy. They were a mixed bunch of hippies and respectables, long hair and short hair, washed and unwashed, smelly and fragrant. They filed past us on and on the crowd kept coming, half an hour on there seemed no let up, and I have never seen so many people. We

Police, Ponies & Husbands in-between

remained linked, tight, and ready to pitch in if needed, 'we were a force to be reckoned with,' we told ourselves. They eyed us with distrust, we sternly regarded them, men and women alike we were stalwart in our aspect.

Just then, I heard above the noise "Suzi! SUE!!...SUE!!" and out of the crowd came Suzanna! We hugged each other but only for a nano second before the weight of the crowd pushed her onward and out of sight. My two friends either side of me coughed.

"Is there anything we should know?" they asked.

"They were my friends. They have come all the way from North Wales"

There had been 300,000 demonstrators for the Campaign for Nuclear Disarmament that day. Suzanna and her friend did not get arrested and unbelievably they got home on their bus before we were released from London. I again spoke to Suzanna on the phone at 1.30am. I had rung her this time to make sure she was okay; of course she was.

***

Hugh and I took a holiday in September. It was a long car journey to Vienna during which we composed the words to 'How much is that doggy in the window' in German, by way of getting us in the mood for the days to come. "Der ein mit zer vaggledee hinter...." We sang out enthusiastically.

Once in Vienna we met up with Hugh's mother and the three of us stayed in a small flat belonging to a friend of hers. There were not enough beds to go round and we took it in turns to sleep on the most uncomfortable armchair/put-you-up. At the rear of the apartment was a Sauerkraut factory and you would have been able to guess this even before opening the windows.

The toilet was along the

corridor of shiny brown tiles where there was on display a wide range of lavatory papers each belonging to the 6 different families sharing the facility. The selection ranged from a floral pink roll of soft perforated wipes to squares of newspaper on a nail in the wall.

But we had the most delicious time, I discovered Wiener schnitzel, and we saw the magnificent performance of the white Lipizzaner horses at the Spanish Riding School.

I was keen to have a riding lesson in Vienna believing that this must be the centre of excellence in all things equestrian. Trudy found a riding school and duly booked an hour's lesson for me. Hugh and I walked down the most unlikely streets for such a place, the austere concrete façade we walked through gave no clue as to the industry hidden behind it.

I was given a lovely looking chestnut and shown into an enormous indoor school where there appeared to be several classes going on all at the same time. There must have been about 30 horses in there. My horse was lame! I pulled him into the centre of the circle and informed the instructor. His English was limited. "He is not lame, he is tired, he works hard, you reconsider, he is good 'orse."

"He's lame," I insisted and the instructor, exasperated, called for a second horse. She was a rather ropey looking bay with one eye but for all that a nice ride, notwithstanding the fact she was stiff and one sided.

"You have zer vong canter," he bellowed at me when it came to my turn to canter to the back of the ride. I knew very well she was on the wrong leg but I was amazed she was able to canter at all being so bent to the outside. We continued to banana our way round the circle until I reached the last horse in the class. She put me in mind of the real live carousel ponies I had seen the day before, constantly trotting the circle in one direction to please the tourists under the famous giant Ferris wheel.

The instructor called us all into the circle and tried to explain the intricacies of the right canter using me as a bad example. An experience I cannot help looking back at with amusement.

When I returned the bay mare to her stall I was met by her groom who took the horse from me and tied her up stroking her sides and illustrating as best he could with sign language how fond of her he was. He was elderly and rather work worn but he was a nice old cock and seemed genuine.

"Ich liebe Pferde" he said several times in case I didn't understand the first time he said it. I didn't!

"He says he loves horses," said Hugh.

I nodded with approval pointing to my chest by way of agreement "And me," I said. He then held out his hand - and I shook it.

"No Sue," said Hugh, "he's asking you for a tip." I looked blankly at both of them.

"Always tighten your girth before riding out of the yard?" I ventured.

"No, not that sort of tip, you idiot," said Hugh, "he wants some money." I dug out a few Austrian shillings from my inner pocket and handed them over to the groom who was smiling toothlessly back at me.

On the way back to the flat we admired the many horse drawn carriages for tourist's city tours. Hugh said they were called a 'fiakre'. "Is that 'PF' as in Pferd," I asked him.

"I don't think so," he said, "Otherwise you would have a pfiaker pferd or cart horse in UK speak."

"The most distinctive thing about a cart horse," I ventured, "is their Olympic ability to break wind." "Mmmmm," said Hugh, "pfarting like a 'pfiaker pferd - interesting." And we walked on in silence contemplating this entertaining thought.

Almost as soon as we returned home Hugh seemed to lose his holiday spirit. Ruth had moved in with us earlier in the summer so she was at home to welcome us back. Lynette had also popped round to help with the reception for the weary travellers.

As soon as the cases were out of the car and in the house, Hugh said he had to go out, he said he had an appointment but he was vague about the details. It had been a long drive back from Dover and he could not even stop for a cup of tea this urge to get out of the house was so important.

"What's up with him?" asked Lynette.

"I don't know," I replied quietly wondering if he was not happy about Lynette being there. But, no, I dismissed that idea. "He didn't say anything about this on the way home" I added. Ruth was bewildered too, but hey, we'd just had a fabulous holiday so what was there to worry about?

Chapter Six: A Betrayal of Trust

One of the first things I wanted to do was to find out how Gemma was getting on. After a few days I had managed to get hold of my 'go-to' expert friend and we had a very chatty conversation. When I finally got to visit I spent a pleasant enough day with Gemma who immediately demanded I rub her bottom for her. She had lost a little of her body condition but she was still too big and strong for this behaviour now and I did my best to stay upright. My friend was quite disgusted.

On one of our days off from work I rang the stable yard for an update on Gemma's health. The 'go-to' expert friend was down with flu and still in bed. It must have been hard attending to the horses when you are a one-man band and no help to call on in times of crisis. She didn't know how she was going to get the mucking out done and even feeding round was proving to be a job too far. Hugh and I jumped in the car and travelled there to muck out and care for the horses for the day. We moved some barrows of muck from the bare mud paddocks and made sure all the horses were fed/watered/turned out etc. Gemma did not look at all sharp. I walked her down the driveway to graze. She was hungry.

***

Life, as they say, goes on and back at Mill Hill the following week I was patrolling in a panda with Michael when we had a call to Hill House in Elstree village. Half of Elstree was on Mill Hill's ground so, along with other officers from Borehamwood, we answered the call which was 'man gone berserk with an axe'. Hill House was some kind of institution and sure enough there was this guy marooned on the stage of a big assembly hall wielding this axe.

None of us were volunteering to tackle him any time soon but after some consideration, and consultation with the carers, Michael drew the short straw and entered the hall while the rest of us peered through the doorway slightly ajar. Alone and unarmed Michael stood at the end of the hall facing the stage. After quite a long silence he began goading the inmate.

Police, Ponies & Husbands in-between

"C'mon then you bastard, c'mon, let's see if you're man enough."

The man became agitated.

"Show us what you're made of why don't ya."

The man got angry..

"You're a bloody wimp, there's nothin' to ya."

The man got angrier. Swinging the axe around in front of him.

"Yeah?" Michael taunted, " c'mon make my day."

The man ranted back "I'll do ya, I will, don't push me."

"If you were any good you wouldn't need pushin.'"

"I'll give it ya, I'll give it ya."

"C'mon then what're you waitin' for," and Michael held his arms out wide and beckoning with his fingers.

The man continued to swing the axe round his head.

Michael continued "C'mon then if you think you're hard enough."

The man jumped down from the stage.

"C'mon then if you think you're hard enough" Michael said again gesticulating with his outstretched arms. Exploding into action the man ran down the hall towards Michael and swinging the axe he flung it in Michael's direction. Michael dodged out of the way with a blink to spare and the axe hit the back wall, chips of plaster came flying off in all directions. I joined in the affray along with three other policemen and we held the man to the ground while medics delivered a sedative to render him no longer berserk. Just another day at the office, I thought.

***

Lady Solitaire will be on her last journey with Molly, one day next week. I am glad that she does no go alone.

Later that week I was compelled to go and see Solitaire, to say goodbye really as she and her best pal Molly were put down the following day. It was the end of an era and I felt very sad about this, so the next day it was a natural impulse for me to want to visit Gemma. It was at times like this that I found I needed to be near her; she always understood.

I was not happy with what I found though. She had lost a lot more weight and this 'so-called' expert admitted she was worried. I removed four barrows of muck from the mud-licked paddocks and when I left, I resolved to return again as soon as I could, hoping that by then things might have improved.

My friend knew I was not impressed. I wanted to know why she was losing weight but it never dawned on me that it was because she was not getting enough to eat. This person knows everything there is to know about horses, I mused, so she must be getting fed. I was extraordinarily bewildered.

I rang for an update a few days later. A member of her staff answered the phone; I don't know who she was, Groom? Cleaning lady? Who knows? "Hold on one moment" she replied to the question, "Who shall I say is calling?"

"Sue Gordon-Bennett" I replied, "I'm ringing to see how my horse is."

I held on, and in the background I could hear the sound of whispering and muttering as if a hand was being held over the receiver. The same voice came back to the phone, "there is no one here at the moment, I think she is teaching."

I left a message for her to ring me back. She didn't and I rang again the following day resulting in a similar scenario. I tried again the next day, and then the day after; I was becoming demented with worry.

Eventually I got hold of her.

"I was waiting to hear the results of the blood tests," she told me as if I should have known this. "They should be back tomorrow, and I have a veterinary surgeon coming too." I began to doubt her expertise, she could always talk a good game using long unpronounceable technical speak guaranteed to make you feel stupid in her presence for not knowing as much as her.

This 'so-called' expert outlined Gemma's other symptoms:

Police, Ponies & Husbands in-between

breathing is not 100% and it's too laboured, she may be anaemic, it might be worms and we don't think she is in foal. I knew one thing for sure, Gemma was unwell for some reason and I was not a happy bunny.

The next day I rang to find out the result of the blood test. "Oh!" the so-called expert exclaimed when she heard who was calling. "I was going to ring you." There was something of a pregnant pause, "You had better inform your insurance company because there is nothing more we can do for her. She may have to be put down due to severe worm damage as a foal."

MY BLOOD RAN COLD.

There was something of a silent pause while I processed this information. Overwhelmed by the treachery of it all my one thought was for Gemma's survival, but I did not explode, my sensible brain took over and I calmly allowed her to think I was taking this lying down. I told myself to let her think I was the gullible fool that she obviously thought I was.

"When you say: she <u>may</u> have to be put down," I finally asked, "what factor will determine this?"

"Well, there are still further tests to be done obviously, but I wanted to be fair to you and let you know the situation as soon as possible. I have invested a lot in this mare and for me to come out of it with nothing is not the best option for me either, so I can assure you I do have her best interests at heart. I'll ring you in the week when I know a bit more"

"OK" I replied brightly and I put down the phone; I was in something of a daze but I was also in the most unspeakable panic. Hugh was asleep because of being on night duty. The tiger in me clawed its way to the surface and I got in the car and went straight round to Pages Farm. "Maggie, I have a big problem," and I told her all about it, "Are you doing anything with your horse box tomorrow, and do you know any sizeable men with muscles?"

"Of course I can help," she said, "We have to get her home, don't we? She can be stabled down the road at Ham Farm, we are full up here." Maggie, bless her, didn't crow about being right all along, she didn't even say 'I told you so.'

"I've just got to get her out of there," I sobbed. "How could I have let this happen"?

"Don't worry" Maggie put her arm round me, "We'll get her

back, she will be all right, let me make some phone calls. Peter is available, I can drive the lorry, leave it with me."

Hugh was on nights and when he woke up at about 3pm, I told him what had happened. "Don't you think you are over-reacting just a little?" He said, and that is all it took for me to explode.

"Over-reacting! OVER-REACTING!! They are going to kill my horse for no good reason and you think I am over-reacting. How dare you, sod your bloody double glazing, I don't care if we are a bit strapped for cash right now, I'm fetching Gemma home, and I'm doing it tomorrow!"

"I'd rather not get involved," said Hugh, "I can understand how you feel, I do, but I would rather not get involved."

"Fine," I said, "Suit your bloody self," and I left to go shopping, slamming the door behind me.

Maggie rang that evening to say we could be looking to leave at about 2pm the following day but in the morning she rang and said, "Can you be ready to leave in ½ hour." I certainly could, the sooner the better.

Hugh dropped me off at Pages Farm so he could keep the car and at about 10.30am Jim, Peter, Maggie and I got into the horsebox and went to repossess my horse. I climbed the stairs to the flat above the stables followed by Peter. Maggie and Jim had gone to find Gemma, we had no intention of asking or negotiating, we were taking her, end of story.

I remember the conversation as if it were yesterday. She opened the door and looked at me. "Oh," she said.

Without further preamble I told her why I was there. "I've come for my horse."

"Well, I can't let you take her," she announced.

"You can't stop me," I replied.

"She is in the middle of treatment with my vet," she protested. "It's most unethical."

"I couldn't care less," I said. "Anything you have to say on the matter is totally irrelevant."

"You can't take her. She is on loan to me, we have a contract."

"No, we don't, not if you fail to look after her properly."

"I won't tell you where she is."

"I'll find her," I said

"This is most unethical, changing vets in mid treatment."

"You say that as if I should give a damn."

"The vet will not be happy about this I can assure you." She jabbed her finger at me.

"I'll take her vaccination certificate while I'm here as well."

"I don't know where it is," and she looked momentarily pleased with herself.

"You can post it to me," I told her.

"You won't get away with this, what will you do with the foal?"

"You said that you doubted she was pregnant."

This took the wind out of her sails, she couldn't deny that is what she had told me, and she struggled to find more words. I tried to remain quietly effective, "I'm leaving this yard now, and I'm taking my horse with me."

"I'd like to see you try" she scoffed, but the bluff was toothless.

"Send me her vaccination certificate," I demanded before Peter and I retraced our steps. And that was the last time I ever spoke to her.

Jim met us at the bottom of the stairs. "She's all loaded Sue," he said, "Are you ready to leave?" The lorry was ticking over, and Maggie was already aboard in the driver's seat and my lovely Gemma was safely installed in the back. We rolled out of the yard quietly satisfied, job done.

***

Once we were on the road home Maggie voiced her opinion of the place. "It's making no money there," she ventured to suggest. "I know it isn't, because I've been there. I've been in that situation, the beds are scant and the place is in disrepair. Did you see the fire buckets full of sand outside all the stables? It is just bullshit designed to make it look like it's in tip-top order, this place is struggling to survive, you can take my word for it."

When we got back to Pages and had unloaded Gemma, Maggie said "Right, let's take a look at her." She ran her hand over her rump fingering the poverty lines, which dominated her profile. Then along her belly, down her legs one by one picking up each foot in turn. She ran her palm across her rib cage, her hand bumping over every rib, which stood out in clear definition. Stroking her head and ears she ran her hand down her neck flattening her coat which was in staring disorder. "We'll soon have her looking good again," Maggie re-assured me.

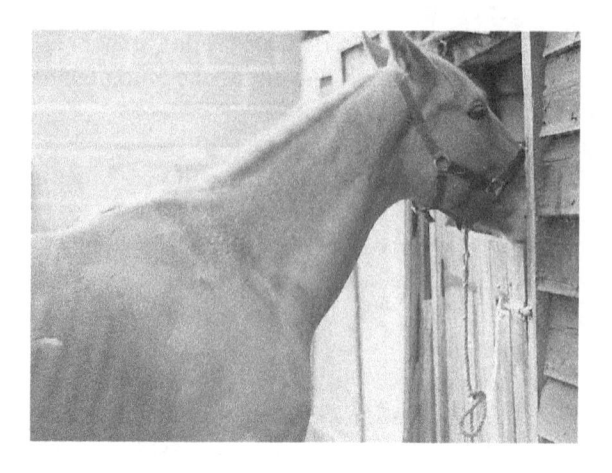

The vet came and tested her for pregnancy passing the verdict that she was, in fact, in foal after all. But this was not what I wanted to hear. I could not understand why the 'so-called' expert would actually consider having her destroyed and I voiced my disbelief. Maggie answered the rhetorical question by saying "we will probably never know the truth."

Gemma was safely installed at Ham Farm in a stable with a nice clean paddock to go out in during the day. She had a bucket feed morning and evening and she thrived. Hugh was not impressed.

Oblivious to his discontent I sat on the grass leaning against a tree drinking in the sight of my lovely horse grazing under the canopy of the old twisted apple trees. The last time I had been in that field was when Ruth had been a toddler. She had her picture taken for The Borehamwood Post while sitting on a pony called Magpie. It had been a memorable day for us all those years ago because, as the youngest competitor, she had won the leading rein class.

I now had to face the oncoming battle of wills with this 'so called' expert who had thought it was okay to put my horse to sleep. The letters began to fly back and forth. I was threatened with legal action if she was not returned. I reminded her she only had a claim on the foal, which she could have, if I was reimbursed with a proportion of the cost of keeping it until it was weaned. Then finally, the last communication I had from her stated that if the mare did not return to her yard forthwith then she had no further interest in her or the foal.

Great! Thank you very much, I thought to myself. As far as I was concerned the matter was now closed and I began the schooling and breaking programme for Gemma before she became too heavy in foal. I reintroduced her to the saddle with ease and rode out round the lanes. The marvellous potential of my lovely horse really did begin to blossom, all was rosy. She was at full livery at Pages Farm and all I had to do was go and enjoy her, which I did, blissfully unaware things were not at all good at home.

Chapter Seven: Paradise Lost

We had a new sergeant at Mill Hill. One of the first things he wanted to do was take a look at the manor he had been posted to. He asked me to take him out in the van and show him the sights. "We'll start with going to Hendon for a cup of tea" he said, "that is the other outriding station to Sierra Whiskey, isn't it?" I replied to the affirmative.

Hendon was a very old traditional station correctly positioned in the centre of the High Street where it could best serve the community for which it was built. There was a very small back yard in which to park our police vehicles heralding the days of little transport other than a horse drawn prison van. We had our cup of tea and met all the boys and girls working there and then I had the unenviable job of reversing the van out of the yard. Skipper insisted on seeing me back but as often happens, if your all-round visibility is good then the addition of someone instructing you can often be a distraction. The back gates were narrow and the van wide, there was barely a fag paper to spare on either side and predictably I clipped the offside wing mirror and broke the glass.

"Deary me," said Skipper, "this is a pretty pickle we are in, and it's Sunday afternoon, are there any car spares shops open on this manor?"

"No, don't think so, Sarg."

"Mmmm. OK, let's head back to Mill Hill and think about this – no, we won't - isn't there a prisoners' property vehicle pound down at West Hendon?"

"I believe so."

"Right, that's it, while I make myself known and meet the guys and dolls there, you can have a poke around and see if you can find a wing mirror to match."

"Really? OK if you think that's best."

I looked around the impounded vehicles but couldn't find anything matching the Sherpa, not even close, and I must confess I was not sorry. When my Skipper finally surfaced he came with a plan B.

"I know somewhere on Kentish Town's patch where there is a

car spares shop open all day on Sundays. We'll go there." He announced as if it was just round the corner but this was no small joy ride.

Sure enough though, true to his word, there was a shop open for business with a big basket of bargain wing mirrors out on the pavement, £1.50 each. I found the right size, paid my money and we returned post haste back to Mill Hill where I was given the task of replacing the broken mirror. It was not a difficult job, but having got the new glass into its housing it became apparent this was not wing mirror glass. It was not convex, it was just flat like a compact mirror, and the image you saw was a blur. Because it was on the driver's side the mirror was a mere foot or two from the driver's eye level and it shouted 'wrong mirror'. I'll get found out in no time I thought, the night duty will know it's down to me for sure, so I did the only thing I could possibly do under the circumstances - I swopped it with the nearside mirror. Simple.

***

Christmas was upon us sooner than you would think and Maggie invited Hugh and me to her house for supper on Boxing Day. We had a nice enough evening but I was fiercely aware that Hugh was not with me, not with me in the sense that if I tried conversation with him he avoided it. He interacted with Maggie, Peter and Gina in his usual animated way but cut me dead whenever I presumed to join in. My head was spinning with bewilderment; I did not know what I had done.

I turned my attention to a bottle of wine, which looked in need of company. Peter's car was blocking our exit and he suggested we sort the cars out before it got too late so Hugh and I were good to go when the time came. Hugh tossed the keys to me, "I'm in no fit state," I protested. He ignored me and turned back to his conversation with the girls who seemed enthralled with his tales of amusement. Going out to move the cars with Peter, I felt weary, I felt bored, and I felt just a bit tiddly. I hit the gatepost trying to reverse out and put a dent in the nearside wing. Hugh was not best pleased. If he didn't have a reason to treat me with disdain before, he had one now. "Bloody Christmases! Bah Humbug!"

***

Hugh had always been a wonderful husband, funny, charismatic, caring. He liked cooking, which I didn't and in every sense he was the man of my dreams. I considered myself very fortunate to have him as my partner in life but on 2nd January 1985 he left me, for good.

I was devastated, bewildered, angry, and I mustered all the pride I could when he told me on the phone a few days later, that he was not coming back. "Bloody right you're not" I blurted out, while inwardly my heart was breaking.

Hugh did not come back and there were many demands now being made. Maggie had helped him move out all his belongings, which included our double bed and the car.

I could not be there at the house when he set about clearing out his belongings. As it happened, I had been approached by my friends at Mote End Farm to consider standing for election as District Commissioner for the Pony Club. So I attended their meeting without saying a word about my husband leaving me. I pretended I was a woman with social standing and nothing was wrong with my world. I was not elected. It was probably just as well.

Then there followed more gutty divorce stuff. I bled, not the skin and bones that make my mortal shape but the abstract part of me, my inner being, I felt like I was an open wound and the treachery had made me raw with despair. My colleagues at West Hendon and Mill Hill were all very kind to me. My good friend Geoff, now the Scenes of Crime Officer at Wealdstone had always been a good friend too. A calming 'father figure' of a man whom I had known from the days when I worked at the Graphics Department at Hendon Training School. In those days he had been an instructor at Hendon Driving School. He rang me as soon as he heard to ask how I was.

"It's so stupid of him," Geoff had said, "and all over a little slut like that."

I froze; it never occurred to me there was another woman. "Who would want him?" I exploded!

"Oh I'm so sorry, Sue," Geoff was horror struck, "Didn't you know?"

"Who is she, Geoff?" The line went silent "Who is she?" I raised my voice. "Geoff tell me!"

"Um, I thought you would know."

"Who is she, tell me NOW!" I was on the war path. Properly cornered Geoff told me.

"The bike from Harrow?" I exclaimed. "Stupid bastard, everyone has been through her."

"I know, Sue. We've all tried to tell him."

"It's not your fault, Geoff," I said calmly as I could "Don't worry about me, I can handle this. It is what it is, I'll cope, I always do." - - - - - I didn't.

I first met Geoff in the days when he instructed the Overseas Motorcycle Course. He was a very funny man. He had me in stitches most of the time but he was a bit of a renegade. He taught himself a smattering of several languages thinking it a good policy to impress the recruits from round the globe who came seeking the expertise of our world famous Driving School. There was one occasion when we had some such students. Their English was limited, and one of them asked Geoff how they should address the Chief Superintendent. What was the correct procedure? Geoff explained the rudiments of protocol in such a situation and when the opportunity presented itself, during a 'welcome to our foreign visitors' reception, the Officer approached our Chief Superintendent, stood to attention clicking his heels together, he executed a superb salute saying those immortal words:

"Hello Sailor."

The entire room collapsed in laughter. This sort of prank had Geoff's signature written all over it.

He used to put reports in for consideration, one was requesting that he be spared the purgatory of taking any annual leave. "Nothing ever happens at home," he argued, "This is where it's at, work, this is where the action is." He is the only policeman I know who was ordered, on pain of disciplinary proceedings, to take his annual leave. He even sent a report up to the Commissioner's office suggesting that serving officers should receive more annual leave when they first joined the job and this should decrease with service. The suggestion was never implemented.

He told me more than once that I was to fill my life with adventures, "Life is not worth living if you don't have adventures, even if they do make you late for tea," he had said. I have always done my best to follow this advice.

Geoff made me laugh at a time when I had little to laugh about, as did many other of my colleagues, and in the aftermath of Christmas and New Year came the Police Pantomime. Michael, the man of the axe disarming fame suggested I take part in the Christmas Panto, which was currently taking place at Bushey Sports Centre. I was already installed as the scenery painter, and he suggested I go with him and get more involved as one of the warm-up clowns, they found me a costume and up onto the stage I went. We all did our own make up and not without a little irony, I painted a large teardrop on my right cheek. Behind the mask I pretended everything was okay, and actually I did make quite a go of it, I enjoyed being a clown. I am an infernal 'show-off' anyway so here was a chance to be exactly that and the escapism was good for me. I was sorry when the pantomime season finished.

***

I felt myself spiralling down into the abyss. Hugh's sister Pat said I needed a holiday and she organised a week in Tenerife for the two of us. Pat was an airline hostess for British Airways and this was only the second time I had flown. She arranged for us to go into the cockpit during the flight. It really was the most amazing experience, but I was in a daze. I tried my hardest to make the best of it and not let my personal feeling spoil a lovely holiday, but I was in the shadow of a wrecked life which was hanging over me like a cancer.

When we got back I stayed one night with Pat but I was desperate to get home. I had to see if Hugh had come back. I had to get back to what I knew and heal my wounds. I wanted to see Ruth and Phillip, I wanted to cuddle up to Sylvester and wanted to see Gemma. But once back at home, on my own, I fell into a bottomless pit, a dark hovel of a place where demons of the past and present gave me no peace. I would stand for ages under the shower hoping the hot water would wash away the pain, but it seemed nothing I could do would take it all away. The feeling of loss, and the memories of the heart-breaking days of my first marriage, all mixed together, they were self-winding in my head, and sometimes I felt like a coiled spring. My insides were in an emotional knot constantly tightening and I felt like an open wound prone to bleeding if metaphorically prodded.

If I had one salvation, it was Gemma, she was my 'sanity saver,' and thank God, I had not taken my father's advice.

***

I clawed my way ahead to keep it all together and thankfully the adventures at work were a great distraction. A young lady with her little boy hailed my panda to pull over and she complained to me that his push bike had been stolen and what's more, she knew where it was. She said it had been taken by some children from the rougher part of Graham Park Estate. Was there any part of the Graham Park Estate that was not rough I wondered. I went to investigate and sure enough there was a bicycle matching the description being ridden about by a lad who looked as if he was too small for the size of it. There were other boys playing about with him and I recognised young Shane who was about six years old. He had lived next door to me until about two years ago and I spoke to him in my usual friendly way asking him who was on the bike. He laughed at me saying, "That's my bruvver, Freddie, you don't recognise im do ya."

"So it is, Shane, I'll have to have a word with him, I don't think the bike is his."

Freddie looked up in my direction spun the pedal cycle and sped off on it as fast as he could. I jumped in the panda and gave chase. Being joined by another panda meant we could cut him off and he was soon captured. My way of dealing with this would have been to give him a talking to, return him to his mother, Doreen, and restore the bike to the owner. But with the other officers present, that was not going to happen and Freddie was soon bundled into the back of the other panda and taken to West Hendon. I was keen to follow them quickly and as Shane had come hurtling round the corner to catch us up, I said to him: "Shane, go straight home and tell your mum we have Freddie down at the station and could she come down; off you go, there's a good man," and he galloped off.

Down at West Hendon I went into the charge room to see how things were ticking along. Freddie was not co-operating at all and the sergeant was getting exasperated. I thought I had better tell the sergeant a few facts. "You do realise he is only about nine years old, don't you?" I told him.

At that moment I heard one almighty commotion going on in the front office. I opened the charge room door and peered across the space to see Freddie's mother, Doreen, she was going ballistic. "You fucking filff are all the same, arrestin' my Freddie an' sending my Shane, to tell me. 'E's only seven. Ouws 'e spoce to know" she ranted on. "I wanna see my boy, I wanna see 'im now, I know my rights and you bastards are goin' to let 'im come 'ome wiv me. Fucking coppers 'e's only nine. I know 'is rights and you lot are a load o' scum..."

Doreen then spotted me in the doorway. "SOO!!" She shouted "Fank gaud you're ere! I'll get some fucking sense now, these bastards av arrested my Freddie. Fuck knows why, somink about a bike, an' I wanna see im now, poor little kid, 'ee's only nine. 'E's never been in trouble, 'e's a good kid, whatever it is they say e's done, 'e in't done nuffin, I know my Freddie, Where 'av they got him 'id Soo?"

Police, Ponies & Husbands in-between

"Doreen, I'm so sorry, it was me, I brought him in, he stole a push bike, or, he was riding on it anyway. I caught him red handed, Doreen."

"The little bastard, where is 'e, I'll show im fucking getting into trouble again, that kid's been nuttin' but trouble from the day 'e was bored, where is 'e, Soo?"

"Follow me", I told her, "you can come through here," and I lifted the hatch in the front desk. She grabbed Shane's hand, I hadn't seen him hiding behind the tall front office counter, and they followed me into the charge-room.

"FREDDIE!! You fucking bastard, dragging me dan 'ere when I got betta fings to do," and Doreen landed one across the back of his head with the flat of her hand, knocking him off the bench onto the floor. "Get up you little fucker," and she caught hold of the back of his collar and hauled him back up. "You wait till I gets you home, being a load o' trouble to these nice policemen."

The charge sergeant looked from me to Doreen and back again.

"I think they can go home," he said, "You can give them a lift Sue, just get them out of here."

"OK Sarge, c'mon Doreen, Freddie, Shane, I'll take you home."

Back to Graham Park Estate we all sat down to a nice cup of tea and a chat about old times. I steered clear of talking about her ex-partner, Ozzy, and the occasion when Shane knocked on my front door one day and asked if his 'Dad' could borrow a hacksaw.

"Sorry Shane, I haven't got one." I lied.

A couple of days later I was chewing the fat with George, the rag and bone man who lived across the road and he told me he had lent them a hacksaw and he was cross because they had broken the blade. "There you go George," I had said, "You won't do that again in a hurry."

Some weeks later, George showed me the local newspaper, "Look at this Sue, did you know about this, you're the law," he said thumbing through the pages. There was a report from a recent court hearing, saying Ozzy had been had up in front of the beak for attempting to rob a post office with a sawn-off shot-gun, earning him a spell in the clink. "Do you remember that hacksaw I told you about?" George reminded me.

"For goodness sake! What are folks like," I said, "It's one thing borrowing the where-with-all to doctor the shotgun needed for the robbery, quite another trying to borrow it from the copper who lives next door."

"I thought I hadn't seen him for a bit," George laughed.

Chapter Eight: Sink or Swim

Interestingly, I didn't really blame Hugh. I blamed her, God knows, I blamed her. "What did she do to get him?" I asked Geoff.

"Trip him up and throw herself underneath before he hit the ground I expect!" He replied with his usual 'off the cuff' humour.

I continued to spiral though. Holding it all together as best I could and caring for Gemma, but one of the problems I had with visiting her at Pages Farm was that Hugh was still very good friends with Maggie. I bumped into him just the once, it was an awkward moment and I didn't want to bump into him again. This made me very wary about visiting Gemma.

There was nothing else for it, I concluded, I would have to move her yet again. I had been spending a great deal of time at Bricket Wood and Ronni had room for her so it was the obvious choice. Ronni had an outdoor manège, and really fabulous hacking. I could just about afford part-livery for her as the distance was prohibitive for DIY, but I had no doubt I would be happy there with people I knew, including Lynette who was a regular visitor.

***

There were occasions when a little smile would creep up on me. I was in at Mill Hill for a tea break. Tom, the garage man was sitting on the edge of one of the desks, swinging his legs and downing the dregs from his mug, when he mused absently; "There's something wrong with the near side mirror of that van, I can't make it out?"

My ears began to flap as I spat out a mouthful of tea back into the mug.

"I can't put my finger on it but it's not right, the reflection is a blur." Everyone looked bewildered and equally dumbfounded. "I think," Tom continued, "someone has hit that mirror on something, and they have hit it so fast, they have bent the glass without breaking it. That's what I think."

I said nowt.

***

Police, Ponies & Husbands in-between

I was still marking saddlery and someone kind made me a lovely 'table high' wooden saddle horse with a flat top so I could mark both saddles and bridles more easily. I designed a device (effectively an anvil) for stamping postcodes in two sections instead of having to use the dyes individually. I had a precision company make one for me and I submitted the idea to New Scotland Yard and received £100 reward for the idea. With the help of the Graphics Department at Hendon I made 4 x A1 rigid posters to display the message for my Crime Prevention show stand. I could not resist including a photograph of Hugh holding a young foal by the chin and staring into its face. I gave it the only caption I thought appropriate: 'You can't tell them to "never go with strangers." But the irony was lost on anyone else.

I wrote several verses, which the Graphics Department artists illustrated for me and the Publicity Department at New Scotland Yard had printed on to card. They read as follows:

> Your yard holds many treasures for those outside the law,
> So my advice to all of you is simply this: 'Secure Before.'
> Is your gate on sturdy hinges that cannot be pulled away?
> Are your padlocks hale and hearty, so when locked they stay that way?
> Is the tack room bricks and mortar? Plus the roof, is that secure?
> And so you don't assist these thieves, don't put 'Tack Room' on the door.
> Can you lock it up with confidence your property will not roam?
> So fit a proven heavy duty lock like your own front door at home.
> Is your saddlery security stamped with all your other stores?
> And are your horses freeze marked to prove that they are yours.
> With 'marked property' stickers on the gate no thief would want to snatch it.
> And on the horsebox, windows, doors, the cat if you can catch it!
> Are you friendly with your neighbours, do they understand your fear?
> Would they call the police if needed, a drink would keep them sweet m'dear?
> When darkness envelopes your yard and no-one is in sight,
> You could hang a lamp and keep it lit, they won't steal in the light.
> And so if you 'Secure Before' this crime wave can be halted,
> There's no point shutting the stable door, after the horse has bolted.

***

The phone rang one morning early. It was Ronni. "Um, it's Ronni. I've rung about Gemma – she's slipped the foal. I'm sorry, can you get out here?"

I left immediately. Gemma seemed in a state of depression sniffing the pretty dead foal every so often. "She thinks it will get up in a minute," said Ronni. It was perfect, still encased in its birth sack, dark bay and a star like Gemma's. I felt the life had been sucked out of me as well, I felt her loss."

"Is nothing going to go right with me?" I whimpered.

"I'll get a spade," said Roger, and he disappeared off to do the manly thing of digging a hole.

"I've called the vet like you asked me to," said Ronni, "It's not a bad idea, she probably wants checking over."

"Better leave the foal where it is until he comes" Roger suggested.

"Oh Roger; isn't it so sad," I cried.

"You can't have livestock without having dead stock," he said philosophically, "but, yes, it is very sad."

Ronni returned from the feed room with a warm bran mash for Gemma, "We can remove the foal from the stable at least, she won't notice if we do it while she is eating this."

The vet came and gave Gemma a jab to help dry her milk up, saying that the foal looked to be full term and if the sack failed to rupture then it would have just drowned. He said "It couldn't be helped, even if you stay up all night with a mare, they are so canny, they have their foals while the groom nips off for 2 minutes to visit the loo or get a cup of coffee."

When he had gone, and when the foal had been buried, Ronni and I took a break and sitting down with our mugs of coffee we reflected on the morning's work. Ronni got out a packet of cigarettes and lit one up. "Here" she said, "this might help." I took one and lit it from hers. It's not the worst thing I have ever done, but it was a stupid thing to do. I had not smoked since before I married Hugh. "I'd rather you didn't smoke," he had said to me one day when we were courting, and I packed it in, just like that, overnight. I could do the same again any time, no bother. Anyway, just one little fag won't hurt, would it?

"Right," said Ronni the next day, "shoes on for Gemma, I think. Let's get this horse out and working, it's high time she was a riding horse, you have some lost time to make up, and the farrier is here tomorrow. Does her saddle still fit her?" I fetched it the next day and no, it didn't, but Ronni had one that did and she kindly lent it to me until I could get sorted.

It was truly wonderful riding Gemma, she was great in company but rather nappy on her own so we did have a few managerial discussions but generally she was great. I made good use of the manége and Charmian was always on hand to offer advice and answer my endless questions. Things were beginning to go well.

***

There was always an adventure to be had when I was out driving a Panda car. It's obvious really, as like any other policeman I was out looking for trouble, it's what we do. One wet Wednesday afternoon I was with a fellow home beat officer, Ian, and neither of us were expecting much action that day. When I say it was wet, I do mean wet, it was hammering down and had been for some hours. Drainage systems were beginning to struggle and rapids of water were tumbling along the gutters looking for the next drain. Wherever it was level ground the water was gathering into small lakes. One of these lakes was at the roundabout at the end of Mill Hill Broadway having gathered excess water from the hill up to Apex Corner. The water was causing no small flood on the nearside and getting ever deeper by the minute, so much so in fact the traffic was inching its way in single file in the outside lane as they entered the island.

Now, I have always been a positive driver and I have been several times on the Driving School skidpan, thanks to Geoff, but there is a small matter of failing to appreciate consequences and downright impatience. We were not in a hurry, I don't know why I could not wait in line with the rest of the traffic but for reasons I can only guess at, I didn't. "What a bunch of pussies," I remarked as I headed for the nearside of the queue - at speed. I noticed Ian's grip on the seat of his chair tighten and into the pond we went with one hell of a splash.

SPLASH!!

It was impressive. Not so impressive was the fact that the Panda ground to an almost immediate halt with hot steam billowing out from under the bonnet. "Bugger," I said. "OK, Ian, out you get, give us a push."

"I'm not getting out" he said haughtily.

"What? You have to."

"No I don't."

"But I have to steer."

"I don't care, you got us in here, you can get us out," and he grinned at me the cheeky blighter.

I kicked off my shoes, I've always been precious about shoes, and opened the driver's door whereupon water immediately began to tumble over the sill and into the well of the driver's side. With a resigned sigh I very gingerly got out in my stocking feet and began to push the panda out towards dry land while steering at the same time with one hand through the driver's open window. At least it had stopped raining. Ian sat there in the passenger seat waving to the gathering crowd like the queen might have done while sailing down The Mall during a ceremonial. I could have done without folks taking photographs. Traffic Division came and towed the Panda back to West Hendon and the Traffic Sergeant came a few weeks later and rapped my knuckles.

***

The rain played a big part on another occasion I booked out the sergeant's panda, it was a good second choice to the Sherpa van with its main set radio. But I could only have it if the sergeant wasn't on duty and or he didn't want it for himself. It was one such day and I heard a call to Bury Farm where there was a little hatchback being driven at speed up and down the muddy track towards the A41. Most likely they were just joy riders I thought, volunteering to take a look. The information was half an hour or so old so there was not much chance of any action, but you never know. It was a very wet bank holiday Monday following the Easter weekend and so we were thin on the ground, police officer wise. It was always good to work on a bank holiday. We got paid double time, and if a bank holiday was your day off, and it was cancelled with less than 8 days' notice, you got double bubble and another day off in lieu. But that did not happen very often.

There were a couple of interesting features along the muddy track, a large bomb crater was one of them but also at the end of the track there were the brick archway remnants of a half-built underground. If it hadn't been interrupted by World War II the Northern Line would have gone on to Borehamwood.

When I arrived at the bomb crater, I found a blue car upside down with the back end sticking up. Everything was quiet, the car looked like it had been there for a little while and I scanned the surrounding fields for fleeing joy riders but saw none. Anyway, the heavens had opened and it was simply bucketing down. Without getting out of the car I did a check on the registration number which confirmed the car was stolen, so I reported the location and I left the area to go back to the station as they were calling all cars in for tea.

At West Hendon they would instigate the call by rattling a spoon in the cup and saying the name or call sign of the station brewing up. In West Hendon's case the call sign was 'Sierra Whiskey.'

At Mill Hill they favoured saying the words to describe the sound that the spoon made. "Ching, ching, Mill Hill" I heard Pip's jolly voice over the radio. The sergeant on duty was catching up with some of his paperwork all day which was why his panda was available. "What was the result of that possible stolen car," he asked me as he was tying up loose ends on the day's log.

"Stolen" I replied.

"Stolen and abandoned, OK, good."

"Stolen, abandoned and upside down in a bomb crater." I said.

"Anyone in it?" he asked, looking up at me.

"Ummm, I don't think so."

"What do you mean, you don't think so. Didn't you look?"

"I didn't actually check, it was upside down, and it was raining, Sarge." It was still raining, as we were speaking, and hammering down onto the roof of our little pre-fab police station with deafening proportions.

"RAINING!" he laughed. "I've heard it all now and mimicking the female voice continued *"I can't get out of the panda car, Sarge, because it's raining!"* The rest of the crew laughed too, mimicking a stupid WPC, me! I saw the joke and held the palms of my hands skyward in a 'what shall I do now' kind of a way.

"You'd better go back up there and check."

"I'm off duty in 20 minutes, Sarge."

"So?"

"It's double bubble." I grinned.

"Get out of here," and he thrust his arm out with his index finger indicating the exit door. I ran for the panda dodging the spots and returned to Bury Farm.

When I arrived back at the bomb crater I was not all surprised to see it had filled with water and all you could see of the car was half of one of the rear wheels poking out of the surface. I reported the fact back to the station on my radio. The rain was beginning to ease up but I still stayed in the car. The sergeant who had sent me had now gone off duty and Sergeant O'Mally was late turn. I explained the history to him and he said he would come out and take a look. There wasn't much to see!

He arrived over the brow of the hill and as he got out of the police car he looked at me accusingly, "So that's where my panda is." We looked at the hole, now a small pond. "We'll have to call the Underwater Search Unit, and that won't happen in the next half hour. Come on we might as well both go back to the station. I want that car off you anyway, but you're not going home, I want you to stay on duty for the continuity of evidence."

"Thank you, sergeant," this was good news indeed.

The Underwater Search Unit pantechnicon was parked at Lambeth police depot. The Sergeant had to ring Scotland Yard who in turn had to ring the authorised frogmen, who had to leave their homes to be called on duty - with less than 8 days' notice mind you. They then had to go to Lambeth from wherever they lived and collect the vehicle and equipment before travelling across London to Edgware. Sure as hell, it wasn't going to happen within half an hour! When the pantechnicon did finally appear over the brow of the hill the entire late turn were there with me to watch the action.

The underwater crew were all hanging out of the windows shouting as they pulled up, "Thank you, boys,". Even putting on their frogmen outfits didn't wipe the smiles off their faces; I was a very popular little WPC that afternoon. The underwater search was very interesting but revealed that the car was empty of car thieves after all that fuss, but some of us went home that night very happy little bunnies.

The incident didn't cure me of nicking the sergeant's panda if I could get it. I was out and about driving it for the very last time one morning and passing by Colindale Tube station I heard on the radio that there was a shout over on the other side of Graham Park Estate, 'burglary happening now'. Keen to be part of the action I attempted to reverse into a handy driveway so as to effect a speedy turnaround. In my haste I reversed straight into the gatepost denting the bumper. BUGGER!

And I could have done without the good people in the bus queue across the road laughing and pointing. Dismayed that I had dented the sergeant's Panda I didn't answer the shout but took the vehicle to a well-known panel beater to ask for his help in straightening out the bumper before I booked off duty.

The lock-up was locked up so I spent the next 4 hours examining all other lines of enquiry to put right the wrong. In the end I had to put up my hands and confess, owning up to the accident and changing nothing other than the time it happened. Traffic Patrol came and rapped my knuckles, but I wasn't suspended from driving. The Sergeant's Panda was taken out of service because of its mileage and all of Mill Hill mourned its passing because they did not replace it.

Chapter Nine: Joy-riding

I was very happy having Gemma at The Old Forge in Bricket Wood and I got to know some lovely people. Clive was one of these notable figures and he had a number of horses stabled there including a point-to-pointer which Ronni was training for him. One day Ronni told me that she had booked to go on a sponsored charity ride in Windsor Great Park with her young horse, Maybe. Ronni had bought her as a yearling and she was given the name when Roger repeatedly sang 'Maybe it's *big horse* I'm a Londoner' everytime he saw her.

As the day drew nearer, she realised she would not be able to go on the day and she asked me if I wanted to take her place. It would cost me £25 but the rules did say that you could not substitute a name and so she explained I would have to go as Mrs Stubbs. We had all been friends during our teenage years.

"I never thought I would get to be Mrs Stubbs." I smiled cheekily. "That was such a long time ago Cath." Ronni mused.

Police, Ponies & Husbands in-between

We had the most wonderful time Clive and I, and the jumps were not difficult with easy and harder options. Gemma jumped like a young horse, far too high for the fences, but she cleared everything I put her at and her abilities won me a bronze rosette. My right hand rein broke when I was halfway round but she pulled up for me and was as good as gold while I tied a knot in it. The little metal 'billet hook' by the bit had snapped. I could never have seen that coming. Windsor Great Park really was the most wonderful place to ride. The old gnarled trees in the park, the new plantations and the vast stretches of grazed parkland all made the experience a day to remember. We journeyed home tired and happy; I fairly hugged myself with pleasure at having such a wonderful horse.

I rode Gemma everywhere I could think of that was a bit different. One of the other memorable rides we had together was when I crossed over the A405 at the bottom of Lye lane. It was a dual carriageway even then but nothing like the traffic on the road now. We took the bridle path leading over to where they were building the new M25, it was a Sunday and I wanted to check it out. I found a place where we could slip down on to the mud flats of the new carriageways and took in the scene in both directions of the new road. We were obviously on a section that was to become a slip road so we walked westward until we came to the main motorway which was about five times wider. Dumper trucks and construction equipment lay dotted about, abandoned and quiet. If workmen were working anywhere on the motorway that day, they were nowhere to be seen here. The going was firm and there was enough of the flat areas to get up some speed so long as you stuck to the parts of the carriageway not pitted with deep ruts and construction debris. I walked Gemma eastwards as far as some pillars that would become a flyover. I turned her west, "What do you think, Gemma?" I asked her.

"Looks good to me," she replied.

"You'll have to listen to what I say," I warned her.

"You'll have to listen to what I say." She replied getting all jittery.

"Don't cheek your mother, shall we go?" It was an active trot to start with before she broke into a canter and then a gallop - she flew.

With the wind in my face, I blinked against the force to check the safe pathway steering her on. Tears dribbled from the corner of my eyes and across my face with the exhilaration and her speed swept us up the carriageway. It was WONDERFUL!!

The roadway was slightly uphill and when we got as far as the intersection that would become the junction to the M1, I asked her to steady up and she obeyed, finally trotting, and at last a walk. I let her have her head and she blew great snorts of satisfaction on to the London clay beneath her feet. "That was fun," she said.

***

I rode out on Gemma regularly, sometimes with Ronni and sometimes on my own. She was a lovely horse, calm, responsive and willing to please. We had some wonderful adventures together. One day I took a detour away from my usual beaten path, and ventured into 'bandit country.' This was not by accident, I was doing a bit of spying, I just loved the idea of being a sleuth.

The previous week I had been to Borehamwood Police Station to deliver some pantomime tickets to the Detective Chief Superintendent. There was a horsebox parked in the back yard and as curiosity killed the cat I popped along to see the collator and ask him the story behind it all. "It is prisoner's property" he told me, "a burglar among other things, he's out on bail at the moment, lives over Radlett way. I looked at the address.

"I keep a horse in Bricket Wood," I told him, "do you want any information, car registrations, anything like that, I can easily ride past,"

"Good idea, if you don't mind, we are always looking for information, it's what we do."

So, Gemma and I rode down the icy bridle path to the remote farm house. There were lots of cars and I wondered how many registration numbers I could hold in my head when a German Shepherd came at speed out of his kennel towards us.

"EEK"!!! Gemma said, and the dog got right up to us before the chain tightened and held it back, with the dog kicking off as only German Shepherds can, Gemma spun and danced and I struggled to keep us together, she was a young and impressionable horse.

Then the front door opened and out came the man himself. "Caesar! Come 'ere" he looked apologetically at me, "Sorry darlin' e's a good dog, it's wot I keep im for, e's only doin' is job." He

Police, Ponies & Husbands in-between

dragged the dog to a barn and shut it in.

"That's OK," I said breathing a sigh of relief, "I'm glad you came out when you did,"

I rode on immersed in thought, now then, what were those numbers? Um.... GWJ 665? Or was it 656, there was a 34S reg. I searched the files in my brain thinking, it's in there somewhere, bugger, I'll have to come again another day.

***

With the police Metropolitan Police Annual Charity Pantomime to think about there was little room for any other activity. We had the most remarkable man leading the way. He was the producer, the director, the casting secretary and the press officer, and had been for donkey's years. If there ever were short-falls in acting ability you could be sure that he would demonstrate to the rest of the cast how it should be done. He was a perfectionist and the productions were always top notch. I remember one dressing down he gave to Michael once. In exasperation he said to him "If Bruce Forsyth was here, he would be on that stage captivating the audience immediately, he would have their attention without having to be constantly nagged how to do it."

"I'm not Bruce bloody Forsyth," Michael shouted back. "I'm a police officer, and being a police officer is what I do best."

He drove us all mad, even me, who up to then had only painted scenery plus a little clowning around. But if the scenery wasn't right, you could rest assured he would say so. We took the criticism and the flack because we knew the show would be good, we knew we would make a lot of money for charity and we all knew, without exception, it would be fun.

The following year he said he was too busy and so there would be no pantomime. Everyone was really upset and not a little angry with the assumption that if he was unable to lead the way, then the pantomime wouldn't happen. There is no denying that to commit to that responsibility year on year is a massive ask and I was not surprised he wanted a break. But he didn't like it when, true to form I piped up "I'll do it." Having no experience whatsoever, we went ahead with the pantomime anyway, the usual crew, bless their hearts, were happy to support me.

It seemed a travesty to me allowing the potential to raise money for charity to fall by the wayside, but how dare I, nasty little upstart that I was. We made several hundred pounds even though the press reviews were appalling. I'm saying nowt, but we suspected the reviews were all thanks to the loyal journalist friends of the redundant Director, in fact you could almost hear the dictation. But I was hurt, the cast were furious, we'd tried to do the best we could and got kicked in the teeth for our troubles. I had to admit, I am not an entertainer, I thought I was, but I'm not. I'm a police officer, and being a police officer is what I do best.

***

Geoff was right, work is where it's at, that's where all the adventures are if you care to look for them. Taking my crime prevention passions to another level, I heard about a marvellous Metropolitan Mounted Policeman who took an active interest in all things associated with equestrian crime. They called him the 'Gentleman Gypsy', he was an expert in the saddle and a seriously good thief taker. Every Wednesday, he was on duty at Southall Horse Market getting to know the dealers, the auctioneers and the punters, he read the reports of stolen horses and equipment and he inwardly digested the information, acting on it whenever the opportunity presented itself. Unlike many horse sales the Auctioneers paid out on the day for the horses going under the hammer, so it was easy to peddle pretty much anything, legal or otherwise.

This was something I wanted to be part of.

I contacted him and offered my help. I was able to organise my duties so I was free to go to Southall Market almost every Wednesday. I loved it, I mingled with the crowds and the travellers, the dealers and the hawkers, and obviously the horses too. I learnt so much.

"I'll need you to stay with me, Sue," he said as we crossed the Broadway from the police station. "I want to have a word in the earhole of someone, and you just hang by my side, I don't want you to say anything, but while I'm asking awkward questions, you will be a distraction. He'll avoid my questions, I know he will but just let me do the talking, that's all." I thought this was so much fun.

Other officers from the Mounted Branch also came from time to time and I got to know most of them and they welcomed my interest. There was a fish and chip stall where you could buy the most wonderful fish and chips, and jellied eels, with hunks of thick cut white bread plastered with butter, and great big mugs of hot tea. There were the stalls and tethering places where all the horses of all shapes and sizes, stood waiting for their turn with the auctioneer.

***

I filled my days with things that interested me to keep as busy as I could blotting out the loneliness and the demons within that waited in the shadows to haunt me. It was in a gross moment of weakness one day I was reading the personal ads and there was a man advertising for a companion. I was seduced into thinking life could improve for me if I could find someone nice to share my life with, so I plucked up the courage to ring the number.

I discovered that this person was the same person who had rescued Gemma and me from his dog in Bricket Wood. I knew what I was going into, I knew this person was the wrong side of the law but I had my police hat on again and simply couldn't help myself.

I saddled Gemma up and set off down the same bridle path. This time there was no dog and he came out smiling to greet me as I arrived, I put Gemma in a rather dark and dingy stable next to his own black cob and we went into the house where he made me a cup of coffee. He told me all about himself and his plans, a whole pack of lies probably, and I told him all about myself and my plans, a pack of lies most certainly.

"I'll show you round" he said and I followed him from room to room. It was all very charming. As we were climbing upstairs my brain screamed 'NO!' I was ushered into what I took to be the master bedroom. 'NO!' the voice in my head was loud and clear, I shouldn't be in here! How could I be so gullible!'

"It's beautiful," I said hastily, and as I turned towards the door to leave he grabbed my arm and threw me ...

..."Oooooooooofff" the air escaped from my lungs as I landed on the bed. It was a waterbed!!!! The liquid parted as I displaced it and I sank even deeper into the abyss, but as the waves returned the pressure lifted me up onto something of a crest. I saw him launch himself into space aiming to land on me, but the crest of the wave allowed me to roll away from him and as he in turn displaced the water it pushed me back up onto my feet before he could stop me.

"I must go," I said and I rushed out of the room.

"Must you?" he called after me.

"Yes, I must," I replied over my shoulder as I descended the stairs.

"You could stay,"

"No thank you, things to do, people to see." I pulled on my boots.

"I've got more to show you,"

"I bet you have," I muttered, and I was out of the door. Lordy, what a thing to happen when you're wearing jodhpurs, that was a seriously close shave. I left him standing on the doorstep and I rode out of there with a purpose never to return.

While visiting Lynette later in the week I asked Libby if he knew this chap seeing as they were in the same line of business. "Him?" he replied "Yes, I know him, I wouldn't cross the road to piss on him if he was on fire."

***

Clive and I were off to the Lions Club Charity Sponsored Ride at Windsor Great Park for the second year running. This time I could go in my own name but money was tight, I was still on a motor bike and I was only able to go because Clive did not want any money for transportation and my darling colleagues paid the sponsorship money for me to go. "It's a worthy cause," they had said, "and it will do you good." How kind they were and I had the most wonderful time.

I loved Windsor Great Park with the magnificent castle up on the hill in the distance and The Long Walk stretching right back to Snow Hill and King George III's magnificent statue, known as The Copper Horse. The ride always began and ended on Smith's lawn where we could picnic in the sunshine after the ride. These were magical moments.

***

Out of the blue came a letter from the Archdiocese of Westminster.

Hugh's relationship with his bit of slap & tickle had developed further and now we were divorced they intended to marry. She was a Roman Catholic, and she wanted a wedding in the house of the Lord. To do this, Hugh had to have his marriage to me annulled, you know? Pretend it never happened! The letter was asking for confirmation that I had been married before and because the divorce was by civil proceedings, (they always are) the Catholic Church pointed out that they did not recognise this, therefore I was still married. Consequently, using their Canon Law, my marriage to Hugh was not binding and this is how they could nullify it.

What an outrage! I was horrified, I really and truly loved Hugh, and I had signed up for the long-term. I had committed my loyalty to him and only him and he had made me the happiest woman alive and it had been a beautiful and positive experience. Even though it had come to an end and I was managing to move forward, but I still held the memories dear. Now they were trying to say it never happened, I was in shock, grabbing my typewriter I replied with no uncertain words.

Dear Sir,
I have indeed been married before and our divorce was by civil proceedings which you say you do not recognise. However, we had been married in Burnt Oak Registry Office which is also a civil ceremony and so, by your own Canon Law, you would not recognise this either.

Therefore, using your own logic, I would have been a spinster when I married Hugh Gordon-Bennett. We were married in a Baptist Church, which, being of a Christian denomination I assume you would recognise. As my divorce to Hugh Gordon-Bennet was also by civil proceedings wouldn't you agree that I am, in fact, still married to him?

It may interest you to know that he is now living in sin with Little Miss Legg-Over which, as you are aware, is in contravention of the seventh Commandment.
       Yours sincerely
       Susan Scott-Blackhall

My letter, it seemed, cut no ice with the purple robed canons in their ivory tower, and I had a reply thanking me for my time and pointing out that the Catholic Church likes to make the rules up as they go along, - or at least that is, in a nutshell, what they were trying to say. This came as no surprise to me having been educated by the Dominican nuns at Rosary Priory; I do believe that we have much to thank Henry VIII for.

Hugh and that woman were married before the year was out; it was a white wedding.

Chapter Ten: Changing the Rein

It's funny the triggers in life that plant the seed that grows. I took time out from West Hendon to visit Mill Hill one day following the call on the radio that tea was brewing. "Ching ching Sierra Lima," Pip's jolly voice called through the airwaves.

With a steaming mug in my hand I settled myself down in the main office with Tom, Ian, Michael and Pip. I picked up a copy of the twice weekly publication, "Police Orders" which had just arrived through the internal post from New Scotland Yard. Absently I flicked through the 'Persons wanted on warrant' pages and before I got to the current lighting up times on the back page my eyes fell on the 'situations vacant.' More specifically, these were for applications to a variety of police departments. Among those listed, there were volunteers invited to apply for the Mounted Branch.

I read the report out to no one in particular. "It says here that you do not need to have any previous experience with horses, well, that's a plus for me I suppose, but I do wish I had had a go."

"I've never understood why you haven't" replied Pip.

"Too late now, I'm too old"

"Is there an age limit then?" asked Tom.

"I believe so, unofficially," I said, "Thirty I think."

"Huh, that's a laugh," Ian chipped in. "When were you last thirty?"

"Exactly," I replied, "I'm thirty six."

"You could give it a try, you never know," Pip was always encouraging.

"Nah. I'd never get in, there's no point."

"You certainly won't get in if you don't apply," Pip insisted.

I turned the conversation over and over that evening thinking there was some logic in what he said, and maybe I should apply to join. I didn't have to expect too much, all I had to do was just stick in the forms and see what happened. So, on 1st May 1985 I put in my application to join the Metropolitan Police Mounted Branch.

***

A week later I rode Gemma back to Mote End Farm, a total of about 8 miles snaking my way through the byways round the back of Radlett to Letchmore Heath and Elstree village. It was a lovely ride; the dappled sunlight on the road was beautiful coming through the trees yet to fill the canopy of shade because the lime green leaves were not quite fully open. We took a shortcut through to Edgwarebury Farm where we stopped to take tea with Maggie and Clive. Gemma box-walked for most of the time while we were there. "You should have been resting," I told her, "we are only half way."

"That's easy for you to say," she replied indignantly. "Are we going back to Bricket Wood now?"

"Certainly not," I said, "We are going back to Mote End."

"Bums," she replied.

We slipped down through the quiet residential streets of Mill Hill and finally reached our destination after a relatively uneventful journey. Mote End Farm was like home to me and I was pleased to have her stabled near by.

***

Having ruminated on my application over the weekend, I decided it was at least worth giving it my best shot. So I visited the police stables at West Hendon to pick the Sergeant's brains. He strongly advised me to get in touch with Imber Court, the training establishment for both officers and horses. "Go and make yourself known. Show an active interest," he told me, "let them meet you, let them see your enthusiasm." I thought this was sound advice so when I was back in the Home Beat office, I dialed the number for Imber Court. The dashing Sergeant Forester answered, an officer I had previously met at Southall Market.

"Oh, good morning, can I speak to the officer in charge please?"

"You're speaking to him, what can I do for you?"

"I have put in an application to join the branch and wanted some advice on how to pursue this." I explained.

"Sorry, you are asking the wrong person, you have come through to the patrol section, You need to speak to Inspector Walker, I'll transfer you."

"Hang on," I interrupted, "did you say you were Sergeant Chris Forester?"

"Yes, who am I speaking to?"

"Sorry, I should have introduced myself, it's Susan Blackhall, um, we have met before at Southall."

"Sue, yes I remember you, I had no idea you wanted to join us?" and he suggested I visit Imber Court and he would make sure I met all the right people. "I think all the applications are in now and our clerk is sorting through them at the moment. I'll take a look at the progress for you and let you know."

Chris put the phone down and without further pre-amble he went straight over to the office. "Are those the applications for the new intake you have there?" He asked the clerk.

"Yes, a good number this time." he replied without looking up. He was reading through the application reports putting some on a higgledy pile to the right, these were the 'maybes', and some on a pile to his left, they were the possibilities, but most were in the waste paper bin which was on the brink of overflowing.

Chris picked up the first pile, and looked through it, straightened up the edges and put it down. He picked up the second pile, looked through it, tidied the stack and put it back down. "Have you had an application from a WPC Scott-Blackhall?"

The clerk looked up and considered the question. "Oh yes, it's in the bin."

"Oh? Why's that then?"

"Too old," he replied. "Too old by a long way." Chris picked up the bin and sifted through it, taking my screwed-up application, he flattened it on the desk and put it on the pile of possibilities. "She's worth taking a second look," he said.

"Whatever you say Sarge," he replied with no small degree of surprise.

***

I was collecting some bags of horse food for Gemma from Bury Farm at the weekend and Maggie told me they had heard of a pony that had been stolen from a field in Elstree village the day before. This was not a time for delay, so the following day I began my enquires early in the morning, even though I was not due to start until the afternoon. Settling in the home beat office I first rang Borehamwood and got the owner's details Then I rang the owner who gave me all the information I required including a description of the pony, it was called Fudge. Being a Wednesday and the day of Southall Market, I sent all the details to the Collator at Southall and the Mounted Branch at Hammersmith before heading there myself on my little Honda 90, arriving at 11am. There was no sign of a pony matching Fudge's description but I did see some of the travellers I knew from a council site not far away from where the pony lived.

I had to leave at 1.30pm and arrived at West Hendon in time for my eight hour shift at 2pm. Having cleared my desk of things outstanding I booked out a Panda and headed north to the very edge of the Met where I visited the petrol station. Knowing the garage was open till late I thought there might be an outside chance the pony had been seen by one of their staff.

The son of the garage owner told me he had been at work that night, "As you know we close at midnight, and just before we shut up I did see some kids from the site, they were riding what looked like a small pony. I was wandering round checking stuff, I didn't take much notice of them." I thanked him thinking 'that's enough for me.'

I had arranged to meet the owner at their field, so I couldn't waste time. She and her friend were there when I arrived, I knew them both but they did not appear to recognise me. The owner had given me and Lynette riding lessons at one time and her friend, Mrs Morris I knew from the Woodcock Farm days. In fact, the last time we had spoken was with threats and unkind words, so I did not enlighten them as to my identity.

She told me that at 9pm on Monday night she had received a phone call to say her ponies were loose on the road. She had found Dazzler grazing by the roadside but there was no sign of Fudge. The fence had been cut and her four-year old daughter was inconsolable. I told them there was a glimmer of hope and we would have to see what happened later. When I returned to West Hendon there was a message waiting for me from Southall to say that a trader from the nearby council site was currently in custody at Ealing Police station ready to go before the Magistrate's in the morning. First thing the following day I rang the Mounted Branch at Great Scotland Yard and asked one of the Southall boys if he was able to meet me at Ealing to interview this traveller. It's always better with two and he said he could make it, thanks to the kindness of his Sergeant.

Once we were down in the Police cells we told him that we knew he could help us and failure to do so would bring the entire weight of the Metropolitan Police down on his outfit like the Monty Python foot - or words to that effect. We couldn't, but he didn't know that. He said he would ask around and ring me by the following day. At 8.30am on Friday morning his expected phone call came and so in full police uniform, driving a panda car, I went - on my own to the council site. There had not been a policeman in there since 1979 and on the previous occasion it had resulted in one humdinger of a punch up labelling the area as a 'no go' for the police. But that was Wealdstone Police Station - what do they know!!

"If I'm not back in a couple of hours," I told my Sergeant, "send in the posse." I was just a little apprehensive.

It is quite an intimidating thing really, to drive into a traveller site, especially if you are in a police car, and you are alone. Caravan doors opened as I opened mine and burly men silently stepped out and stood watching me. They were menacing, and I began to question the wisdom of my actions, 'what the Hell am I doing here?' I thought to myself. Some of them, with folded arms, extruding testosterone, spoke much with their eyes both in my direction and to each other. I posed no threat, I thought. What can I do, a little girl like me, all on my own. I was about to ask for the whereabouts of the man I was looking for, when one of them spoke.

"What do you want with us, Misses?" he asked approaching me all thick biceps and string vest.

"Hold your tongue," came a sharp retort and the man I was looking for appeared from his van, "she's 'ere to see me and the boys. It's OK."

"Arh, thank you for ringing me," I greeted him.

"Lo Missis, I'll show yoos what we have found," and I followed him to a ship's container. "It may be yours, it may not." He said opening an unbelievably heavy doorway he revealed Fudge looking bewildered and forlorn with a couple of other miserable specimens that passed as ponies. "My boys found him in Bushey" he continued. "We'd lost three of our own and we was lookin' for 'em."

"Yes," I said, "that could be the pony we're looking for."
"Can you deliver him back to his owner for us, please?" I asked.
"Yus, Missis," he said.
"How did it go yesterday at Ealing?" I asked
"I got a fine Missis, bugh nuttin' I can't pay."
"That's the way of the world, I'm afraid," I said philosophically.

Smiling at me in a most friendly fashion he said. "If yoos ever wants to call in when yoos passing by, my van door is open."

"Thank you, I might take you up on that."

We delivered Fudge back and it was a thoroughly happy ending. The ladies would like to have seen an arrest, but hey - what's more important? I got Fudge back safely.

Reunited

TIIER again: Natasha and her friend Fudge, after the anxious days. Photo: B

I did go back to the council site, shortly afterwards and a couple of times again later. I enjoyed a hot cup of tea with the family and even arranged a doctor's visit for Granny who was unwell on one occasion. She was a lively soul, she told me some stories from her traveller life and I would retell them now but I can honestly say I did not understand a single word except that the tale was interspersed with Says I and Says Ee. I can only hope I laughed in all the right places!

***

I could not stop thinking about my application for the Mounted Branch and ambling back from the field having just turned Gemma out, I dreamt idly of what my life would be like if I was accepted. I dreamt of Changing the Guard at Buckingham Palace, talking to enthusiastic children clustered round the stall with a police horse in it and riding bravely into a violent crowd of football hooligans to clear the Queen's highway. The air was full of escaping think bubbles. "I'll have to be fit," I thought to myself, "fitter than I am now and I'll have to give up smoking, yes, that's a must, if I am accepted there will not be much time." I ambled onward. "I'd better start soon! I ruminated on the whole scenario and concluded that there was no time like the present," and I broke into a brisk trot. Being in jodhpurs and top boots is not the best idea and given that the ground was undulating, and I am unbelievably clumsy, I tripped, falling arms first into the gravel. Gosh, my hand did hurt and I really did not want to report sick but the following day when a thick yellow line had travelled half-way up my arm I decided it was time to visit the doctor.

Antibiotics and a magnesium sulphate poultice on the fingers worked wonders, which is just as well because the following day I received the invitation to have an initial riding test at Hyde Park with a Chief Inspector Petter. I had less than the week and I was still off sick but I managed to persuade the doctor to issue me with a certificate of fitness so I could keep the appointment.

My mother was in Stanmore Orthopaedic Hospital at the time having a knee replacement. "Can I borrow your car please, Mum?" I asked her as I was still on a motorbike, and I would have to travel in riding gear.

She protested, "I'm not sure, Sue."

"Why ever not, pray."

"Well, I've lent my car to both of your sisters and they have both had accidents in it."

"That's stupid," I argued. "I'm the only daughter to drive professionally and I'm being penalised for the mistakes of my sisters. It's not fair."

"What do you mean 'drive professionally'? Mother questioned me.

"I drive a bloody police car mother," I insisted, "How professional do you want it to get?"

"Oh alright" said my Mother. So I borrowed my Mother's car to go to Hyde Park.

In Kilburn High Road a large lorry reversed into the side of me!! I was devastated. All mounted interviews and riding tests drained away from my imagination and I felt I would not even get to Hyde Park, let alone on time. Anyway, how was I going to tell Mother? Disproving the theory that you can never find a policeman when you want one, I spied a disgustingly spotty youth in a uniform on the other side of the road. I exchanged details with the lorry driver and asked the officer to contact West Hampstead and ask them to ring ahead to Hyde Park and tell Chief Inspector Petter I would be late. I was, in fact, still ten minutes early!

I took the test riding round in circles showing the Chief Inspector what I could do. He was a kindly man and not at all the gruff individual I expected him to be. The horse was a bit stiff compared to my lovely Gemma, but he was nice enough. Then I was asked to perform a half pass, which is a dressage movement whereby the horse moves at 45 degrees sideways in the direction he is facing. I had never done this before but I knew the aids and my horse performed the movement beautifully, well, he went sideways at least. All that crowd control I suppose, it pays off if the horse knows his job. I was told there and then that I would be recommended for a further interview which put me on cloud nine. But every silver lining has a cloud and I returned home dreading the altercation with my darling, and long suffering mother. She was remarkably understanding and the insurance company for the lorry paid for the repairs. Thank the Lord.

***

Out of the blue Chief Inspector Walker from Imber Court rang to invite me to attend the main interview and riding test on Monday 24th. I mulled over the plans I would have to make for Gemma, Sylvester and that rabbit, Lé roi. So this was it, make or break! I held my breath; it was really scary.

Then I was off to Imber Court early next morning, it was now all down to me. I rode as well as I ever could and the interview was okay, I think, but they were not giving anything away. There were some nice hopeful ladies there with me and all embarrassingly much younger than I was. Oh well, I would just have to wait and see.

    I had made several lines of enquiry with regard to Gemma hoping to loan her out, and finally a nice young lady came forward, who worked for Ronni in Bricket Wood and she had always shown an interest in Gemma. I would still pay for her food, forage and rent if she could keep Gemma shod and in work and look after her daily needs. Sylvester would have to come with me even though they had stipulated 'no pets allowed,' what is the point of rules if they can't be broken, I thought. A friend of mine said he could look after the rabbit and my children could still come and stay with me as I would be allowed home every other weekend. So, just in case, we were all set.

***

The following Saturday, I retired to bed early leaving Phillip watching a film. At 10.45pm, the phone rang and the Chief Superintendent told Phillip to let me know in the morning that I had been accepted for the Branch and I was to report for my six months basic riding course at Imber Court on 15th July. Well! Who'd have thought it?

Chapter Eleven: Game On

The last day I was to serve as a Home Beat Officer at West Hendon was a week before my starting date of the basic equitation course of six months training for the Metropolitan Police Mounted Branch. I spent the day happily enough clearing my locker and making the tea, I even trotted across the yard to the stables and had a cuppa with the late turn shift. They featured heavily in my thoughts later that evening while I was sitting in the rabbit hutch of an office where the home beat officers conduct their affairs. It was all quite unexpected really, with only 35 minutes left of my time at West Hendon one of the officers came bouncing into the office with the news that one of the police horses was loose and causing havoc. "Do you think we should investigate." he said.

"Is anyone down there sorting him out?" I replied.

The Station Sergeant from the front office has gone to the stables."

"Oh for goodness sake, what does he know?" I said. "Come on, we'd better go down."

We entered the stables, the Mounted Branch stables, where cobwebs were kept swept, windows cleaned and floors washed to a standard never seen in any private yard that I knew of. There was mayhem. The horse, General, had rattled his door open and in his keenness to pinch all the hay in the stalls of the other horses, bedding and horse poo had been scattered hither and thither. A new bale waiting to be used had been broken open and a box of cabbage leaf treats had been strewn everywhere leaving splinters of wood and slippery leaves across the passage.

General was still loose and the Sergeant and other colleagues were drawing straws as to who should catch him and put him back. I grabbed a head collar and I put it on the big grey horse. Putting him back into his stable I asked the Sergeant if he intended to make a report. I shut the door and added a knot of string to make sure he stayed there. The skipper wasn't sure, but I suggested that as there was no real damage and there did not appear to be any injuries then probably not, and he could leave the clearing up to me.

I was just finishing off and wondering if my sweeping technique would come up to speed in Surrey, when one of my colleagues happened by arriving for night duty. He was full of congratulations to me for transferring to 'The Branch,' and said he imagined that I was well pleased with leaving West Hendon. "I bet you are glad to be out of this shit hole?" he said rhetorically.

I looked at my surroundings, I looked at the broom, I looked at what I was sweeping and I looked back up at him. "Is that a serious question?" I returned the rhetoric.

***

I made the most of Gemma the week before handing her over to her new carer and I was also able to have Ruth and Phillip for a couple of days and a bit of quality time with them.

Imber Court was steeped in history as well as being a fascinating place visually. An archway led to the remount stables, the patrol stables and the school stables. There was a prefabricated office building, a small indoor school, the section house, classroom and a rather nice little museum. There was also the largest indoor school I have ever encountered. It was simply huge! There was an overspill for school horses in the temporary loose boxes past the garages used for storage, and several round pens, a flight of steps for training and an electric horse walker and two lunging arenas. There were the rugby pitches, and football pitches, the pavilions and the cricket pitch with its own little club house. On the Esher side of the river, which we had to wade through to reach the 40 acres of open land with a cross-country course and paddocks for horses at rest, plus another rugby/football pitch.

I entered the establishment through the 'ranch style' white gates the evening before the first day of my six months training. At last I had a car and I drove up to the section house at the end of the drive. Falling up the uncarpeted stairs I cracked my knees and this made me realise that walking on air did not make me any less accident prone. I had with me all I would need for my stay including one large black and white cat which I smuggled up to the top floor where I was billeted along with the other girls.

I was the first to arrive and chose one of the two bedrooms. It was sparsely furnished, no pictures on the walls and a ceiling covered in midges.

I got out a framed picture from my suitcase of Ruth and Phillip and set it by my bed. I got out a picture of Gemma and put it on the window sill. I fed Sylvester and settled him in with his own bed and some of his favourite things and wrote a note to put on the door asking the other girls to please keep the door shut so he could not escape. Back downstairs I could hear movement in the house and found other successful young men settling themselves in on the first floor. In the kitchen there was a note on the large centre table:

<u>Welcome girls and boys, tea, sugar, milk for your use.
Love from Brenda.</u>

The first of the other girls arrived, she was all bubbly and full of anticipation. She introduced herself, she cannot have been much impressed with me because she took the other bedroom. Liz was close behind her and elected to share with me. She was a quiet lady, but with an infectious dry sense of humour. A couple of students who lived locally, did not appear on the first evening, but arriving in good time the following morning. The girls were really cool about Sylvester living with us and we agreed to keep him a secret and flat bound for the duration. There was a balcony where he could get some fresh air and I had no doubt he would be just fine.

After those precious initial introductions we ventured across to the bar of the club house where we met some of our other class mates. The same club house where many a rugby victory had been celebrated in those distant days when I shared my life with Hugh.

I slept with difficulty and resolved to go home at the first opportunity to collect my own duvet and pillows. In the morning, all of the new intake were told to gather in the kitchen where we would be introduced to each other and our instructors. There were 16 of us, 12 young men and 4 ladies, twice that of most other intakes. Our two instructors could not have been more different from each other. Sergeant Allister Blamire was tall, dashing and witty, the other instructor was a serious man, an excellent jockey and he took his duties on with great conviction.

I looked around the kitchen at all the other probationers. Liz was being remarkably quiet watching and learning. Maggs was sharing a joke with anyone who fancied joking; and another lady was having a quiet conversation with someone she already knew from her foot duty days. We met Brenda, our house mother and Sergeant Blamire told us what our daily routine would be for the next six months. We were split into two classes, one starting at 7am and the other starting at 2pm with one hour overlap between the two shifts. Sergeant Blamire was popular, he was one of the boys, always laughing, always ready for a bit of fun. His teaching techniques produced bold confident riders even though occasionally a probationer got broken.

[Illustration: rider on a bucking horse with speech bubble: "Is this what you mean by leg yielding, Sarge?"]

We were ushered into the classroom opposite the section house to await the various introductory talks. The classroom was a fascinating place dominated by a complete skeleton of a horse, or should I say 'ex-horse'? There were sloping glass display cases all round the room containing various exhibits from farrier's tools to balling guns and other veterinary artefacts. There was a collection of large glass demijohns containing several stages of the developing equine foetus pickled in aspic, well, they were pickled in something anyway. There was a lectern at the front on a small stage with a rolling blackboard. Having been talked 'at' by both our instructors, and a dishy Chief Inspector, last of all we had a pep talk from the Governor's groom, a man of many years' service, and one of the 'old school.' He had come to enthuse us with a passion for the Branch saying we had to be 'Cavalry men;' we should grow moustaches and walk with a swagger, ride our horses as if going into battle even when we weren't going into battle. We were expected to be 'Cutlass Rattling Rapists'. BLIMEY!!

***

The museum was part of the same building as the classroom and there was a little entrance area neatly decorated with posters and pictures to tempt you in and learn the history of the Branch. It had been put together almost entirely by the dashing Sergeant Forester who had an unquenchable passion for all things historical. He was also the Editor of the twice-yearly Mounted Branch Magazine, appropriately called 'The One One Ten'. It was named after the manpower make-up of a mounted serial for demonstrations at its time of creation. One Inspector, one Sergeant, ten Police Constables. This was just my kind of thing and I promised cartoons and articles for the next issue. I had in fact already contributed to the One One Ten during my days of equestrian crime prevention.

By the following day I felt as though I had known my class mates for months, and we started training in earnest beginning with the mucking out. All the horses were kept in stalls, so this was not a difficult job.

"All this clean straw here," Sergeant Blamire began his instructions while poking the unsoiled bedding with the fork "we keep to put back in the bed. All this crapped on straw here," he continued poking the wet bedding and the mangled turds therein, "we put in the wheelbarrow and take to the muck heap. All other soiled straw we dig out, and what do we do with it?"

"We take it to the muck heap, Sarge," we all said in unison.

"If the horse is a gelding," he stopped mid-sentence, "what's a gelding Miss Collishaw?"

"A castrated male," said Liz.

"Correct. Gentlemen, you can uncross your legs now! If the horse is a gelding, he wees in the middle, see there? His willy hangs down towards the back of his tummy, so all the wet straw is in the middle of the bed," and he gave Cranwell's willy a little poke with the handle end of the mucking out fork. "Have you all got that?"

"Yes, Sarge."

"If the horse is a mare. That is a lady horse. She wees out the back because she has ladies' bits, under her tail," and he lifted the tail of one of the mares to show us all her ladies' bits, in case we were in any doubt. Giving Flame's bits a little wobble he asked, "have you all got that?"

"Yes, Sarge"

"When a horse wees he often groans and grumbles, he's not in pain, he's not sick, he's just enjoying having a piss, OK?"

"Yes, Sarge."

"We get the mucking out done as quickly as we can, the less time we spend mucking out - the more time we have to sit around and drink tea. Right, let's get on with it then."

"Yes, Sarge."

We girls were all horsey so mucking out came as no shock to us but some of the lads had hardly ever encountered a real horse before; some, probably, coming no closer than a picture on a tin of biscuits. A visit to the famous muck heap at the back of the classroom revealed that no one there had thought to keep it neat and level. We girls dug in and quickly had the sides steeped up in a vertical wall and the top flattened out. When we returned to the stables for the next load I was interested to notice the horse, Falcon, was bucking and lashing out in his stall as Ian was attempting to move his dirty bedding. God he looked dangerous, were we expected to ride him?!

John Hyphen-Pename, a broad Mancunian, and ex-Household Cavalry officer, stepped in to help out. "I can do him, Peppy," he said, immediately labelling the lad with what he thought was a suitable nickname. "if you want me to, that is. 'Eee means no arm, some of the cavalry 'orses are like this," and HP got stuck in ignoring the flying legs just as if it wasn't happening. "C'mom Falcon, you know yer loves me really." The bond was forming and believe it or not, from such unlikely beginnings, HP and Falcon were a match made in heaven; he loved that horse, he truly loved him.

Sweeping up was to become something of a daily chore. We had to sweep the yards right up to the muck heap, about 100 metres, with some of the class pushing the straw and rubbish sideways ahead of the main crew pushing it forwards.

After breakfast we saddled up and filed into the little indoor school. I was on Galleon, a very good looking grey with a naughty streak. Apparently, he had been issued to Brian on the patrol section before retiring to the school. He had previous convictions for rearing and bucking among other things. On one occasion Brian and Sergeant Forester had ridden him into the main ring of the Surrey County Show to escort a dignatory, when Galleon, for no good reason, lay down. I think this is what sealed his future.

Sergeant Blamire had us going sedately round the outside at a walk while he explained the rudiments of riding. Then he asked us to trot. Lordy how those boys stayed on I'll never know. It was okay for those of us who could ride a horse and even better if you knew how to rise to the trot. That was all to the good because rising to the trot was more comfortable. For those readers not familiar with how a horse trots, I'll quickly explain. The trot is a gait of two time, the horse bounces from one diagonal to the other, okay! A diagonal is one front leg and the opposite hind leg. So, the horse springs along like this and it can be very bouncy but if you rise forward in the stirrups every other beat you find it is much more comfortable.

"Why are you posting to the trot, Miss Scott-Blackhall?"

"Posting, Sarge?"

"Posting! - or 'rising to the trot' in your mincy civvie language,"

"Sorry Sarge, wasn't I supposed to?"

"No one else is posting are they? Arh, with the exception of all the other little Lucindas. He held his brow in mock despair, "God save us from horsey girls! Oh!" he exclaimed slowly, "and also Police Constable Hyphen-Pename You're a big girl HP, what are you playing at, you should know better."

"Sorry, Sarge"

"Right, you can post when we can all post, OK?"

And we bounced around the school with our brains being shaken to Kingdom come while we wished we had never applied. Then Frederick, an unassuming big grey horse came out of line into the middle of the school, bucked the lad off on to the dirty shavings with a thump, before returning to the gap where he had come from.

Look at that," shouted Sergeant Blamire, "He's an automatic horse until you get on him." Obviously this was not the first time Frederick had done this. "OK everyone, waaaallk, waallk, w a a a a a a l k, W A L K!"

The front three horses walked but most of the others didn't so there was something of a domino effect. It was a good job Falcon was at the back, I thought, but then HP knew what he was doing.

The lad on the floor climbed back on to Fred, shaken but not stirred. Then before we knew it the lesson was over and we were giving the horses their lunch before settling down to ours back in the section house kitchen. That afternoon was spent cleaning our kit, saddlery in mincy civvie speak, and afterwards we 'knocked the horses over' or to put it in more familiar words - giving the horses a nice groom. The list of differing terminology went on and on.

The two classes took it in turns to work weekends and for those on duty, the horses would be ridden without saddles each Saturday. On Sundays they had the day off. We each had two horses to exercise and having no saddles to clean, eased the workload. We threw folded blankets over their backs instead and secured each with a surcingle. We called this activity a blanket ride. If Sergeant Blamire was on duty the rides were good fun; we played a game with a yellow duster. It was a kind of 'tag' game, the aim being to get the duster off the possessor of it, who would have it tucked into the top of their boot. It was every man for himself on some occasions, and sometimes we were in two teams. It was fast and furious and made for good teamwork. A must for serious riot situations. On Sundays the horses were rested, we got the mucking out done in record time and spent the rest of the day sitting about and drinking tea. Just as Sergeant Blamire had said we would.

***

One week into the course and I had a phone call from my friend who was looking after the rabbit, Lé roi. My friend told me he was not prepared to look after him any longer. There was nothing for it but to collect him and his hutch and bring him back to Imber Court with me. Sylvester was still in hiding and though he was not a happy cat his secret was still a secret. What's one extra rabbit? I thought and decided to squirrel him away behind the temporary boxes. Okay, 'rabbit' him away to be strictly accurate. I made him a little harness so I could take him for walks, but did I really think I could keep a rabbit on the premises without anyone finding out.

Sergeant Chris Forester, as the curator of the museum, was in and out of the Section House area all the time. We became good chums and I confided in him that I had a rabbit living on the premises. All my class mates knew anyway. Chris was walking out to the top field one day with one of the Inspectors, who did a double take on seeing the rabbit hutch, "What's that doing there?" he said in a surprised way.

"Oh, that's Susan Scott-Blackhall's rabbit" Chris said blandly.

"Oh, fair enough," replied the Inspector and no more was said, but as Liz pointed out, my credibility was taking something of a hit when I was seen each evening taking a rabbit for a walk on a lead.

Chapter Twelve: Mirror, Mirror on the Wall

Liz did not do mornings. She was the grumpiest person I have ever encountered as the early morning sun broke through our bedroom window. But that is when I am at my best and I usually awake punching the air with the enthusiasm to get going. If you happen to be the sort of person who likes to take the wake-up process slowly then, having someone in your bed room chortling a merry 'Morning Campers' into your lug hole will come well short of improving your mood.

"Liz?" I piped up one morning in a jocular fashion. "Are you going to ride Arabella today?"

From under the covers came a predictable reply: "SUE!!! It's six fifteen in the morning - I don't want to ride at all!"

Arabella was a beautiful bright chestnut with a long white stripe down her face. She was the tallest horse in the school, probably thoroughbred and not much else. She was an unpredictable ride and even more unpredictable in the stable. She was unbelievably ticklish and to watch someone groom her was an entertaining spectator sport. She wasn't nasty, but she was the sort of horse who woke up every morning and thought to herself: "Oh my God I'm still alive."

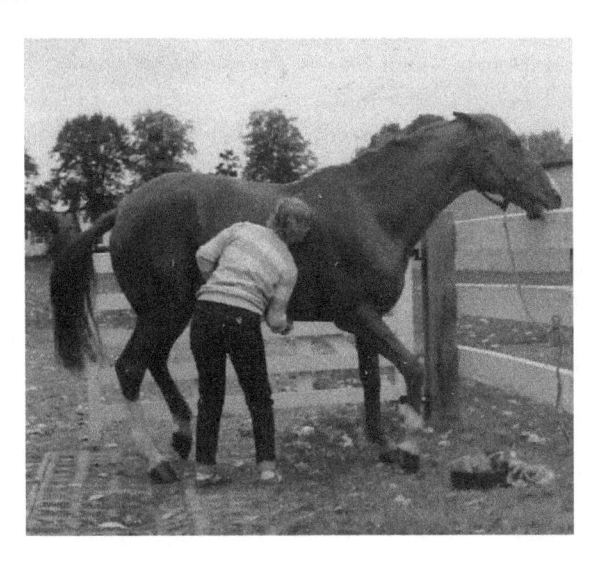

All the school horses were there because they were no good on the streets of London for one reason or another. Dresden, for example, was an exceptional copper but his feet were too brittle and they just would not stand up to the hard roadwork.

We got to ride all the horses over the first sixteen weeks and during that time we developed our favourites. Maggs really liked Cranwell and my favourite was Galleon, the one who had a talent for lying down and rolling in the most inappropriate places.

One Sunday Maggs and I decided we would take Galleon out of his stable for a bit of a play. He was inclined to be something of a handful on Monday mornings after his day off. Neither of us wanted to ride him but we thought we could take the edge off him by giving him some loose schooling. He trotted round the school happily enough but he was a horse to get easily bored so we thought that we would just let him do his own thing. We knew we would have to keep an eye on him given his passion for rolling on the floor, Galleon was as white as the driven snow and we didn't want to spend good tea drinking time cleaning him up.

We stood and gossiped under the gallery while he trotted about investigating his surroundings, sniffing the ground where other droppings had been and generally looking as though he was having a good time. Then, quite suddenly we had to break our conversation because Galleon was going down. We leapt into action shouting and waving our arms and he 'jack-in-the-boxed' to his feet and hurtled round the school bucking and farting in protest.

"That was close," said Maggs.

"I can't believe how quickly he gets down, and without any warning either," I mused. We continued our conversation, when Galleon suddenly dropped to the floor again!

"We can't take our eyes off him," Maggs said.

"I think it is when he believes we are not concentrating. Did you notice, we were actually looking at each other, rather than at him, on both occasions?"

"Oh yes," Maggs agreed, "I think that's right; let's put it to the test."

"How are we going to do that?"

"We'll face the wall."

"Ok, how do we know if he rolls?"

"Ha ha, I've got that covered," she laughed, "and walked across to the corner where there was a mirror,"

Police, Ponies & Husbands in-between

"Of course," I said, "I've got my camera with me too, this should be fun."

We faced the mirror and in no time at all Galleon just fell to the ground, we spun round and shouted at him and this brought the usual lap of honour at a canter accompanied by bucking and farting. We faced the mirror again, and we noticed that Galleon did not take his eyes off us either. He went down again and as soon as we turned with vocal protests, he was up on his feet and trotting a quick circle of protest.

"We'll just look at him next time he does it," Maggs suggested. "Just to see what happens eh?"

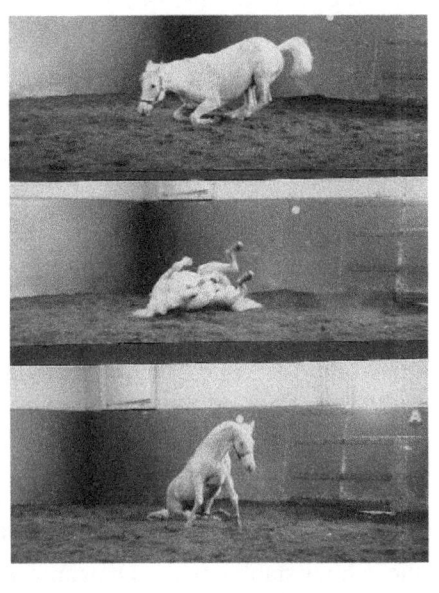

We faced the mirror again, this time when he dropped to the ground we did not attempt to say anything at all, we just turned and looked at him, and he got up immediately with a shake of his beautiful head.

This happened two or three times, then Galleon did the most remarkable thing I have ever seen. He walked calmly to the other end of the school where there was a smaller mirror on the wall so riders could check their positions as they came down the long side. He stood still as a statue right in front of it, looking back at

105

us. We looked at him through our mirror and he looked at us through his. We turned and looked at him, he turned his head and looked at us. As I type this, believe me, that is exactly what happened and I have the photographs. Sadly cameras didn't do videos in those days.

It was as if he just wanted us to know, that he knew, that we knew, what he was up to. I just wish we had let him perform the stunt again with one of the senior officers to witness the experience and prove we were not making this up. As a reward we allowed Galleon to have a good old roll about and we cleaned him up afterwards with our cups of tea on the side.

***

Everyone in the class knew about Sylvester as well, the word had gone round as some of the lads might visit us girls in the evening up on the top floor, purely socially you understand. But that is where Sylvester lived and he was a big cat. "What's that," they had said amazed at my cheek.

"Oh, that's Sylvester," we said as if it was perfectly normal. Then one fateful day I was on early turn and mucking out down in the school stables when Duncan came in and said to me: "Sue, is your cat fluffy and black with four white feet and a white bib under his chin?"

"Yes?"

"He's just jumped off the balcony!"

"What! That's two floors up, is he alright?"

"I don't know, he hit the ground running."

"Oh my God," I left the mucking out and ran up to the back of the Section House but he was nowhere to be found. "Puss puss, puss puss puss - puss puss, PUSS PUSS!!! Oh Sylvester where are you?" I was dismayed. But the upshot was, if he had been a secret beforehand, he sure as hell was no secret now.

As soon as I had finished work I wrote out some little notices and put them round on all the lampposts locally. I waited for a phone call to come in to say that he was safe. None came. After about ten days I had given up hope but then out of the blue, while I was cleaning my kit one afternoon, Glyn came into the harness room and said to me "Sue, is your cat fluffy and black with four white feet and a white bib under his chin?"

"Yes?"

"He's outside the Section House now, crying and trying to get back inside." Glyn continued. "We've tried to catch him but he just runs off."

I ran as fast as I could up to the Section House calling him. And there he was! I was just overwhelmed to see him. I picked him up and hugged him. I was thrilled skinny, as they say, and Sylvester was thrilled skinny, too, but it was a different kind of skinny. After that episode everyone agreed we could prop the front door ajar with a brick so he could come and go as he pleased. He wasn't brave enough to come through the kitchen, you know what cats are like, but the front door was always quiet. He could slide up the back stairs to the top floor where there was always a welcome for him.

***

Many of our riding lessons took place over the stream in a big field they called the 'Forty Acres'. The lesson was often quite fast and furious; making good use of the cross-country obstacles including a bank and a drop fence. We learned how to negotiate these challenges at a cracking speed along with tent peg training and other skill at arms.

Sometimes I saw Sylvester prowling about doing what cats do. "Hello Sylvester," I would greet him from the back of my police horse. "Are you having a lovely day?"

He would look up at me startled beyond belief. "Bloody Hell!

Police, Ponies & Husbands in-between

What are you doing up there?" He said, every time he saw me.

***

The weekend of the Annual Mounted Branch Horse Show was fast approaching. It attracted a huge crowd from members of the public and competitors from the Constabularies. As probationers we were a ready source of labour, after mucking out and lessons we had the rest of the day to pitch in and help with refurbishments. The buildings were given a spruce up where needed, cracks in the tarmac weeded, licks of paint on peeling paintwork, the classroom scrubbed and dusted, and the Museum sorted to an order fit for the finest visitor. The Metropolitan number one football pitch was to be the main event ring, it was mown, weeded, neatly edged and manicured to perfection. The marquees were erected and 2000 blue chairs were spaced right round the outside of the main ring with proper upholstered chairs with arms and cushions uniformly arranged at the top end of the arena in readiness for visiting dignitaries. Maggs and Liz looked immaculate in their foot duty uniforms in readiness to usher important people around the pavilion. Every year at the Horse Show we usually had some dignitary come to open the show and this year it was Her Majesty The Queen. They don't come much more dignitary than that.

We were all given specific jobs to do on the two days of the weekend. The strong young men on the course were ring monitors mostly, erecting the jumping course and replacing fallen poles during the action. I had shown an interest in the museum and Sergeant Forester was looking for an assistant, he had such a dry sense of humour, which had me in stitches much of the time so I readily volunteered to help him. Because of this post I did not get to see many of the events in the main ring but I was given time out to visit the refreshments on offer in the beer tent.

There were quite a lot of preparations to be made getting the museum ready for the show and I reported for duty to find Sergeant Forester pulling out the contents of a rather cluttered cupboard; you know the sort; chuck something in there and shut the door quickly before it all falls out. "There is way too much junk in here," he complained. "Half of this can be thrown away." Holding up a beautiful saddlecloth I noticed the Royal crest emblazoned on it. "I would really like to display this. It's quite a trophy" he continued. "But the Palace don't know I've got it so it is a bit risky!" and folding it up he put it to one side in readiness to be hidden away in the cupboard again when he had tidied up.

Many of the items in the museum had been donated, borrowed or stolen from other departments. All manner of goodies were put together in display cases making the whole project rather impressive. One of the few legitimate pieces of equipment was a full-sized fibreglass horse, which had been bought from the Imperial War Museum. He was fully saddled up wearing the police kit. It had the military style police saddle with a long white stick housed in its leather case hanging from the rear of the saddle on the right-hand side and a pair of leather wallets hanging one each side at the front. The head kit was thick tan English leather with a head collar section that was separate from the rest and a large chrome ring under the jaw. Attached to this there was a chain that hung in two lengths dividing to encircle the horse's neck at the shoulder. In those days they were useful if the reins were cut during violent clashes in a demonstration, but they don't wear them now. There were actually two pairs of reins that we were expected to operate, attached to a universal reversible port mouthed Pelham, or elbow bit. H-P with his previous Life-Guard experience, was in charge of cleaning this kit and the result was just outstanding. The horse looked magnificent in all its finery.

We finished all the work that had to be done in good time. "Great," said Chris. "They can let the punters into the museum tomorrow. We are all ready for them." We had all sorts come into the museum; sometimes it was very crowded and sometimes not. A Chelsea Pensioner came in wearing his wonderful scarlet coat and tricorne hat. He was a lively soul and I tried to persuade him to stay with us as an exhibit.

While I was sitting at my post, I was approached by a woman I knew from 'Back in the Day'. It was Mrs Morris, you may remember her from chapter ten and the little stolen pony, Fudge? "Hello, Mrs Morris," I said.

"Do I know you?" and she leaned right forward over the desk and stared into my face, "Do I know you?" She repeated the question.

"Yes," I said, "You do." She clearly did not recognise me from last year or even back in the day at Woodcock Farm. I considered this to be a good time to remind her, as I stood there in full uniform. I cut a dash and was a far cry from the downtrodden low life she would remember me as.

"You may remember me," began. "You kept your ponies in Barnet Lane and I lived opposite your stable yard, at Woodcock Farm. You would have known me then as Cathy."

There was silence while she digested this information. Finally, she spoke, "So you are, so you are!!" and standing back to take a better look at me she continued "Well, well, well, Sandra, look at this," and turned to her daughter, "Look who it is"

"Hello," said Sandra.

Police, Ponies & Husbands in-between

"Hello," I said smiling. I felt deeply for her daughter. Her parents had bought her a fantastic pony when she was just a little girl and she won prizes everywhere. Then as she grew out of the first little pony, they bought her another to match her development, bigger and better, virtually unbeatable at County level. Sandra was a super little jockey. She was as cute as a kitten as a youngster and now she was an attractive young woman. I had been told at the time by a mutual friend, Sandra had never been allowed to 'have a go' on her ponies. Her acivities were confined to winning rossettes at prestigious horse shows. Gymkhanas and pony clubs were something only other children did. Noisy, unruly, common children, just like the ones at Woodcock Farm.

"I would really like to join the Mounted Branch," she said. "But I don't know where to start."

I advised as best I could although joining the police force is no guarantee of getting the posting you would like. "But," I told her sincerely. "You can do anything you want." I echoed the advice given to me many years ago.

It's true, everyone knew me as Cathy in those far off days. When I had been accepted into the Metropolitan Police Force in 1974, my father suggested that I returned to the name I was brought up with. "None of these people will know you and you can wipe the slate clean and start over again," he told me. "Imagine," he began, "when you have made it in life and you are in the Royal Enclosure at Ascot, and The Queen spies you through the crowd. How much better would it sound if she said to The Duke of Edinburgh, 'Ooh look, Phileep, there's Sooo, hello Sooo, do come and join us."

I grinned behind a cupped hand, the idea was so preposterous.

"It really would sound so much better, just imagine if she were to say, 'Eer Phil, there's our Caff, yoo hoo Caffy, come over 'ere."

Those wise words continue to echo whenever I look at the mirror image of myself in those far off years, and I had found that against all the odds, he had been right.

Chapter Thirteen: Blue Sky Days

September was with us and our spare time was taken up helping with the preparations for the One Day Event on the Waynefleet Estate just round the corner from Imber Court. It was a large plot of land near Esher, I don't know how big, 150 acres maybe? It was sandwiched between the river Ember and the main line railway.

The dressage arena had been marked out, the grass had been mown and it was our job to rake up and remove all the long grass cuttings. The day was hot and dusty and there was a good crop of hay from the mown rectangles, if anyone on the staff had the inclination to conserve it. But they didn't, so instead they piled the raked heaps on to a trailer and secreted it somewhere out of the way to rot. It was a really fun afternoon peppered with the occasional grass fight amongst the lads full of high spirits. We certainly earned our pint in the clubhouse that evening.

We were all to be jump stewards come the day of the One Day Event. I longed for the opportunity of seeing Gemma compete one year with its course of challenging cross-country fences. I was posted with Liz to a drop fence over a substantial log. Ruth had come down for the day and we marvelled at these brilliant horses all strutting their stuff, with many of them being regular police horses.

We watched the 'Gentleman Gypsy' of Southall market fame, going strongly and clearing the fences one after the other in magnificent fashion. The following week he would be on the same horse at Chelsea football ground keeping the opposing fans apart. We ask so much from our amazing horses, a challenging cross country course one day, crowd control at football matches the next. From violent demonstrations and generally patrolling the busy London streets to performing in stately ceremonial grandeur.

The fence we were monitoring had the advantage of being at the point on the course where it looped back to run parallel for a few yards in the other direction towards the finish line. If there was a lull, it was possible to walk a few strides and watch another section of the course. It was entertaining to say the least. There was a peppering of hopeful prospective candidates, helping out where they could, and keen to curry favour with the bigwigs and facilitate their success on the next probationer's course.

***

Sergeant Blamire had a plan for our passing out parade at the end of the course. We assembled on our horses in the big school to practise the formations we had to memorize, all set to music of course. Crossing alternately in the centre and making circles and loops and weavings all went to make for an impressive display. He then pulled us in a line down the centre of the school. "Right" he said, "put your hands just behind the saddle and feel the horses back." We did as we were asked. "OK now, just so you know, we do not put any weight on this part of the back,"

"This is an odd time to have a lesson in saddlery fitting," I thought quietly.

"Put your hand further back on the horse and you can feel where the rump rises up." He continued. "We can put all our weight here because it is directly over the hind legs. This is a strong part of the horse's back." We all looked at each other bewildered. "Now, we are going to try something a bit different, class! On the count of three, dismount…THREE." We dismounted on the count of three, though it was hardly a count. He continued "Push your horses up closer together so there is no air between them," Sergeant Blamire spoke to the probationers at either end of the line. "C'mon push your horse over from that end," he pointed to the left, "and you push from your end" he turned facing the right hand end. "Closer class, they have got to be much closer together. ....For goodness sake Peppy look at the gap there between Flame and Cranwell, get these horses butted up... Right, that's more like it. The closer they are to each other the easier it is for you lot..................OK, I want one man holding two horses on the end. H-P, you are the spare man so on the count of three mount the end horse and stand on its rump...THREE"

"What Sarge? Stand on the rump, Sarge?"

"THREE!! I said," he barked back.

H-P mounted, and stood on Falcon's rump, quite confidently, I thought.

"OK, good. Now what I want you to do, is run along the horse's rumps until you get to the other end where you will jump to the ground and take the end horse."

We looked on in stunned amazement, or at least I did. We just stared at each other in disbelief.

"The quicker you run the easier it is, just bounce from one rump to the next, how hard can that be?"

H-P ran first, he was amazing, he just seemed to float from one rump to the next and at the end of the line he launched himself into mid-air and landed neatly on the ground bending his knees as an act of suspension. We all clapped with appreciation... and nerves.

"Right, take the end horse H, and you can all pass down so we have another spare man on this end. Duncan, you're next, on the count of three...THREE"

Duncan climbed aboard Falcon and prepared himself for the coming challenge. All the horses knew what was coming now and they were jigging about a bit. Duncan ran, he was a man of smaller stature but he bounced athletically down the line and landed with ease on the ground at the other end. "No applause for me then," he questioned us.

"Nah! That was crap" we said, all laughing.

I was inching my way down the line as each pupil took his....or her turn. Maggs was visibly nervous, as was Liz, but they both did

OK. They were bloody marvellous actually, in my opinion. Then it was my turn. I mounted Falcon and slowly raised myself upright to look along the row of wriggling bottoms in front of me. God! They were wriggling about like a row of little girls, their eyes fixed towards the back of their skulls watching keenly for the next man to assault them. I set off leaving Falcon's rump to land on Frederick's, then up on to Arabella's and on to Cranwell's. As I approached each horse they ducked slightly with the anticipation of the Monty Python style black boot landing on them. Flame was next and she was much shorter in height than Cranwell, plus she had a scrawny back end, plus she could duck for England and her butt seemed to practically disappear. No stopping now and I landed on her and slipped! One leg disappeared between her and Galleon which brought a gasp from the class, but I recovered my position and continued. I continued right to the end and jumped to the floor thinking, "Don't land on the right leg, just don't ....don't ......don't." I did, and the metal plate seemed to sing like a tuning fork up my shin. Bugger.

"Well done," whispered Liz who had run just before me. She moved down one horse and I joined the end hopping as H-P took his turn for the second time.

When we had all succeeded in doing what we thought could not be done, Sergeant Blamire addressed us once more. "That was good, well done all of you, we will do it all again in the pass out, and it will look good." Oh, my God! NO!!!

***

October was with us before you could say 'knife' and with it came the Horse of the Year Show at Wembley. The previous year I had instigated a Crime Prevention stand specifically tackling stable crime if you recall. I completed a form 728 asking if I could be released to attend there again. The Crime Prevention Officer at Wembley Police Station was game to continue this but said he would find it easier if I was there with my know-how on the equestrian subject. As it turned out the whole class was going to be on duty at the show as ring stewards for the activity ride which was being performed as one of the attractions. There were close associations between the show committee and the Mounted Branch. The permission was granted to me and though I loved the work there, talking to members of the public about horses, I did envy the rest of the class out there in the main ring, wearing their blue fatigues and looking like they were having so much fun. We all bussed in and out each day from Imber Court and it was like a jolly school outing.

Maggs and Liz suggested one evening that we make enquiries about the Spanish Riding School coming soon to Wembley.

"They might even give us complimentary tickets" Maggs said hopefully.

"They're not going to give us tickets, for goodness sake," I said.

"I bet they will," argued Maggs. "All we have to do is ask them."

"You can ask," said Liz. "I don't do asking."

"Um, I'm not sure how we go about this." I was hesitant.

"Come on," said Maggs. "They can only say 'no'."

So the following day we climbed the steep stone stairs to the administration unit, and I bravely asked the question. To my utter amazement they gave us six tickets.

A couple of weeks later, what had become a clickly little group, Maggs, Liz, H-P, myself and Alistair were at Wembley watching the Spanish Riding School performing at their best. What an inspirational evening it was. The beautiful white horses were just as spectacular as they had been when I saw them in Vienna with Hugh.

***

With November came the colder weather and we began to muffle up around the stables, although the hard work kept us warm. I noticed a flurry of growing excitement among the Remount staff and the Patrol Section, and I became aware that rehearsals had started for the Annual Metropolitan Police Mounted Branch Pantomime. Me and my big mouth, I got talking to the lovely Sergeant Forester one morning, and I boasted about my experiences painting scenery at Bushey Sports Club.

"Really, Sue? You painted scenery? I think they are stuck for scenery this year, I'll put your name forward."

There was no 'saying no.' If duty called, you answered, and so before the week was out I was given special dispensation to paint their scenery for them. It was all housed in the garages between the temporary boxes and the isolation boxes barely 50 yards from the back door of the Section House. Now there's handy.

The rest of the class all came and put their noses round the door to investigate what I was doing. Just about everyone came to investigate, Chief Inspector Walker, and the other Governors, as well as the pantomime cast. Their Director/Producer came by on a regular basis to give me his advice and share his thoughts. He usually came along with the officer who traditionally played the dame, he was a bear of a man, and therefore the obvious choice. This year it was Aladdin and I thoroughly enjoyed the brief I was given. Wishy Washy was due to be put through the mangle and I had to paint a huge elongated cut-out of his mirror image so it could appear on the other side as if he had been flattened. I recall the lines when he was asked by the dame what time he was due to visit the dentist.

"Tootherty" says Wishy Washy.

"I know you have tooth achey, idiot Wishy Washy, what time are you going to the dentist?"

"I told you, twoth 'irty."

Arh! The old ones are the best.

I enjoyed watching their rehearsals in the evenings. Volunteer officers came from almost every stable in the Met to perform as a character, or help with some task or other. They performed a much more traditional pantomime to the ones I had experienced in North London. I preferred the traditional, you cannot have too much of "Look behind you" in my view.

***

The last big event of the course loomed fast. For the passing out parade we were allowed to choose the horse we wanted and I chose Galleon. H-P had his beloved Falcon and Liz had Arabella. Maggs rode Cranwell and Peppy was on Flame. We sent invites to our families, polished and scrubbed our kit to perfection and 'practice – practice - practice' made the display good enough to perform on the big day.

As we entered the big indoor school all our loved ones were sitting with smiling faces and their hearts thumping with glowing pride, as ours were. We circled the school a couple of times, then we performed smaller circles and divided into two rides crossing over in the middle. We trotted the exercises, and we cantered them. We lined up in the centre of the school and for the second time only we did the 'run along the rumps' thingy. Just as scary as the first time, I slipped on Flame again, bloody mare, but regained and continued. Everybody gasped, I gasped, 'Damn it!' Then we concluded the display by lining up at the end of the school facing our audience in readiness to canter towards them. Galleon knew what was coming, and he reared, I stayed on him as best I could, then with a lunge forward he snatched at the bridle and I felt like I was trying to hold a steam train, and we were off towards the watchers, comfortable in their chairs, before pulling all of the horses up to a halt - even Galleon …just in time.

It earned us a most enthusiastic applause, some standing up to add impact to their appreciation. I was so proud to see Ruth and Phillip there jumping up and down and my mother who looked on in amazement. I felt I had earned her admiration at long last, after all I had done as a young girl to disappoint and distress her. It was a special moment.

***

I was told I would be going to West Hampstead where I would be, what they called - a 'Strapper'. You were 'on probation' for 6 months, swabbing the decks and making tea. I suppose the name

Police, Ponies & Husbands in-between

comes from grooming the horses for other officers. There was a particular technique called strapping. To strap a horse is a way of vigorous grooming, traditionally used with a wisp, which is a twisted plait of hay. The idea is to rhythmically thump the working muscles of the horse, shoulders, rump etc. As the horse anticipates what is about to happen, a Nano second before each thump, it flexes the muscles with expectation and this is believed to be quite a good 'work out' for the horse. It certainly is a good 'work out' for the one doing the thumping!

I was sorry the course had come to an end. We had all had so much fun, The teamwork of sweeping the roads every morning. The rides out in formation over Esher Common, and cross country instruction in the Forty Acres. The high jinks with blanket rides on Saturday mornings, the gossip, the practical jokes, the togetherness. Lounging about in the evenings on the girl's floor, sharing bottles of wine and a slug of scotch with H-P, Maggs, Liz and Alistair. These were all things in the past.

Now my working days were to be spent at West Hampstead where I was the rooky, the new kid on the block. I still had many visits to Imber Court though to complete the finishing touches to the scenery before the pantomime performances started. Time away from my new stables probably didn't win me any Brownie points and I found the other officers there a bit unforgiving. This whipper-snapper skiving off and not pulling her weight, ideas above her station, and a woman to cap it off.

As soon as the pantomime was out of the way, I settled down to service at West Hampstead, and I found it was not as easy as I thought it would be. There was an element of chauvinism to which I did not react well. The sergeant had been such a good ally at West Hendon, over the altercation I had with that bully of an Inspector, and I had looked forward to serving with him. He continued to be a considerate skipper, although some of the things I did must have made him exasperated. There was a horse there called Condor and when I got him tacked up to ride out on patrol I could not tighten the girth enough for what I considered to be safe, in fact I could actually slide my hand inside the girth at its tightest, 'that'll never keep the saddle in place' I told myself and this did worry me because I seemed to be asked to ride Condor quite a lot.

I asked if there was a shorter girth I could use and the other officers treated the question with derision.

"I've never had a problem," one of them told me.

"That's tight enough" another said on inspection.

So, I solved my problem in the only way I knew how by going to a local saddler and buying a girth that fitted him properly. It was a leather balding girth, just like the one he already had. It was not cheap.

The skipper was cross with me. "I come here to earn it not spend it," he had said in bewilderment at why would I have done such a stupid thing. I just was not on the same planet as the rest of them.

Riding over Hampstead Heath was good though, and the views of London from the top of the hill were breathtaking and Old Hampstead was the quaintest place.

Lynette and I had spent many a late night in a little café called 'The Great American Experience.' We watched the world into the early hours, and once saw the dawn break over the Heath. Lynette was a really good friend and I remembered all this as I rode past the café every time. It looked so different from the back of a horse and who would have predicted that my life could have taken such a turnaround from those uncertain days.

She and Libby now had a family, a small child called Amy, they lived not far from the stables.

***

Gemma seemed perfectly well cared for with Kelly looking after her for the six months I was at Imber Court and I didn't think I needed to intervene. I continued to pay the bills for everything she needed and Kelly did me an incredible service looking after her every need for all this time.

I did think Gemma looked rather fat when I visited, and the shavings in her stable looked as clean as when they came out of the bag new. She was going through clean bedding like I've never known before and I did feel it needed a mention. Kelly was horrified that I should think six bales a week was excessive and said that to manage her bed any differently would mean she was just sleeping on shit. She was in charge so I paid the bill without complaint.

Kelly had enjoyed Gemma's company very much but now I was back at home full time there were going to be changes to our arrangement. I have to admit that because I was now strapping at West Hampstead the task of looking after her was going to put pressure on my work load, and at that stage I was not sure what it would be. I could see Kelly was sorry the agreement was coming to an end so I suggested that I could let her have Gemma on loan for another six months but I would expect her to pay for her now as I no longer really needed anyone to look after her for me. She was delighted and readily accepted the offer and I felt very happy for both of them.

I still kept in touch though and visited Gemma regularly. Sometimes I saw Kelly and sometimes I didn't, but that did not matter to me, I was visiting Gemma. She was growing into a magnificent horse and she looked a picture, better for not being so fat now Kelly was paying. It did not escape my notice either that the colour of the shavings in her stable got considerably darker, which is how it should be. I couldn't help smiling to myself, there were obviously different rules when I was paying the bills.

Chapter Fourteen: Square Peg, Round Hole

While I toiled at trying to be a good mounted policewoman, there was a chain of events taking place in the capital city. Rupert Murdoch had moved his print empire, News International, from Fleet Street to the new high technical plant at Wapping with new working agreements and many redundancies. On 24th January 1986 talks with the Sogat union broke down, the redundancy pay-outs were rejected and 6,000 workers came out on strike. These protests continued almost nightly for the next year and would bring changes to the way the Mounted Branch dealt with violent disorder. I was aware that mounted serials were being deployed for twelve hour shifts and the manpower of the branch was being stretched to capacity. Backed by Maggie Thatcher's government our objective was to keep the peace and the gateways clear for the TNT Express couriers to transport the newly printed newspapers from the plant in the early hours of each morning. I was also aware that it would only be a matter of time before I would be joining them, but it did not happen while I was at West Hampstead. I had continued to be in close contact with Sergeant Chris Forester, we had become really good friends. He kept me up to date with what was happening in the East End and it wasn't pretty. It all began gently enough, but we could have predicted the changes in the strategy from the strikers, and as sure as eggs are eggs, the protesting became more proactive. As, indeed, did we.

Police, Ponies & Husbands in-between

***

West Hampstead was a fairly sleepy place to police, but one of the most memorable occasions was on the 6th February when the Royal Horse Artillery had a police escort to Green Park to give a 21-gun salute in recognition of the Accession Day of Queen Elizabeth II. In those days the barracks were based at St. John's Wood just down the road from our stables.

Watching this smart regiment preparing for the ride into Central London was quite something, they mounted together moving as one on the command from their sergeant major. Having got the left leg into the stirrup, they stood with both legs straight, suspended in mid-air holding their balance on the saddle, and on the bark of their sergeant all swung their right legs over simultaneously. It looked very smart. The jangling of the gun carriages on the metal roads made for a very inspiring display. In fact, it was fantastic, there was a healthy covering of snow and as soon as the ponies were unhitched from the guns they were galloped away to a safe distance from the impending explosions. The spray of the snow that the ponies kicked up behind them was simply magical, and the whole ceremony was very moving. Our own horses stood like rocks obviously. They were police horses after all.

***

Getting to work became a challenge when I began to have trouble with my car. It was running hot and I discovered there was a slight leak in the radiator. One morning, while on the way to work the leak had expanded so much, it was touch and go as to whether the radiator would empty before I got to West Hampstead. I knew with all certainty that I would have to get it sorted out before I was able to return home. When I got into the mess room at the stables, I rang Lynette because she lived just around the corner I thought she might know of a friendly mechanic who was local to the stables. Lynette was not at home but her husband answered the phone. "You might be able to help me, Lib," I said and I asked him the question.

"I can sort you out," he said, without hesitation, "can you meet me up the road?" he paused before explaining further. "I ain't coming into no police station."

I smiled to myself and said "Yes, I can pop out for a short while."

"Meet me at the top of Ajax Road." He instructed. I told the skipper the problem I had and he gave me the go-ahead to meet a man who could help. I didn't tell him that the man was known to the police in the gravest of circumstances. I put on my civilian jacket over my shirt sleeve order and headed out on to the street, my black riding boots and spurs clicking away as I walked. I waited at the top of the road until Libby turned up very shortly in a white Transit. "Hop in," he invited me.

I hopped in, "Where do I sit?" I was a little bewildered.

"On the chair, obviously," he said. It was literally that. A simple metal kitchen chair trying to fill the space that was void of any original seating put in at manufacture. Libby pulled out of the parking space and set off. I sat thinking how ridiculous this was.

"Where are we going?" I asked him.

"I said I'd sort you out didn't I?"

"Sorry, yes you did, um thank you."

"Well, I'm sorting you out. Sit tight."

Sitting tight was all I could do, steadying the chair by holding on to the dash board. There was no stability and certainly no seat belt. "Sitting tight is what I do best," I said making light of how I was feeling.

He took me to a lock-up where various vehicles were being repaired. "This is a friend of mine, Sue," he introduced me to a mechanic who looked to be the greasy-rag-in-chief. "She needs a new radiator but she needs it as soon as possible. She's a police officer," he really didn't need to tell him that, I was standing there in half blues, and I had 'copper' written all over me. "Can you help her?"

The mechanic eyed me up and down clocking the boots and spurs poking out from beneath my coat. "I can get it done by the end of the week," he said "This is really pulling out all the stops for you, Lib. You can see how much work we have on here."

"Ok, that'll be good, the car is in Hillfield Road by the nick, can you collect it from there?"

"You don't half ask for some favours, Libby. What's the registration?"

"I have to get to work tomorrow," I said handing over the ignition keys. "How am I going to do that?"

"Don't you fret, Treacle," said Libby. "If I said I would sort you out, I'll sort you out." He took me back to Ajax Road, "What time do you finish work?" I told him and he said: "I'll see you back here then, and I'll take you home."

Libby took me home, and the following morning he picked me up and took me to work, returning me home later in the day. The morning after Lynette came and picked me up and took me home again. One bloke I didn't know from Adam came and picked me up. They did this every day until my car was ready to collect. You cannot ask for better friends, I felt very privileged.

***

Back at home one evening I noticed Sylvester was rather quiet. The following morning, he was clearly not a well cat. I was on duty that day, in fact we were starting work really early because we were needed on the outskirts of London where there was some trouble at a laboratory for animal research. We were to be boxed to the location to help keep the peace and prevent an invasion from the demonstrators who were gathering en masse.

I bundled Sylvester into a large box and took him to work with me. It was about 5.30am. Once at the stables I put him in the WPC's changing room and told the skipper. "My cat is far from well Sarge," I said, "I didn't know what else to do, I couldn't leave him like this at home. I'll have to find a local vet, and hopefully they can collect him from here. Is that OK Sarge?"

He was a good Sergeant, and very understanding. "We are leaving here at 8am sharp, so as long as you can get things arranged by then, there's no problem."

As the horses were being led up the ramp I was still on the phone, but in the nick of time I finally got through to a local veterinary surgery prepared to come and collect him. There was nothing else to do but leave Sylvester trapped in his box awaiting attention.

The demonstration was not a violent one but the demonstrators obviously thought we were being cruel to our horses expecting them to perform crowd control. "You're wicked, you lot, treating your horse like that. Look at that poor creature with foam coming from its mouth, how dreadful, you bastards," they said, or words to that effect. They clearly did not understand that for a horse to salivate in such a way is a good sign, an indication that the horse is happy with the bit in his mouth and he is gaining much pleasure from mouthing it properly. They also didn't know that I had moved Heaven and earth to get my poorly cat sorted out.

Wearily we returned to the stables in the early evening. The first job before going home was to collect Sylvester who was recovering from his operation and the effects of the anaesthetic still keeping him dopey.

The vet explained. "The problem is the dried cat food you have been giving him. They sometimes don't drink enough water, even if it is offered, so it fails to break up and collects in lumps inside their gut. It can be fatal." He did not seem to be best pleased with me. "If we had seen him any later, he would have died." Clearly this was something he felt strongly about. "You did the right thing getting him to us though," he conceded, "this would have been an ex-cat if you hadn't."

"I don't like to think of Sylvester going hungry," I explained. "I do shift work and sometimes the hours are long," but on the vet's assurance that he would be fine, I never fed dried food to him again.

***

The six months had nearly passed since Gemma had been in Kelly's care with a proper loan agreement in place. I was in no rush to take Gemma back from her as commitments at work were so heavy and they were clearly getting along very well. Rippling under my skin was a rather uncomfortable feeling about the lack of bonhomie when I took time out to visit her. I didn't always see Kelly but when I did I was made to feel most unwelcome, as if I was interfering.

Amazingly I considered selling her to Kelly and tentatively suggested this, but she didn't want to buy, or couldn't. But then why would she, she had her all to herself at the moment anyway, for free. Even so, she was clearly very fond of her. I suggested a more long-term loan and I was surprised when she hesitated, saying she would have to give it some serious thought.

This situation would have to be resolved, I felt I was dangling in limbo waiting on someone else to make the decision and Kelly was in no rush. Although it would be a challenge, I considered the only way forward would be to have my horse back again and with this thought in mind I visited her a bit more frequently. When I did visit, however, I was still getting the impression that she did not appreciate the intrusion, I suppose she and Gemma had been together now for over a year, and it seemed to me Kelly had lost sight of who actually owned the horse.

One weekend Gemma was nowhere to be found and Di told me Kelly was having a lesson just down the road at Totteridge Common. She gave me directions where to go and I toddled off to watch Gemma performing. I was really looking forward to seeing what she could do and leaning on the rails of the school watching the remainder of the lesson, I was not disappointed. She went well for Kelly and looked a real picture. I was so proud of her.

The end of the lesson came and for some reason I thought Kelly might introduce me to her instructor as Gemma's owner. I thought we might have a jolly little chat about what a wonderful horse she was. There was no such introduction. The instructress looked at me a bit bewildered, and clearly, she must have wondered who I was. Kelly glared at me, clearly she was angry, and as she rode past me out of the school she hissed "I'll see you back at the yard,"

Because I had my car I got to Mote End before her and I was waiting in the yard when she and Gemma arrived. Kelly wasted no time in letting me know what she thought. "What do you think you were doing coming down to Tessa's yard when I was having a lesson?" She exploded.

"I just wanted to see my horse performing," I explained to her. "What possible reason can you have for not wanting me to do that?"

"Well, it was very off-putting, I take these lessons very seriously, I'd rather you gave me prior notice before you come in future," she said "Just turning up when you feel like it is thoroughly inconsiderate of you." And she swept down the passage dragging Gemma behind her. I didn't stay to bandy words for no good reason and left the yard without further preamble. This was going to give me much to think about over the next few days. I couldn't help it but I was full of malice.

Ronni at Bricket Wood knew Kelly better than I did and I wanted reassurance that I was not being unreasonable. "Has she forgotten who Gemma belongs to?" Ronni had said when I told her of my problem.

"Yes it seems that way," I replied.

A few days later when I had thought it through I went back to Mote End at a time when I knew Kelly would be there. She greeted me with characteristic abruptness. "Hello" she grunted, passing me without stopping on her way to the feed area.

"I've been thinking about the offer that I made to you with regard to you taking Gemma on loan more long term," I began as she retraced her steps with a bucket of grub for Gemma.

"Well I haven't decided yet," she announced, as she passed me without looking back.

"Well I have," I said to the back of her as she swept down the passage. "I think it is now time for me to have her back."

She came to an abrupt stop and turned to face me. "I thought I had the option." She was clearly taken aback.

"I also have the option," I told her, "and I think I have waited quite long enough for you to make up your mind."

"We haven't discussed it."

"I've tried, God knows I've tried."

"When were you thinking of?"

"As of now."

She looked absolutely stunned and struggled to find something to say, failing miserably.

"Thank you for all your help with her," I continued, "I do appreciate it," I was also struggling because I didn't want to appear unpleasant. Although, it has to be said, being pleasant was the last thing I felt.

Kelly was very hurt, and maybe I should not have been so harsh, it must have come as a bolt out of the blue, but I was just so angry that she clearly was not prepared to include me in Gemma's life. The horse I had owned since birth, and fought for and loved. So for the second time in Gemma's life I had to re-possess her.

At least the summer time was an easy time of year to look after a horse and I had plenty of time to organise her winter routine. I'll worry about that when the time comes, I thought. One thing was for sure, I was done with lending my horse to people I thought I could trust. Never again, I vowed, never again.

I moved Gemma to live out on the lush grass at Bury Farm. Her education was going remarkably well, even if I did have to fit it in between the commitments at work and visits with Ruth and Phillip. But I muddled along and Gemma took to this haphazard routine like a real trouper, I'm not so sure about the children. Gosh! Children? Ruth was now nineteen and Phillip was sixteen.

***

The end of my six months at West Hampstead had come to an end and our Chief Superintendent asked me where I would like to go when the postings were given out. I told him I would like to go to Hammersmith, but Hammersmith didn't want me, they already had two women Officers and they didn't want any more, thank you very much.

In actual fact, I was becoming mindful that women in the branch were a constant bewilderment to many of the men. Any expression of enthusiasm I showed was met with derision and I found this a bit debilitating. I wrote a poem, and that made me feel better.

<u>Mounted Patrol</u>
Feed, muck out, knock over and change
Breakfast, kit up, adjust stirrups and go.
Alone with the public the feeling is strange
So, you talk when they stare at you, smile, say "hello."

You feel rather elegant, high in the air
And delight in the jangle of chains with each shake
Of the head from your beautiful mare
And the sound that her rhythmical footfalls can make.

Gazing idly at cars that are parked in the road,
You see several windscreens with tax out of date.
So, you pull out you note book and give them what's owed
And report them for process, a total of eight.

Police, Ponies & Husbands in-between

"Where shall we go now?" you might say to your horse
And you head for the Heath and the wide-open space
Where you jump a few logs between bushes of gorse
Or open the throttle with the wind in your face.

Don't tell the old sweats you've enjoyed your day
They'll damp your delights and refuse to discuss
That the job can be fun, and will probably say
"Wait till you've been mounted the same time as us."

Chapter Fifteen: Great Scotland Yard

I was posted to Great Scotland Yard in Central London. It was a fascinating place and had some amazing history. The name originally came from the tradition of housing Scottish Royalty and diplomats in the area during the reign of the Tudors. Great Scotland Yard, synonymous with the Metropolitan Police, had also been the home of John Milton, the blind poet after whom my father's charitable organisation had been named.

The entrance was just off Whitehall, with a large archway leading into the building with an electric portcullis which could be operated from ground level as well as from the back of a horse. It led into a small yard and all the horses lived on the first floor where there were nine stables and ten stalls. There was a ramp to the first level that swept round three sides of the yard. Our Sergeant had the rare quality of being conscientious towards the welfare of his troops. If I did anything wrong, which happened with regular monotony, I always felt as though I had let him down.

The mucking out was every morning; and we had the most convenient of systems. A lorry from the Royal Parks would arrive just as we had finished dragging the sheets full of muck out to a hatchway in the floor of the balcony that hung over the yard below. It parked underneath and the muck would be whizzed down the hatch to fall into the back of the lorry beneath. Brilliant!

There was a harness room, a feed room and a large tearoom which also doubled as a men's changing room. Some of them, quite rightly, objected to changing with women present in the room. Meanwhile we girls were unfazed by the regular dropping of trousers. We had our own changing room two floors up which was a bit of a slog but it kept us fit. Our changing room was extremely small for the number of girls, being four others besides me.

The tearoom was the hub of activity. The duties board on the wall told us where we should be and which horse we should be riding. Plus there was a desk for the sergeant, although he also had an office on the ground floor, as did the inspector. There was a large table in the centre, so large in fact you could not easily touch hands with the person sitting opposite.

There was a small kitchen area in the corner of the tearoom with a sink and a microwave, a kettle and cupboards full of mugs and plates. We all had our own mug, which was closely guarded, and it was a cardinal sin to use someone else's mug without permission, let alone damage it.

On one unfortunate occasion I damaged the Sergeant's mug; in fact I broke it into small pieces. "That mug was very special to me" he complained bitterly disappointed at his loss. "It was from the Ada Cole rescue centre and I doubt I will find another one."

"Sorry, Sarge," I said, but that doesn't say enough really. Anyway, by lucky chance I was planning to visit my sister in Harlow at the weekend and I knew from previous visits that I drove right past the Ada Cole rescue centre. What I didn't know was that the centre closed at 4pm and I just missed the deadline. Not to be thwarted, I climbed over the locked gate, with great difficulty, it was a big gate, and set off to find a member of their staff.

"Good evening," I began. "I am sorry, I have gate crashed."

"I should think so," said the staff indignantly. "We are closed."

"But I have a minor emergency and I wondered if you could help."

"No, I think you should leave." They told me angrily.

"Please hear me out," I begged. "I'm just asking a small favour."

"You have no right to be here, I'll see you out." She folded her arms and glared at me.

"Please, can I just explain?"

"Whatever you say will not excuse this trespass, who are you?" She demanded.

"I am a mounted police officer in London and I have committed the sin of breaking my Sergeant's favourite mug," I continued without preamble.

"Oh I see," she said, visibly re-valuing my status, "and how can we help with that?"

"Well, it was one of your mugs and I wonder, could you sell me a replacement?"

The mood changed as if by magic and I was awarded a generous smile. "Oh yes, I should think so, wait one moment, I'll get the key to the gift shop." They sold me another mug, and I gave it to the skipper on Monday morning. I didn't tell him the full story but he was still very impressed, and rightly so, but there is nothing like a Brownie point or two to see you through the day.

***

The first and foremost commitment for the day in Central London was the Changing of the Guard at Buckingham Palace. It was not so much the changing of individual officers as changing the regiment. Officers from Great Scotland Yard were responsible for escorting the retiring regiment from their guard duties at St James's Palace, while those at Rochester Row were responsible for escorting the new regiment from Wellington Barracks. Every day there would be one of the Guard's regiments swapping their duties with a visiting regiment. Among the most memorable of these regiments was the Gurkhas, so proud were they to be in London strutting their stuff down the Mall, holding high their colour. I have escorted the Royal Marines, unbelievably smart in their ceremonial uniforms with white lanyards, belts and helmets. There were sometimes smaller visiting regiments from the more rural areas of the UK like the Cheshire Regiment, and those regiments from the Highlands north of the Border, bringing with them their particular tartan and, of course, their bagpipes.

Security and protection from terrorist attack was always one of our objectives, with the power to divert the troops in order to avoid a dangerous package or vehicle and take an alternative route. Police intelligence was always an advantage and thankfully these occasions were rare but not unknown.

Our daily hindrance was crowd control as some tourists liked to run amongst the marching soldiers for photo shoots.

There were three noticeable sections, at the front was the regiment's band, and I have to add here that it takes a good pair of horses to march in front of a band, be it bagpipes or brass. Next is the regiment's flag emblazoned with all the battle honours, known as 'The Colour.' Then bringing up the rear is a small contingent of soldiers with a pair of police horses following on.

Once the two regiments had entered the Palace forecourt to perform their handover ceremony it was then our other task to keep clear the three front gateways. This could be no easy task given the public were often seven or eight deep, all along the railings. Not surprisingly they all wanted a good view of proceedings. Everyone was out for a good day and the whole operation was performed with good humour. Being so high up you could better anticipate how best to operate your crowd control and sometimes we had to have a one-way system in operation. There were always people wanting to cross the gateway, which was quite acceptable, but they were not allowed to linger, their crossing over had to be done in an orderly fashion.

During the ceremony a small contingent of soldiers would leave the palace to relieve the outgoing regiment at Clarence House. Two mounted officers would escort them and this was a task I always enjoyed. It was a bit of a change of scene from the busy hustle and bustle of Buckingham Palace.

When the hand over ceremonies had been completed the two regiments would then leave through the centre gate to go either to St James's Palace or Wellington Barracks. We completely closed the road around the Victoria Memorial, or, as we called it, 'The Wedding Cake' and I liked to stand at the bottom of Constitution Hill holding the traffic at a standstill. If I saw an opportunity for those turning left to go up the Mall they could do so up until the movement of the new guard going to St James's Palace. I would stand beside the nearside lane of traffic and speak to each driver in turn to make sure that they were indeed going left. Sometimes I might get a car turning right in which case I would pull him to the front so the cars behind could go about their day. It was always nice

Police, Ponies & Husbands in-between

to talk to members of the public, anyway, and they appreciated my efforts to help them.

While performing my duties on one occasion outside the Palace, I was approached by a Russian lady who had a few other Eastern Block tourists with her. Now, we didn't see many Russians in the mid 80s so I felt I should do my best to give a good impression of the English Bobby. I answered her questions as best I could and she translated to her friends. I was patient and polite and we got along famously. Within moments she was thrusting a small gift in my direction and I did my best not to receive it. It was a highly colourful wooden spoon painted in a traditional Russian design. I could find no way of refusing this without getting cross so I accepted the spoon gratefully and stuffed it in one of my saddle wallets. We exchanged smiley faces and in no time one of her friends wished to give me a gift also.

"Please, please," I begged them, "No, I cannot accept."

"You must" she insists. And I accepted a little wooden painted cup. Then another gift came my way, and another and another.

"No! Enough!" I protested, trying to push back the nest of Russian dolls, and then a small Russian saucer, but still they kept coming and other people are starting to take notice. I was running out of room in my wallets and pockets so in an attempt to break this wave of 'bonhomie' I had an idea. "Would you and your friends like to come and visit our police horse stables?"

They were delighted to be given this opportunity "We are not all here at the moment," she explained. "There are a few more of us, is that OK?"

"Yes, certainly," say I, and I gave them the directions and what time I would expect them to arrive. Back at the stables I waited eagerly hoping they would turn up as I had forewarned the skipper as I didn't want to look like an idiot.

Forty-two Russian souls walked under the portcullis much to the dismay of the other officers. As I had promised, I showed them all around and we toured the stables and the harness room, and admired the horses, and I told them everything I knew. They seemed to enjoy themselves while my colleagues hid in the tea room completely baffled as to what I could have been thinking of inviting half the tourist population back. Good job done, I thought, going home I was thoroughly pleased with myself.

Police, Ponies & Husbands in-between

***

It was customary for newcomers to the branch to start with an older horse and then as your experience grows, so you could expect a younger animal, the pinnacle of achievement being to be issued with a remount. To be issued with a remount was a real privilege and it was the ambition of most young officers new to the branch. I was issued with my first horse, Ultra, a delightful, pretty little grey horse. Being an older horse she did not like to walk at the side of the road near the gutter because the slope of the camber was uncomfortable for her joints. But she did the job well and was a pleasure to ride. She had one little quirk when we were performing our duties Changing of the Guard. When I parked her in the gateway near to Constitution Hill, no sooner had we come to a halt and she would spread her legs out and pee, a long and yellow stream hitting the tarmac with some force and splashing out in all directions. This made tourists leap for cover, not to mention staining her legs yellow. It was a cast iron way of moving the crowd anyway! I tried taking her on to the grass in Green Park, but it made no difference. Eventually, at some point, I might have to return to one of the gateways, and that was the only trigger she needed. It was embarrassing, to say the least.

I didn't get along with our Inspector at Great Scotland Yard. Like me he was vertically challenged which gave him much to put up with in this world of tall men. He took a great deal of ribald behaviour from his peers but to his credit, he took it all on the chin with good humour because that was the sort of man he was. At the time I did not see this quality in him and to be honest, it seemed to me that he never lost an opportunity to call me to his office for some misdemeanour. I don't think I reacted well.

I was hauled up in front of him on one occasion for not saluting him when I passed him in the street. I stood to attention in his office and received the rollocking due to me for such a crime.

***

I wrote a book review for a few issues of the One One Ten and I attempted to launch a regular piece on retiring police horses. I considered it to be a noble idea to pay some sort of homage to the

Police, Ponies & Husbands in-between

service they had given but I found it quite difficult to obtain the information I needed from other officers. Police horses rarely retire; generally they are humanely put down and therefore would pass into the pet food industry mainly for dogs. As an amusing aside the 'Dog Section' and the 'Mounted Branch' were viewed by those in the ivory tower of New Scotland Yard as being similar in skills. If you can walk a dog you must be able to ride a horse and vice versa. I gave the first piece I wrote the unsavoury title of 'Transfers to the Dog Section'. This was a step too far for many officers and I found it difficult to write about lost horses when information about their service was not forthcoming, not to mention the stick I took for my 'gallows' sense of humour.

So I turned my attention to cartoons. I did not see the dangers of making disparaging pictures and incidents about people which, by the very nature of cartooning, was less than kind. In any case, I had not been there long enough to 'take the piss' and I chuckled to myself when a new idea gave me inspiration. I was 'hauled over the coals' constantly in the aftermath of each new issue of the 'One One Ten' leaving the printing presses. 'Stick your head over the parapet,' I thought to myself, and someone will take a pop at you.

As any cartoonist will tell you, a chink in the armour of a personality will provide the artist with all the material they desire to characterise any ordinary God-fearing person. My long-suffering Chief Inspector came in for much of my attention. I was ruthless, but then so was he, and I suffered many sleepless nights worrying about how I could find a way to earn his acceptance. Drawing wicked cartoons of him, however, wasn't one of them.

***

As the Wapping dispute became more violent so Mounted serials were deployed in substantial numbers. The demonstration ran through the evenings into the night and each shift for us was twelve hours. At the beginning of the dispute, they issued us with 'Noddy Helmets' to shield us against the violence that was sometimes unleashed: they looked ridiculous! The horses wore clear Perspex blinkers on their bridles but this only protected their eyes from missiles coming from the side. By the end of the dispute the horses had Perspex visors right around the front to their faces and thick leather shields to protect the length of their delicate nasal bones at the front of the face. The horses also had kneepads in case they fell on the rough going of roads strewn with house bricks, tyres and other debris. For the first time Police Officers had Nato helmets, although initially we had to find one that fitted from a collection of helmets piled on to tables in the underground car parks serving as muster stations.

We were later issued with our own made to measure helmet and body armour and arm pads for the protection of elbows. If you came off your horse you had no chance of getting back on board. I imagine Medieval Knights in armour had a similar problem. Most of the time we were kept in reserve around the back streets in our serials of one Sergeant and ten Police Constables. We sat there, hour after hour, in the dimness with only the light pollution of the city to help us see.

One night we settled ourselves to our positions looking at the 15 foot wall around the print works with its curls of razor wire along the top, it was simply hammering down with rain. We had our collars up and our heads down and a torrent of water cascaded off our helmets and into the lap of our long overcoats at the front of the saddle forming a puddle. Eventually you had to lift the garment to evacuate the rain but it refilled again in no time.

"Lets' have a game of 'eye-spy,'" piped up one of my colleagues.

"Eye-spy with my little eye, something beginning with 'W,'" said another.

"WALL."

"WALL."

"WALL."

"WALL."

"WALL." shouted five or six of them at the same time. And then there was silence because no one could think of anything else to say.

I fumbled in my wallets for my personal Walkman for some soothing music to listen to. No word of a lie, this is true, I placed the ear pieces into my ears and turned the set on, it immediately played what is often referred to as 'Air on a G String' or more correctly Johann Sebastian Bach's Orchestral Suite Number 3 in 'D' major.' You know the one, it was used in the Hamlet cigar advert, but maybe you are not old enough to remember.

Chapter Sixteen: A Change of Scenery

I was hankering to move house. I considered the time was right to start anew and leave the old memories behind me. My neighbours had changed a few years ago, and they had changed for the worse. A nice lady with her daughter had moved in but there was also a son serving time for shooting a police officer. He was now due to be released and I must confess it worried me. Being posted in Central London meant I could live anywhere around the M25, although, because my family was in the North, South was out of the question. I looked at the Surrey/Berkshire borders and found an ex-council house in Englefield Green between Staines and Windsor. It was the only house I looked at and immediately thought 'that'll do' and bought it.

I then began to look for stables which proved more difficult. There were lovely up-market yards I couldn't afford, and scruffy dumps I could. Fate took an interesting turn in my change of direction and, as is so often the case, a solution to my problem came rather unexpectedly at The Horse of the Year Show.

The summer had come to a close and Chris, the Crime Prevention Officer at Wembley, once again contacted me to ask if I could join them at The Horse of the Year Show with the Crime Prevention

Stand for the third year. This did cause some bewilderment among my colleagues: what was I thinking of, trying to be so different from everyone else in the Branch! The time of the show approached fast and I detected uneasiness among my peers. After all my job was to work at GSY and ride my horse and pull my weight. If I was not there, someone else would have to do my share of the work, my share of the commitment to the Guard Change plus the riding of Ultra.

One morning over breakfast another officer asked me if I could get hold of some recruitment application forms for his sister who was thinking of joining the police force. I wasn't sure how I could do this and suggested he rode down to New Scotland Yard where I was sure he would have no trouble getting everything he wanted. He appeared irritated that I was so unwilling to help. Why couldn't I bring the papers back with me from the stand at the Horse of the Year Show, he argued, amazed that I was being so difficult. I tried to explain that it was not a stand for recruitment; it was a Crime Prevention Stand. I am not convinced he understood the difference, and I began to feel that I must have 'skiving little shit' written across my forehead.

When I joined the Branch I felt that my interest in Southall with other officers from the Branch had stood me in good stead and there would be the opportunity to be more involved in the same. In fact, the opposite was true. The officer who worked such wonderful miracles had driven the whole inspiration for me, but the Mounted Branch was an organisation with a different remit altogether. This was crowd control mostly in the form of ceremonials, football games and demonstrations. Horses are, in fact, second to none and so whenever there is a large number of people who require controlling, the horses do come into their own. But I could still feel the residue of my passion and off I went to the Horse of the Year Show at Wembley for a whole week without a backward glance.

It was another good show, even though we were squashed under the stairs again. Opposite us was the public face of Harvey Smith with his 'Team Sanyo' selling Harvey Smith T-shirts, fleece jackets, books, cards and any amount of memorabilia. When Harvey was present on the stand signing everything from books to polo shirts, the walkway became thick with jostling people like bees round a honey pot. We picked up on much of that success and as always, found the horse owners were keen to talk about their own fears and situations, and hopefully they took on board the advice we had to offer. In addition, across the way from us was the bookstall for the equestrian publisher J A Allen which was also a popular stop for customers and the efficient assistant looked as though she was having a good week. It was not unknown for me to pop round to their shop at the back of Buckingham Palace in Grosvenor Place while patrolling on Ultra. If I knew the book I wanted, and it wasn't too big, the cheery assistant would happily find it for me and bring it out to the street where I waited in the road, my payment at the ready.

People loved to talk about their horses and we were good listeners and it was my lucky day when a nice young lady called Louise happened along to speak to us. As the conversation developed it transpired that she kept her horse, 'Squire', in Englefield Green. The stables she was at were not on my list to visit because it was a private house and apparently, they were quite particular about whose horses they had stabled there. Louise enthused about what a wonderful place it was to keep a horse. "It is a bit more expensive than some yards but it is worth every penny," she said. "You have Windsor Great Park just down the road and for £60 you can get a permit to ride anywhere in the park for a year." She said she would make enquiries on my behalf and we exchanged telephone numbers.

***

I had an unbelievably busy run-up to Christmas. Gemma was happily turned out in the fields at Bury Farm and Maggie agreed to keep an eye on her. I said goodbye to The Meads in Burnt Oak and all the sad memories and moved to Hazel Close in Englefield Green near Windsor on 20th November 1986. Having taken the week off work I lost no time in getting the new place organised. One of the most pressing objectives was to purchase a cooker and a fridge. So, the very next day, I was shopping in Staines to see what I could find. I enjoyed the excitement of a brand-new kitchen and made my purchases, expecting the delivery the next day. Catering-wise, I could whistle and ride till then. As I came out of the shop into the covered shopping mall, my head was in the clouds with excitement, anticipation and anxiety, all at the same time. I was not concentrating on where I was going as much as I should have been and I collided, literally, with a lady pushing a small child in a pushchair.

"Oh!! I am so sorry," we both said at the same time.

As we looked briefly at each other, mutual recognition came to us like a thunderbolt.

"Erika??"

"Cathy??"

"OH MY GOD!!! It's you!!" And we hugged each other and bounced around in a circle in a thoroughly girly way while baby Edward peered up at us from his push-chair.

Erika had kept her horse at Woodcock Farm twenty-one years earlier and we had not been in touch since those days.

"Come and have lunch with me," she said immediately. "I only live round the corner. It's just a pork pie and some pickles but do come."

"I would love to, I would so love to, yes yes, where are you parked?"

"Follow me." And we left the building for a good old-fashioned 'catch up'. Erika had a lovely house with the River Thames at the end of the street. There was a dog, of course there was a dog, and there was a husband too, Teddy, who was working at Shepperton studios. He was a freelance cameraman for the film industry and worked whenever there was work. Like most freelance professionals there were weeks when there was barely time to breath and weeks when he waited for the phone to ring, although I don't think Teddy ever did much waiting.

Erika and I were in fine form. It was just as if the years melted away and we picked up where we had left off, although I did tell her I had reverted to my original name and she embraced the change without hesitation. She was involved with Egham and District Riding Club and she had two ponies, 'Beau', who was a Welsh Cob, and a dinky little pony called 'Highwayman'. Life in Surrey was going to be good and I was filled with eager anticipation for a new start in life.

***

Police, Ponies & Husbands in-between

The Mounted Branch had a reunion every year at the beginning of December. It was usually some sort of 'it ain't half hot mum' style of concert party, put on by anyone who felt they could do something inspirational. Wendy came up with a cracking idea. In those days women police officers came in for some stick from their male colleagues and it seemed to her that now was the right time for a bit of payback. Digging out the LP she had of the sound track to film 'South Pacific', she painstakingly copied out the lyrics, and rewrote them.

"Hey girls" she announced through the internal post. "I've got some spanking new words to 'There is nothing like a dame.' If you are up for a bit of a sing-a-long at the reunion this year, we are having rehearsals at Imber Court next Thursday evening. Do come, the more the merrier." How could I not go? I also knew there was a new intake of recruits in the Section House and wondered if any of the girls would like to join in. Only Linda was at home as the other girl lived out. "That sounds like fun," she said when I told her.

"Come on then," I encouraged her, "you are one of us now."

When the reunion date came, we were all prepared and the words learned. The boys put on the usual skit designed to take the Micky out of someone and this year it was our turn, us girls. A group of them including Brian and Alistair came on to the stage in drag. Each was taking the character of one of us 12 lady-mounted officers. To my horror I discovered that Brian was supposed to be me. ME! For goodness sake, what had I done to deserve such attention? But my friendship with the dashing Sergeant Forester had been noticed and the inevitable innuendos that followed made me feel really uncomfortable. "You know when you have arrived in the job," Chris whispered to me, "you've arrived when they take the piss out of you, take it as a compliment, I have."

Then the time came for the girls to retaliate and we did it in style. We appeared out from behind the curtains to a pleasantly surprised

144

male audience. We were wearing our black Police jackets, shirt and tie, foot duty hat, tights and high heels. No skirt, no trousers. We were a sensation.

It began:
> You got body brush and curry comb and dandy brush and all,
> And most of you have got a horse that's standing in a stall
>> You got head kits, you got saddles, you got lots of mounted games,
>
> And now at last, - you got us dames.

And continued in good form, ending thus:
> If it wasn't for us lot here today, you down there would all be gay
> So thank us girlies, womanly, female, – D-A-M-E-S.

"You can see now which of our girls have got bottle," I heard the pantomime dame say to one of his mates. It really was a stroke of genius on Jacko's part.

***

The festive season now in full swing there was talk of this year's annual Mounted Branch pantomime. Mick had directed the panto for a number of years and he had done wonderful work raising large amounts of money for charity. He now wanted a break from the organising of the whole show. So yet again; a successful pantomime was threatened with closure. I just couldn't help myself and I stepped in like Corporal Jones, in Dad's Army. "I'll do that," I shouted from the rooftops. "Let me! I want to be the one to direct the Pantomime!"

There was not the grief I had from the foot duty pantomime at Bushey. Mick was helpful and supportive, as were the other members of the crew. In the past they had been a travelling show going to various venues including institutions with disadvantaged children. I could not quite reconcile myself to travelling even though I was told that Lambeth would send a box van to tour with all the scenery and equipment. I decided to have a static event in the clubhouse at Imber Court, as this was what I knew and it was tailor made for the job, as Bushey had been. So in between moving house and Christmas and New Year celebrations, the regular crew and I got on with the task of putting a show together. We rehearsed endlessly a production of 'Sleeping Beauty'. An old friend from West Hendon wrote the script for us and the Graphics Department at Hendon, where I had once worked, did the artwork for the posters and the programme.

***

Along with the days before Christmas, came the anticipation of the fancy dress party at Great Scotland Yard. How would I dress? Schoolgirl, I thought. That's the ticket, I'll go as a schoolgirl with long plaits. I had always wanted plaits as a schoolgirl being insanely jealous of those girls who did and were forever being chased by the boys. I could lisp too. I had a bad lisp as a girl and my parents spent shed loads of money trying to cure it, which they succeeded in doing but I could turn it on at any time. "Thoothan likth thothagezz," my wicked elder sisters taught me to say. It was, however, a spanking good do with officers coming over from Hyde Park Stables and Rochester Row. We all met initially in The Clarence on the corner of Whitehall and cut a dash in our flamboyant costumes. We seemed to be viewed with amusement when sensible customers learned that we were the local fuzz in drag. I became extraordinarily popular with my overinflated bust and short gym-slip.

***

The following day I was delighted and relieved when Town Green Farm agreed to take Gemma as a new livery. Louise was very excited when she told me. "It's going to be so fab," when she rang with the good news. "I have been the only livery there for quite some time so it will be great to have someone to ride with."

"I'll get Gemma up here as soon as I can, hopefully this weekend," I told her. "I'll speak to Maggie straight away." And I rang her as soon as I had put the phone down to Louise.

"I'm OK for Sunday," Maggie said "but I have to cover the shop on Saturday, Clive has got some deliveries to make."

"Great, I'm late turn today, so I'll speak to my skipper and try and get the day off. I'll ring you later, OK?"

Steve stood in front of the duty board and considered the manpower for the day. It was the eve of the eve of Christmas Eve so riots, demos and footballs were on a bit of a hold. The Changing of the Guard was just every other day, provided it wasn't raining, but there was skeleton staff on duty. "Yes, OK," he said after a few moments, "don't say I never do anything for you." I fairly skipped into the line of stalls to 'knock over' Ultra, before going out to do the Guard Change.

***

The 28th December came soon enough and I arrived at Bury Farm in good time for 10.30pm. I had left a shopping list of forage at their shop and Clive had gathered all my requirements together including 20 bales of hay and loaded it on the lorry the previous day. After a good deal of consideration Gemma decided that perhaps she would go into the lorry after all. This vehicle was new to her and she was proving to be nobody's fool, therefore she would not come to any final decision until she had satisfied herself it was safe. We set off in good spirits for Englefield Green, taking the road through Windsor. The spectacular view of the castle from the motorway thrilled me to bits and I was certain that this new life was going to be just perfect for Gemma and me.

We pulled up outside Town Green Farm and parked the lorry as much off the road as possible. The archway into the yard was only big enough for a car so we had a fair bit of carrying to do, with the hay having to be winched bale by bale up into the loft above the stables. I found a lovely note from Louise:

<u>'Welcome! Hope to see you in the next week.
Happy New Year. Louise & Squire.</u>'

Gemma surveyed her new home from over the stable door and watched us approvingly as Maggie and I were usefully employed storing her hay, which I hoped would last her for the best part of six weeks while I could source some more locally. There was so much to learn about the area and I looked forward to the adventure of it all. There was no storage space for feed bins at the farm, so we had to take everything to my house and store it in the garden shed including the large trunk that I kept for all her bits and bobs.

I helped Mags with her own horses when we returned to Bury Farm. It was a long day but I climbed into bed happy with the anticipation of the coming year.

Louise took me into Windsor Great Park where you could ride anytime if you had a permit. We had a fantastic ride and it was so reminiscent of the Lions Charity Sponsored Ride I had been to with Clive. We galloped and we jumped and as always, the scenery was spectacular. I was so taken with the opportunity and felt so privileged, I wasted no time in getting Gemma a permit so we could be 'legal' and I could enjoy riding in Windsor Great Park whenever I wished.

Chapter Seventeen: Share and Share Alike

The next thing I did was to put an advert in The Horse and Hound for someone to share Gemma with me. I dreamt of someone to share in both the pleasures and the responsibilities and in any case this was the only way I was going to be able to juggle a full time job and keeping Gemma - doing it all myself, not to mention the family who were now further away. Hmmm, I hadn't thought of that!

So, the advert read thus:

<u>Wanted: reliable person to share my 16 hands mare, 6 years old. Unspoilt with impeccable manners. Kept at DIY yard in Englefield Green, owner works shifts so flexible help, plus financial contribution required. Must be sympathetic rider - Tel 0784 85268</u>

I had one enquiry to my advert, and as it turned out this was the perfect person to share Gemma with. On the 31st December 1986 I opened the front door to Mandy, who had come in answer to the advert. I saw a nice-looking young lady wearing smart breeches, long socks and trainers. "Come in, come in," I welcomed her and over a cuppa we got to know each other. Mandy was a Nursing Sister working in a retirement home just round the corner. She was also on shifts so this could all work out rather well. I liked her immediately and we wasted no time in getting ourselves along to see Gemma.

Even though I had given her two and a half hours in the park that morning to make sure she was not too fresh, she still managed to prat about with me when we took her into the outdoor manège. So much for the perfect manners! Undaunted Mandy climbed aboard and she behaved perfectly. Hmm! That says much for my riding! Mandy liked her, a lot. In fact, I suspect it was love at first sight and we immediately set about agreeing what sort of arrangement we were going to have. I could spare little time to pre-amble further as I was at work at 7pm. New Year's Eve was always going to be heavy on the manpower commitment so I toddled off to work.

"After all I've done for you," my Sergeant greeted me as I crossed the forecourt, "you treat me like this."

"What have I done now, Sarge?"
"You were supposed to be here at 2pm."
"Ooops, sorry Sarge."
"Get your horse knocked over first, we are looking to go out at about 9pm."

I was posted to Trafalgar Square and the crowds were starting to build up in great numbers. It was good humoured and good fun, and by twelve midnight you could not move for people in the square. They had boarded up the fountains to stop folks bathing in them, as if you would want to at that hour in the middle of winter. But folks do, don't they? I kissed that many people I lost count, and the noise, and the singing, and the general hub of 'Happy New Year' for the coming of 1987 and a general feeling of 'all's well with the world' was a sight to behold. I felt very privileged to be there. Even my Sergeant, Steve, forgave me my sins; he was in such a good humour.

***

Early January brought the unforgiving commitment of the annual pantomime and it was now in fourth gear. Having little time to attend to my own requirements in life I had nothing ready for me to eat when I was due to leave for Imber Court for one of the performances. I grabbed some chicken from the freezer deciding to eat it on the way there. 'It'll thaw as it goes down' I thought to myself as I tugged at the unappetising frozen drumstick. God! Was I ill?! I won't do that again!

I had Gemma clipped out two days before we had the biggest fall of snow enveloping the farm. Roads were so treacherous, my delivery of hay failed to arrive and I had to scat about buying it bale by bale and carting it in the back of the car until the lorry could get through. The arctic weather was well below freezing and the taps froze almost as soon as you turned them off. I kept Gemma's top door shut in my attempts to keep her warm and Mandy lent me some woolly leggings to put on her.

This was not the sort of weather to be working through the night on some persistent demonstration, but that is what I was doing on 24th January 1987. One year to the day the Print Union Sogat had not gone away and was hell bent on a final big push for supremacy against Rupert Murdoch and Maggie Thatcher. I was riding Eve.

She was not a horse issued to me and I cannot say she was my favourite ride. She had a mouth like iron and sometimes I could not hold one side of her. My serial was sent to Virginia Street to be the first on call should the need arise.

The early part of the evening's activities were good-natured enough with the arrival of the marchers several hundred strong, led by a lorry carrying a jazz band playing some jolly tunes. As it came to the mouth of our street the band climbed off and the empty lorry was turned immediately over on to its side. This may have been an attempt to prevent the Mounted Branch from coming into force but we are made of sterner stuff. The mood of the demonstrators changed drastically and bricks and missiles began to fill the air.

A JCB came and towed the truck out of the way but not before the demonstrators attempted to set fire to it. Serials of policemen with protective shields hurried past us to replace the unprotected officers and for some considerable time we watched them coming back past us injured and bleeding to be treated by the medics at the bottom of Virginia Street. This did nothing for the rising adrenalin within the ranks and finally we were given an order to clear the crowds back to prevent further injury.

It was our intention to go up into Wellclose Square and tensions were becoming so heightened and the heavy bombardment of missiles had not subsided. My colleague next to me noticed something across the road, catching the light. He began to try and attract the attention of our skipper, Steve, sitting on Lydia just in front of me.

"Sarge!!" he shouted, trying to make himself heard above the din of confusing noises.

"Sarge! Sarge! Skip! HEY! SKIPPER!! He couldn't get his voice heard above the noise.

I joined in, I have a good voice: **"Oi! SARGE!!"** And Steve turned, half to give the command to clear the street but his eyes fell upon my frantic friend.

"Sarge, look, they've strung a wire between the lampposts across the road. If we go up there at any speed we'll be decapitated."

"Oh my God," Steve exclaimed, "Well spotted." And so we did not go.

A bit later we did enter the affray with a purpose, we trotted purposefully up into Welclose Street towards the Sogat bus. I became separated from my other colleagues and during those worrying moments I was aware that something had struck Eve on the face. Thankfully, with the help of two shield officers I managed to get back down to the rest of the serial in Virginia Street.

I had hardly been there for long and Inspector Petter joined us and gave instructions to clear the crowds in front of the plant. He received a message on his personal radio and immediately relayed what was said to the rest of us. He had to 'SHOUT' so he could be heard over the din.

"THERE IS A SMALL GROUP OF SHIELD OFFICERS TRAPPED BY AN ANGRY MOB ABOUT A HUNDRED YARDS DOWN THE HIGH STREET. THEY'VE GOT THEM SURROUNDED, I WANT FIVE VOLUNTEERS TO GO AND GET THEM OUT."

"I'll go, Guvnor," I piped up enthusiastically and with about four others we hurtled down the road. The mood of the crowd got angrier as we brought the officers back, running in front of the horses at break-neck speed as the crowd cleared a path for us or risk getting trampled.

Demonstrators were scattering in front of us as we negotiated the highway strewn with bricks and debris under the horses' hooves. We certainly had to earn our wages that night and when I got back to the stables later, I found a sharp piece of house brick buried in Eve's visor. It had gone right through the Perspex section and embedded itself into the leather pad underneath. If we had not had protective gear she might have been seriously injured, it may even have brought her down. Who knows?

***

The snow cleared by the beginning of February and I delighted in the Great Park but it was not without its adventures. One of the first times I took Gemma there, we got ourselves on to an open space and I asked for a canter, she put in this enormous buck of excitement and I sailed into mid-air landing unceremoniously on to the chippings just in time to see Gemma disappearing over the horizon bucking and farting in a most unladylike fashion. Picking myself up, I set off to follow her towards Blacknest Gate and home. I was met by a farrier who had come out to look for her rider having caught her as she tanked into one of the many polo yards just round the corner. "She is a beautiful horse," they said to me when the farrier and I arrived at the yard. "She would be perfect for polo if she was a hand shorter," the lady smiled at me and I thanked her for catching her and sending someone to find me.

It was not the last time that happened! Less than a fortnight later I was becoming quite bold and began to jump a few little jumps. There were plenty of logs about and Gemma and I were having the most wonderful time. Pride goes before a fall and I asked her to jump one log just a little higher than my abilities, fully committed I leaned forward ready for the take-off but Gemma, initially going for it, put in a half halt before leaving the ground. The interruption in her flow of movement was too much for me and I shot out of the saddle. Remembering the previous occasion, I hung on to her reins for about twenty yards before the contours of the ground got the better of me. As I bumped along the ground at break neck speed, I thought: 'Your mother used to do this for a living back in the days when she had been a stunt man's horse'. Luckily, we were in the deer park so I knew she could not get out, I just had two square miles in which to find her!

I dutifully recorded all events in Gemma's diary and it is quite unbelievable the things we did in the first couple of months. Mandy's general-purpose saddle fitted Gemma better than the one I had and so by selling it I was able to buy a purpose-built dressage saddle for her. Goodness gratious me, what a crutch hugger.

Mandy wanted to compete on Gemma in one-day events and gingerly asked if that would be okay with me. I considered this to be nothing short of exciting and in preparation for this we began training. Town Green Farm had no other liveries apart from Gemma and me and Louise and Squire. Even so, we had to book the outdoor school and pay an additional fee for the privilege. Mandy had the brainwave of asking the racing yard next door if we could use their jumps and cross-country fences. 'She is certainly braver than me,' I thought as she nipped through the adjoining gate to ask the head groom.

I took Gemma down to the outdoor manège to walk her round in preparation for dressage training and had not been there very long when I saw Mandy by the fence waving frantically, beckoning Gemma and me over. "The head groom is a love," she said excitedly. "He says we can use the facilities, how good is that? Let's take her down there now." And so we did. It was terrific. We laid out trotting poles and we each tried her over them putting up a small fence at the end. Mandy was by far a better jockey than me but I enjoyed seeing someone else on her, it was lovely to see her go so well. "Now let's see if she can jump," Mandy said, and we put the fence up to about three foot. She could. Oh my God! She could! "It's going to be a wonderful summer, Baldrick" Mandy's grin stretched from ear to ear.

"What did you say?"
"It's going to be a wonderful summer, Baldrick"
"Who's Baldrick?"
"Oh, Baldrick? He's an idiot."
"WHAT! Thanks a bunch".
"No, Sue! I don't mean you are an idiot." Mandy looked at me in a 'what-have-I-said-now' kind of a way, "Don't you ever watch Blackadder?" she asked.
"No."
"What never?"
"No, I've seen it in the paper, never watched it though."
"You should, it's with Rowan Atkinson and Stephen Fry," she persisted.
"Who's Stephen Fry?"
"You must watch it, you must."

I looked blankly at her, and now I come to think of it, so did Gemma.

"You should, you must, really, it's sooo funny, it'll change your life."

"If you say so, OK, I'll watch it, when's it on?"

"Tonight, 8.30." And we walked back to the yard to settle Gemma down for the night hoping this new-found facility would not be a 'one off' and we could use the jumps again. It was a terrific opportunity with a gallop and everything, right on our doorstep.

That evening I watched Blackadder. It changed my life!

***

Our first dressage test and we came third with a respectable mark of 86. The second test we had to hire transport as it was a little further away. Chris came with us to watch me, which was lucky because one of her shoes was loose so Chris took it off for us and the people there kept telling us she had a shoe missing, like we didn't know.

***

It was difficult to keep Chris in the shadows when I was doing so much with Mandy but I did not tell Erika he was in my life. I felt so ashamed of myself, much as I loved him. Chris had children, lovely children, and he was fond of them. It was a light bulb moment for me. It was the first time I realised men actually liked their children. Not that I had a problem with my own father but I thought he was special. I thought I was special dam-it. Sylvester and I curled up in bed together and I was lost in thoughts of making sense of it all.

So, John must love Ruth and Phillip, I concluded with much consideration. I had always thought he had just used them as pawns, which I think was true to a certain extent, but he must love them too. It was a good thing that after so many years we were now able to communicate, in fact I would even go so far as to say we had become friends. There were events in which we had to share space. When Phillip was awarded the Chief Scout medal, for instance, we met at Baden Powell House for the presentation. I recalled how much pride I could see in John's face. We were both proud of Phillip.

We were both proud of Ruth too when she joined The Territorial Royal Signals, looking so smart and military for her passing out parade. It was all food for thought.

***

"So, are you on your own now, Sue?" Erika asked as we enjoyed a cuppa in her kitchen.

"Yes," I replied, "you could say I'm between husbands at the moment."

Erika looked pensive. "I wonder?" she muttered almost to herself. "I wonder?" Then she spoke up directly, "My ex-husband, Richard, is on his own. Shall I ask him to take you out for a meal one evening?" I was taken off my perch with a bang. I had already made it clear to Chris that if I got the opportunity of meeting anyone else, anyone more available, then he would have to accept I would take that opportunity. There was no misunderstanding. "Yes, do," I replied without hesitation.

"He's a nice man," Erika continued warming to her theme. "He's a gentle man. We are still good friends, Teddy and he get on well and we never really fell out. I loved him once after all. I love him now, in a sisterly way."

"He sounds nice."

I was understandably troubled; I didn't much like the idea of all that chasing about courting with all its uncertainties. Anyway, with so much going on with Gemma at the moment how could I possibly find extra time for men. But if this Richard bloke did decide to ask me out, well, it seemed rude to refuse. Anyway, I put the thought on the back burner of my brain and got on with life.

It took Erika some time to persuade her ex that a blind date of her choosing was anything like a worthwhile project, but the phone rang one evening and Erika's ex-husband's first words to me were: "My ex-wife has told me I must take you out one evening, and I'm not going to get any peace until I do, so how are you fixed for next Wednesday?"

"Next Wednesday sounds good," I replied. And when Wednesday evening came, I opened the door to a tall good-looking guy who introduced himself to me as Richard Merrill. I liked him, and as the evening lengthened, I liked him even more. But what in heaven's name was I to say to Christopher? He won't like this one little bit, I thought, and I was right; he didn't like it.

Chapter Eighteen: All About Gemma

Mandy was really getting very excited with the prospect of eventing Gemma and thought she would be capable of competing in the British Horse Society Novice standard events. One-Day Events in fact. She was adamant that our own transport would be a must and we set about scanning the pages of The Horse and Hound for a small lorry we could purchase between us. We looked at a rust bucket in Bournemouth and an overpriced Transit in Chelmsford, then on Friday 13th Mandy spotted a little CF Bedford in Alton down in Hampshire. For fear of losing it we drove down to see it the very next day, and we both agreed it was a very pretty little lorry with a maroon cab and wooden panelled sides. Had I realised how talented Richard was with trucks and transport I might have asked him to accompany us. As far as I was concerned, he did something that sounded rather dull at Kensington and Chelsea Council.

Anyway, the little lorry looked just what we were after and so we made the deal, left a deposit and headed back home to go to our various work places both in time for the 2pm shift. Typical girls we talked with much excitement all the way back. Not about how we were to afford this lorry, not about whether or not to re-varnish the wood work, and not even about how we improve the interior to suit Gemma's comforts or ours. Nope, we talked about what we were going to call it!

I didn't like 'Nursey,' which was what Mandy first suggested.

"Because she nurses Gemma, Baldrick" Mandy argued.

Police, Ponies & Husbands in-between

"Why do you keep calling me Baldrick?"

"I don't know," Mandy shrugged, "It suits you. I wouldn't mind a bit if you called me Baldrick."

"Wouldn't you?"

"No of course I wouldn't, so what about 'Nursey?"

"Nah!" I said "That's rubbish. "What about 'Queenie'?"

"Queenie" said Mandy lovingly. "Yes Queenie, why not."

"Why not indeed, Baldrick."

So there you have it, we were good to go, the Bedford had a name, and so did we!! Priorities and all of that eh?

Chris took me down to Alton to collect her and the same evening I gave Gemma her supper inside the little lorry. The next day Mandy and I, and Queenie, took Gemma to Rose Hill where we could hire their cross-country course. We shared the hiring of the course with a friend of Mandy's, who told me I had a very nice horse and should be very proud of her. I was. Mandy took her round the pony club course first and then the big one missing out the fences which we thought might overface her like the Bird Hide and the Water. I did a couple of isolated fences with Mandy's instruction. "This one is a drop fence" she explained, "Drop fences are just the best, it's like flying," and Mandy was right, it was like flying.

The catalogue of events that followed during the summer was extraordinarily impressive. Our feet did not touch the ground. Too right there was no time for men and both Chris and Richard hovered around on the periphery of my interests. Chris was destined to a divorce the way things were going, but not to be with me. If I had taken the time to consider my options, then I would have realised, very slowly, the lovely Richard was becoming a more important feature in my social circle.

Mandy and I shared the necessary exercising that was required to keep Gemma fit and having Windsor Great Park so close was just wonderful, a really lovely place to ride every day, we were so lucky. I took Gemma there for a picnic one quiet day in the week when I had nothing better to do. There was just the two of us, I took a book to read, a sandwich and a drink all packed into a little leather bag designed to fit on the side of the saddle. I tied Gemma to a length of line and attached it to a tree and took her saddle off so she could graze. I read my book for a while, before just sitting and watching the deer in the distance. I moved Gemma every so often to provide her with more grass and the sun beat down on us interrupted only by the leafy trees which produced a wonderful dappling effect dancing on the grass.

Riding back up the long walk I saw a Landau coming towards us with a smart pair of horses trotting out in perfect step. Gemma and I moved over to the side of the drive to make room for it to pass and as it did so, I could see that Lady Diana was one of the passengers. Gemma and I bowed our heads and she smiled at us as I gave her a Mounted Branch salute in respectful reverence. It had been the sort of day that dreams are made of.

***

We were off again shortly after Rose Hill to Russell Farm in Wendover to hire another cross-country course and have some lessons. Gemma jumped like a dream, judging her fences and boldly tackling everything that she was asked to do. "What a clever little horse she is" our instructor said. Encouraged by this success, we took her to an unaffiliated one-day event at Seer Green in Buckinghamshire which was a club event so the cross-country was not too challenging and good practice for our girl.

Mandy had a dressage test at Snowball Farm but I couldn't go due to working late turn. We did know Gemma was a dab hand at untying knots and for this reason Mandy made sure the lead rope was good and secure on the ring inside Queenie before climbing into the cab to struggle into her jodhpurs. It was during this prone position that she heard someone calling to her in an excited fashion.... "Your horse is coming down the ramp." Bootless and trying to do up her flies, Mandy jumped to the ground just in time to see Gemma setting off across the field. Tail up, while bucking and farting, at an enthusiastic canter. Luckily the gate to the road was closed and while Gemma was doing a wall of death safely past it, it seemed the best plan of action was to allow her to settle down. This was fortuitous as running barefoot across the stony pasture was not Mandy's idea of fun. Eventually she put her head down to graze and the capture was complete. It was a recipe for success, surprisingly, as she performed one of her best Dressage tests.

In April I took Gemma to a Sponsored Ride in Aylesbury. He organised the picnic and it was a very exciting day for me. I saw quite a few people there who I knew including Gina from Pages Farm. She was riding her lovely mare who did particularly well in view of the fact that one of her reins had broken half way round. What is it with these sponsored rides that people's reins break willy-nilly, I thought to myself remembering Smith's Lawn with Clive.

We both had some lessons on Gemma at Wokingham Equestrian Centre and on the 22nd April, before Vicarage Farm, our first Affiliated Dressage and show jumping. She was now fully registered with the British Horse Society's Dressage Group and Horse Trials. Then on 3rd May Mandy and I had Dressage tests, it was at the same location as the Fulmer In-hand show Gemma had gone to when she was a baby. A baby with substantial hocks, which had the lady judge all but renting her clothes in disbelief that such a nice youngster should be afflicted with curbs.

Later that day we took a little time out to visit next door and take the head groom a bottle of Scotch as a thank you for letting us use the jumps. He showed us the horses they had there including a nice bay called Brown Trix. He had won the Grand National that year but it would have been a real accolade if he had been accompanied by a rider! I discovered, two years later, he became a game-changer for the course at Aintree when he jumped to his death at Beecher's Brook.

Maori Venture preceded by the riderless Brown Trix, wins the Seagram Grand National from The Tsarevich and Lean Ar Aghaidh.

Then, no sooner had we time to come up for air, The Lions Club of Windsor were again organising their immensely popular sponsored ride in the Great Park. Richard had recently joined The Lions Club of Maidenhead. He joined me for the day and we had a jolly time meeting up with Clive and his daughters. Gemma was always a dream ride and she was becoming more confident as I was becoming bolder, tackling the harder fences on the course.

This was good timing for our first unaffiliated One Day Event at Rose Hill on 10th May. We knew most of the jumps having hired the course earlier but familiarisation did not make The Quarry any less scary. It was a deep bank which dropped down about 15 feet although the landing distance was rather less because the ground sloped outwards. There was a platform from which to launch into space with timbers secured for the take-off so no chance of slithering over the edge. "At least there is no jump before the precipice" Mandy said, "but you still have to jump off the edge into nothingness." I was not able to get to that part of the course to watch her complete it and it worried the life out of me in case Gemma did not tackle it safely. But true to form she took it all in her stride. "She is such a star" said Mandy when we met up again at the finish line and she was positively glowing with pride and achievement. "We are going to have such a lovely summer," Mandy added, I

Police, Ponies & Husbands in-between

agreed and glowed with pride too.

For me, the summer of 1987 my days were all about Gemma and I had the opportunity of taking her to another sponsored ride, this time at Tweesledown, where I had once been before, with Charmian. She had asked me to accompany her to an Affiliated One Day Event two years earlier to help as her groom. I was in awe of the talented horses and riders gathered there and Charmian was kind enough to buy me a beautiful pair of leather riding gloves as a thank you. I should have been thanking her.

A few days later there was more Dressage at Vicarage Farm. Dressage was not Gemma's forte as she was beginning to headshake rather badly. It seemed to be stress related mostly and she expressed her reluctance to comply with the discipline of dressage by swinging her bum inward to go slightly sideways down the long side of the school swishing her tail in defiance. These are all signs of resistance and Mandy and I worked hard at getting her into the ring when she was just in the right mental state. I don't think they know what causes this problem, the increase in the growing of oil seed rape has been blamed and for some time it has been generally thought to be some sort of 'hay fever'. Whoever heard of a horse with hay fever! It had been suggested we stretch a stocking over the nose to desensitise the senses. We found the stocking solution very useful when working Gemma in but it did contravene one of the many dressage regulations when it came time to go in the ring.

I had entered some classes at a show in Guildford on 20th June. We had a working hunter show class in the morning and Show Jumping in the afternoon. I had my mother staying with me at the weekend along with Ruth and her boyfriend David. Not being very enthusiastic about the showing classes I put it to the family that we just go for the jumping in the afternoon. This was quite an adventure really as it took all three of us to get Mother into the lorry. "Can you get that far up Mum?" I asked when we took her out to inspect Queenie and the possibilities of her climbing aboard.

"I'm going to have a good try" she replied.

"I've got a little stool which might help" and fetched it for her. Mum began the struggle to climb in with her knee replacements being the biggest hindrance. "There is a handle just inside the door Mum, hang on to that if you can reach it" she reached for the handle.

"You're doing fine Nan" said Ruth, "I'm right behind you."

"David, run round the other side and grab the other hand."

"I'm there" he chortled as he climbed into the driver's side, "C'mon Nan, give us your hand." David pulled, Ruth pushed and I hovered giving instructions before she was finally seated.

"Done it" she said triumphant and we set off to collect Gemma and on to Guildford. Mother stayed in the lorry all afternoon and watched the proceeding from the elevated position of the cab. It was an extraordinarily hot day and when I entered the ring to jump in my shirtsleeves, I was sent back out again to put a jacket on. Ooops.

Gemma was a star and I felt so happy to have my family in tow. All we had to do when we got home was to get Mother out; she had seized up quite a bit so it was no mean achievement.

On 28th June we had a Hunter Trials and Richard came with me with a hired video camera. Then on 12th July I took Gemma to a Working Hunter class in Hertfordshire. I was told by the judge that her saddle did not fit her properly and she should not be wearing brushing boots in a working hunter show class. She still placed us in 4th though and I thought this quite an achievement in a big class. We came 6th in the show jumping, which pleased me no end. Gemma was wearing Mandy's saddle being better than mine but I should have paid this more attention before and we were going to be asking her to do some tricky fences two days later and this worried me quite a bit. So, the following day I rang the best saddler I knew and booked an appointment later the same day for her to attend their premises for a saddle fitting. Thank goodness for Queenie, I concluded, and armed with my Access card I bought a brand-new G. Fieldhouse general purpose saddle for a cool £314 which I didn't have. I thought it was the most wonderful thing I had ever purchased, I loved it, and felt this was going to give Gemma every chance of success at her first Affiliated One Day Event at Waldridge Manor. It took me months to pay off the cost accumulated on the card but a girl's gotta do what a girl's gotta do.

Waldridge Manor is considered to be a One Day Event though actually it spans over two days. I was working on the first day leaving Mandy to go on ahead. She achieved a fantastic thirty-three points for her dressage bringing her to a position of 6th until the show jumping which earned her five penalty points and her status slipped. Mandy's friend Lindsay put us both up for the night including Gemma as well. We did not get a great deal of sleep that night as they had weaned the lambs on the farm and they were all penned in the yard next to the cottage, and yelling for their mothers. 'Silence of the lambs' indeed, I've never heard such a racket.

The Cross-Country element of the competition the following day was so exciting. Mandy, Lindsay and I walked the course and although the first fence was relatively straight forward, it was big. "Blimey Baldrick!" I said, "Rather you than me." Mandy and Lindsay looked at me in disbelief. We walked to the next which had a longer option over two substantial fences and the quick route being a rather imposing corner jump. "Bloody Hell" I said standing next to it measuring the height against my body.

"It's a rider frightener" said Lindsay, "nothing more, the horses find it easy."

The next fence was a coffin. "This coffin combination looks quite inviting" quipped Mandy looking for support.

"So long as you don't end up in one," I piped up cheerfully. We walked on, Mandy and Lindsay unusually quiet.

We came to the water, "Grief that looks deep" I said, "and she's not keen on water."

"For God's sake Baldrick" Mandy swung round on me.

"What have I said?" - - - - I said.

"I think" began Lindsay "unless you can come out with any encouraging remarks, keep your thoughts to yourself, please."

"Oh." - - - - "Sorry" - - - - - "OK, I'll shut up then shall I?"

"Yes" they both said in unison almost shouting.

It was just so wonderful watching Gemma go round the course, even though she refused three times at a fence bringing her total to a cricket score of 200. Mandy rode her brilliantly and I was awestruck at how talented they both were.

Police, Ponies & Husbands in-between

Chapter Nineteen: Accident Waiting to Happen

Being mindful of the lack of show jumping practice Gemma was getting, Mandy suggested we go to Stoke Poges to a little riding club event where they have clear round jumping. It hadn't stopped raining from the days at Waldridge Manor, surely, we are not going to get the promised 40 days and 40 nights of rain following St Swithin's Day? That would be such a shame with all the effort we were putting in.

Mandy was working until later so she said she would see me there. As I pulled on to the field it was hissing down with rain and for this reason, I decided to tack Gemma up tied inside Queenie. Forgetting how good Gemma is at untying knots I got into the cab for my hat, gloves and some money for the entry. There was a little Anglia van parked next to Queenie and the man who was with it called to me through the rain "Your horse is just coming down the ramp!!" I looked at him in disbelief as I purposely stode towards the back of the lorry just in time to see Gemma step clear of the ramp and head across the field towards the entrance before I could stop her. "Quick! Jump in" he said running round to the driver's side while another lady ran for the passenger side. He started the engine up and began to move forward. I had no option but to jump in the back, throwing myself inside while the van was heading up the field and picking up speed. I looked out between the two front occupants just in time to watch Gemma leave the field and head out on to the road.

"Where has she gone" I asked.

"I think she has gone left"

"Towards those traffic lights? Oh crikey,"

"We'll find her," said the lady passenger, "we'll find her."

"There she is" said the driver, "Oh look she's stopped all the traffic, what a clever girl" Gemma was trotting purposely across one of the busiest of traffic junctions stirrups flapping and one rein longer than the other waving in the wind. Her head was up and her flaxen mane was bouncing jauntily as she turned her head this way and that, I could see she was in no mood for stopping anytime soon.

We crossed the junction, eventually, with the disadvantage of having to wait for the lights to change first, and followed on until we caught up with her through a housing estate, then, thankfully, a more rural setting. The lane was narrow though and we could not get past her, so we just followed hoping the luxury of some nice grass might slow her down. It didn't. Then, up ahead there was a person on a push bike, and presumably she heard the sound of hooves behind her and turned to see Gemma still trotting at quite a pace. Getting off her bike the lady, who did look rather elderly, delved into her pockets as she tactfully blocked Gemma's passing, holding out a palm full of pony cubes as a reward.

What wonderful people they were who had come to my rescue in my hour of need? The man who drove the van, the kind lady with him and the lady on the bike who skilfully caught her. All I had to do now was renegotiate those traffic lights, and my hat was still in the cab of the lorry, as was my purse, ignition keys, etc etc.

I arrived back at the show ground 25 minutes later, in the rain, to find Mandy already there and wondering what had happened to us. Now the excitement was all over, I did enjoy the telling of the tale. We knuckled down to some serious work and Gemma was nicely worked in after our ride back. In the end we were quite pleased with ourselves that she had done this extra work to help build up her confidence. "I'm glad we brought her here now" Mandy said nodding and I agreed it had been worthwhile.

We would not have said that an hour later. Gemma, Queenie and I headed back for home and turning right on to the Uxbridge Road I found myself stuck across the central reservation waiting for the traffic to clear. It was not heavy traffic being 9.30pm or thereabouts and as far as I could see there was just one large van in the fast lane coming towards me on the left. He slowed and flashed for me to come out in front of him which I trustingly did, and made for the nearside slower lane of the dual carriageway.

Suddenly out of nowhere, (don't all accidents begin like that?) a car already in the nearside lane and previously hidden by the presence of the large van, overtook on the nearside connecting with Queenie amidships on the port side. "Where the Hell did you come from?" I asked the driver, and he, pretty much expressed the same sentiment. We were all to blame, in truth. The van driver for flashing me out when a brief check in his wing mirrors would have told him it was far from safe. The car, for overtaking on the nearside, the van wasn't turning, he was just letting me out. And it was my fault too for crossing the line of traffic and because I trusted his judgement rather than my own. I checked Gemma quickly and exchanged particulars with the other driver and headed home. Note to self: forever be mindful that just because another driver allows you to proceed in front of him, does not mean you have to go.

Gemma had a small cut below the nearside front fetlock but Queenie would cost an arm and a leg to get repaired. I settled Gemma into her stable for the night dosing the cut on her leg with a good smothering of Green Oils which is my cure for everything. By the time I got home I was quite upset as I knew I would have to tell Mandy what had happened and I didn't know how she would take the news. "Oh Precious," she said soothingly down the phone, "I can understand why this has upset you, I'll come straight round." She brought with her a comforting bottle of Brandy which we sipped as we discussed the way forward.

"At least Queenie is not off the road" I ventured.

"No, thankfully, it shouldn't interrupt our programme."

"I hope not, we are doing so well, and so is Gemma."

"Thank goodness we have fully comprehensive insurance" said Mandy grasping at straws to find something positive to ruminate on.

"I just hope that we don't have another day like today."

***

Joining the Mounted Branch had opened up the opportunity of seeking out a retired Mounted Police Officer, Geoff Dorset. He was a very good teacher as well as being a British Horse Society examiner. I booked fortnightly lessons to improve my riding abilities as well as all the other events we had planned.

I kept my eye on the event pages of the Horse and Hound for anything low key enough, to be suitable for Gemma and me. I noticed one of the local Riding Clubs were advertising an unaffiliated one-day event. Ruth and David were staying with me at the time and they were happy to tag along making the occasion another jolly family outing.

I made the mistake of working Gemma in for the dressage test by a wooded area in the corner of the field. The flies were in their thousands and Gemma kindly invited them all back to the lorry and having no repellent with me they followed on into the arena. I did not think the test was a good one but the mark was ultimately not that bad.

Unusually the Cross Country came next and Gemma ran out at the first fence. "If you're not interested" she said indignantly, "then don't expect me to be."

"Ok," I told her, "I'll ride the next like I want to" and we were off, I pushed on after the water trough which gave us no problems, then on up the hill where I really let her go. Could I bring her back? I could not! "Whoa there Honeysuckle" I breathed into her ear as we came over the hill to tackle a bank complex at an amazing rate of knots. Then came a sharp right-hand bend to the tyres which was a drop fence, Mandy's words sung in my ears "drop fences are wonderful, they're like flying" she had told me, and Gemma flew! Down to a left turn and then in front of us we saw a double,

"Yikes!" Gemma shouted to me "I can't take a fence at this speed."

"What have I been telling you for the last 600yds?"

Gemma slung out the anchor and sat back on her haunches, still with a strong hold on the bit she leapt it like a stag, one bounce and then the second half. Snatching at the bit she practically took the reins out of my grasp before she was off again tanking across the open space to the pheasant feeder which she cleared with no hesitation. Then on again, over a wide ditch which I doubt she even saw, just taking it in her stride and finally, finally we crossed the finish line with no time faults.

I was utterly exhausted and I still had the show jumping ahead of me. Unbelievabley we had a clear round giving us the overall result of 9th for the day. I was very pleased with that, so were Ruth and

David and so was Gemma. "Didn't I tell you I could do it?" she told me smugly as I led her up the ramp.

***

The daily programme at work was like a well-oiled machine and I was on a spare horse one bright and breezy Thursday heading for a blatt round Hyde Park. Devon was white as the driven snow, and a robust sort of horse with a build more appropriate to pulling railway rolling stock than gracing the elegance of Rotten Row. Parked there in the sunshine was the beginnings of a circus arriving to set up for the week. I wandered over to take a closer look and maybe have a little dialogue with some of the jolly circus folk. There was no-one about but there was the huge trailer of an articulated lorry with one side open. Inside there were four elephants swaying gently and watching the movements around the park. The trouble with me is that I don't properly think things through and gripped by the desire to show Devon the elephants, I went over to take a closer look and they seemed really cool about having Devon visit them, they must be used to horses I thought, they are circus elephants after all.

Then, seemingly without warning one of them stretched out its trunk towards us so the tip was just feet from where we stood. The nostrils quivered for a moment before letting out the most incredible trumpet noise right into Devon's face. I have never seen a more impressive capriole let alone sit on one! Devon let out a kind of shriek, it wasn't a neigh or a snort it was just a shriek, and then, on a sixpence he spun round and tanked off across the park with me hanging on for dear life. Gathering my reins frantically we sped towards the bandstand and I fought to rein him in just in time before we got to the road. I let Devon stretch his neck out as he heaved great breaths of air into his lungs and I was quite shaken too, "Sorry Devon old chap" I said to him patting his sweat sticky sides and neck to soothe him back to normality. He had never been the liveliest Police Horse and I was quite impressed.

"What in the name of carrots were they?" Devon asked me when he had enough breath to say anything.

"Just elephants mate" I replied, "The sort of thing we see every day round here."

"Yeah right." He said. "Well, I'm in no hurry to see them again."

***

Our next affiliated event was at Aston Clinton and it was fast looming up. I had a lesson booked with Geoff beforehand but he was unwell so had to cancel. This did, however, give me more space to nip up to St Albans straight from work to collect my son, Phillip, who was staying with me for a couple of weeks. It was his school holiday time and a rare treat for me. The three of us piled into Queenie on the day of the event and set off for Oxfordshire.

The cross-country course was smashing with lots of options and easy alternatives to the bigger fences starting with a small steeplechase fence. The bank had two options and Gemma took the hardest which was a step up and a three-foot fence over to a drop of a couple of feet on the landing side, and she made it look so easy. Mandy did not ask her to jump the brush fence which attracted much attention because as each rider approached it, a row of fountains spurted upwards so the horse was not only surprised to see such a barrier, but was expected to jump through it. A bottle of Champagne was given by the jump sponsor to every successful competitor who cleared the obstacle.

Gemma finished the course lame and the resident vet diagnosed a puncture to the sole. An antibiotic jab and instructions for the next few days left us a bit worried for the next event at Smith's Lawn in less than a week's time. Following instructions to the letter with poultices and further antibiotic jabs, Gemma ran up sound in the nick of time. I rang our farrier who said that if I could get her to where he was working, he could fit a leather pad under the shoe so we could keep her working. Thanks to Queenie, this was no sooner said than done with just two days to go before the Dressage test that I had entered at Pinnerwood.

I was on early turn at work again the following day and I was having trouble getting hold of a copy of the BHS Test Prelim Number eight. I

Police, Ponies & Husbands in-between

had drawn a blank with everyone I knew who I thought might have a copy, and I had run out of time to order it by post. Having no time to address the problem, I hit on a brainwave and I decided that the only way forward was to go directly to the J A Allen book shop round the back of Buckingham Palace. I knew I would be doing the Changing of the Guard that morning so right in the middle of my duties at the Palace, Ultra and I nipped round the back to buy a copy of the test directly from the shop. The famous Charles Harris was just coming down the steps as I approached, and I knew he was a good friend of Geoff's and, in fact, many of the officers in the Mounted Branch. We engaged in a mutually enjoyable chat and he told me that Geoff was feeling much better and I should give him a ring. He was kind enough to go back into the shop for me and so with this help my problem was solved and I had my Number eight Dressage Sheet. Ultra and I got back round to the front of the Palace just in time to escort the new Regiment back up The Mall.

***

Phillip had been a hard task master helping me to learn my test. I thought I had her just right as I entered the ring at 'A'. She had been performing her circles and extensions beautifully outside the ring and I was so proud to have Phillip there with me watching the performance. As we bounced joyfully down the centre line, I was delighted to see that my old instructor Charmian was judging and she winked at me in recognition as I reached X for what I hoped would be the perfect halt. This was going to be such a proud moment I told myself. I bowed my head dropping my right arm down by my side in the traditional salute. Two seconds and we moved forward bouncing into a neat working trot.

Charmian did not take her eyes off us as she dictated to her scribe what to write in the judge's spaces on the test form.

'Much better move off, stiff and unbalanced at the turn.'
Working trot 20 metres circle at 'C' the instructions read,
'Some better strides but not working through the back'
Working canter.
'anticipating canter' wrote the scribe *'Wonderful flying change against the hand!'* dictated Charmian.
Working trot. *'Rather hurried & unbalanced.'*
Free walk on a long rein. *'Obedient to walk showing tension, some good stretching walk could cover the ground more'.*
Working canter right circle change the rein through working trot. *'Slightly better turn, canter across much better'.*
Down the centre line and halt and salute.
Phew!! That was a long four and half minutes.
Charmian wrote, *'Lots to like but very little really good work shown because of tension & hollowness.* *'Tactfully handled* & she had added; *keep it up'.*
Our final mark was 66 out of 100, what a miserable effort!

***

I felt guilty taking time out to ride Gemma while Phillip was staying with me, it was bad enough that I had to go to work. I could not leave it all to Mandy, obviously. So, I dusted off my pushbike and said to Phillip that I wanted to take Gemma to the Great Park and he might find it a bit of a wheeze to come with me. It was great, the sun was shining and while I rode my horse Phillip cycled and it has to be said, whatever your mode of transport, Windsor Great Park is just the best place to be.

Chapter Twenty: Neglect & Due diligence

We had only one day for respite before the One Day Event at Smith's Lawn. It was good to be somewhere local for a change, although we still took Gemma in Queenie. Mandy's Mum and Dad came to watch the fun. Mandy's new boyfriend also came along. The cross country is always the most interesting element, fence number five was three poles fanned out with no proper landing at the upright end. There was a big double oxer and a simple water obstacle with no jump. Gemma flew over all of them but then there was a brush fence which had a solid pole on the top which she hit quite hard and Mandy came off. I did not see that happen because Phillip and I were at the coffin element waiting with my camera to capture her image as she came through it. I got a lovely picture of Gemma climbing the steps - all on her own because Mandy had fallen for the second time. She was exhausted, Mandy that is, and with a mouth full of sand she climbed wearily aboard and completed the obstacle and in so doing, completed the course.

"Baldrick! You kept taking photos?" Mandy exclaimed when we were all back with Queenie.

"Yes of course I did Baldrick, that was the most exciting bit."

"I can't believe you did that, Baldrick, you are unbelievable."

"Oh don't take any notice of me, Baldrick, I'm just a complete fruit loop."

"You can say that again" chipped in Phillip totally bewildered by all this 'Baldrick' nonsense.

***

I was forever in trouble at work, I tried hard not to be, maybe I tried too hard. I was on a different planet from everyone else, so I must take some of the responsibility. Anyway, it takes a brave person to stand up for the underdog and that brave person for me was Roly. He really looked out for me in his own subtle way, he was my guide as to how to be a good mounted man. He reminded me quietly if I was running late with things that needed to be done like cleaning my kit or getting ready to go out. You could not afford to be left behind if there was some operational duty to perform and we had to be somewhere at a certain time.

Roly was a fascinating man, he served in the Household Cavalry before he joined the Metropolitan Police Force and transferred into the Mounted Branch like so many ex-cavalry personnel before him. He left the United Kingdom with his family to live in Canada where he joined the Royal Canadian Mounted Police. It says much for the man that when he returned to England he was readily accepted back into the Metropolitan Police. His love for the horses saw his return back into the Mounted Branch and luckily for me that he was posted to Great Scotland Yard where I was able to take advantage of his kindness and guidance.

One morning a few of us were on plain regular daytime hours as we had a lorry of horse food and forage due to arrive. A set number of officers were required for the lengthy unloading process.

We were permitted to park our cars on Horse Guards Parade when it was not in use and there were no ceremonials taking place. I arrived on this forage day the same time as Roly, and we walked together through the archway of Horse Guards to cross Whitehall on to Great Scotland Yard. As we walked past the mounted sentries sitting on their horses so immaculate and static, I remarked how sorry I felt for the soldiers being stuck there doing absolutely nothing and putting up with all those annoying tourists. "What a dreadful job" I said to him, not knowing of his history "poor fellows, that would drive me insane."

"Have you any idea how hard these guys have to work to achieve the honour of such a posting?" he asked me looking aghast, but allowing himself a wry smile at the comedian he was in the company of.

"Really?" I marvelled.

"Really" he replied utterly dumbfounded that I could have such a lack of understanding for the way the military worked.

I shook my head in disbelief as we crossed Whitehall, and Roly did the same.

The forage lorry arrived and five of us got stuck in to unload. I pitched in with a will, standing with my back to the edge of the lorry and easing one of the many twenty kilo bags of horse nuts on to my shoulders. I trotted towards the ramp to take it upstairs and Phil's hand caught me by the shoulder, "Take it easy" he said, this has to last us all day, we don't want to get it all unloaded in too much of a hurry."

"Don't we?"

"Good God No, anyway, we don't carry stuff up the ramp that's too much like hard work. You would do your back some damage that way."

"Where do we put it then?" I said, and Phil pointed to the guys who were setting up a platform which was attached by ropes to a winch two floors up where the hay loft was. The platform carried all the bagged feed up to the next floor where the stables were and the hay was stored on the second floor. Everything was pulled through the hatch on the balcony, the same hatch that we dropped the muckings out into the waiting lorry from the Royal Parks every morning. The system was faultless.

***

I was on late turn the following day and chose to ride my second horse in the evening. Ivor was a nice little black cob. The streets were beginning to get dark, as dark as London can get with all the light pollution. I had a local radio on my shoulder and I listened carefully to a report of a recently stolen pedal cycle on The Embankment. Within minutes a bloke on a pedal cycle came hurtling round the corner of Whitehall Court, and from what I could make out in the dark, he appeared to be wearing all the right colours of the description. He did not stop when I tried to intercept his path so Ivor and I chased after him. We didn't have to go far before I grabbed his collar and pulled him from the bike. "Where do you think you're going my ol' son" I said. "I told you to stop."

"Let go of me" he insisted. I didn't. In turn he did not let go of the bike either.

"Let go of the bike" I instructed. He didn't. In turn Ivor was frightened by the bike and began dancing across the road.

"Let go of the damn bike" I shouted. He didn't.

"Let go of me" he shouted. I didn't.

Ivor continued dancing while becoming hotter and hotter as he did so.

There was a stalemate between us, "I just want to ask you some questions" I said,

"Well ask me then" he replied still dangling under my fist. Ivor continued to dance.

At that moment the cavalry arrived in the form of the area car from Cannon Row and it was all over in a trice. Chummy was arrested, and the bike was also taken into custody. I was so shell-shocked I didn't even think to ask for my name to be included on the arrest papers. A valuable opportunity lost in the bid to help boost the Mounted numbers game. But hey! I was glad to get back to the stables and finish my duties in a more relaxed way. Ivor was dripping with sweat, and because he was just beginning to grow his winter coat I did not think it was appropriate to hose him down. Anyway it would have taken him ages to dry, so I thought it was better to let the sweat dry and I could rub him clean before I went home.

I forgot!

I was so pleased to get home after a long day at work. I fell into my bed and I slept. 3.30am I woke for no good reason and sat bolt upright with the horrible realisation that I had not brushed Ivor clean. It was my day off but there was nothing else for it but to go back into London as quickly as possible and see the horse right before anyone else came into work and found him. Ruffling Sylvester's furry back I apologised to him and left for the one-and-a-half-hour round trip. Ivor was no pushover to clean up and I scrubbed and scrubbed at his sweat caked coat until I felt he looked good enough to go out on another day's tour of duty. Leaving the building by the side door I came face to face with Alice the cleaner followed closely by Roly. They regarded me with no small amount of bewilderment, "Good morning Sue" they greeted. "Morning" I called cheerily as I disappeared past them too embarrassed to give an explanation.

When I returned to duty two days later, the incident was largely forgotten but I did detect a questionable comment or two, which I did not rise to, much to the annoyance of those who made them. I am sure that what they imagined to be the reason for my early bird behaviour was far more interesting than the actual truth.

In contrast to forgetting a horse's needs, on another occasion, I stuck my neck out to protect one. I was on my own at work for late turn duties and walking along the back of the horses all lined up neatly in their stalls, when I noticed Lydia, the sergeant's horse, breathing heavily. Her sides were really heaving at a phenomenal rate. Thanks to the instruction on stable management that I had been receiving I knew with all certainty this was not right. I timed her breathing, it was fast. I took her temperature, it was high. She was a lovely horse, something of a Gemma look-a-like and I liked her immensely. Unfortunately, Steve was away on annual leave so I had to ring the Inspector at home. There was nothing else I could do.

We did not enjoy a good relationship and so I felt unbelievably brave and stupid both at the same time. He told me I must be mistaken and to re-do the checks of breathing and temperature. I did this and rang him back with the same findings. He had no option but to come into central London, there was nothing else he could do and I waited for him to arrive with my heart in my mouth. When he arrived he was not best pleased but his findings resulted in the same high temperature and respiration. He called the vet who diagnosed pneumonia.

It was gone midnight before I got home but that lovely horse Lydia was saved and continued to control crowds and perform ceremonials with no lasting damage.

***

Sometimes the two lives that I led overlapped. Erika and I had an exciting day out into central London to visit the Society of Equestrian Artists Annual Exhibition at the Mall Galleries. Erica was expecting her second child and was well on the way to the happy event. Being in this delicate condition she had an urgent call of nature. We were just around the corner from Great Scotland Yard where I worked. "We'll pop across the road and go there" I suggested cheerfully.

Our Skipper, Steve, was on duty and I chatted happily to him while Erika was upstairs, apologising for the intrusion and explaining that needs must. The tearoom door opened and Erika came in chuckling to herself and saying that it was a good thing she had a sense of humour. A past life as a film extra had trained her well for the jolly japes that sometime happen in a man's world. Steve and I looked at her in puzzlement. "Someone," she began "had balanced fire crackers under the rubber studs fitted underneath the lavatory seat." I was also used to this kind of Tomfoolery so it came as no surprise to me. "I suppose I'm lucky there was no cling film stretched across the porcelain seat as well." She quipped,

Steve looked thoroughly embarrassed but no one was blaming him.

"Your baby could have come early," I said, "That would have created an incident to remember."

"Who said it won't" Erika laughed.

***

With Smith's Lawn out of the way, Mandy asked me if I would mind if she took Gemma down to the New Forest for a week and I readily agreed saying it would be good for both of them. So off they went, Gemma, Mandy and Queenie, and I got on with a few other tasks.

Ultra was not at her best. I could tell she was struggling when I took her to Hammersmith for shoeing, and in anyone's book it was a good distance for a horse her age. I made noises to the Inspector but he was not convinced and called over the Chief Inspector from Hyde Park. To be a horse light in the stable would give them operational problems, it's true, but my bringing to light her problems merely earned her a slot on the duty board for a day at West Ham football stadium. There is no doubt in my mind that this was a way of punishing me for my insubordination. All the others were against the posting and did much muttering behind hands. I imagined that they thought I was responsible for speaking out, and I should have kept my head down and said nowt. I continued to fight her corner and I refused to lie quiet on the subject until she was taken off the West Ham roster and placed on duty Changing of the Guard at the palace instead.

I did not stay quiet, I knew that she was not right, so the Inspector finally conceded, just to shut me up, he agreed to call the duty vet and get her looked over. I knew this was not going to end well so the following day I rode her straight down to one of the green spaces along by the Thames. I dismounted and loosened her girth, removing the bit from her mouth I allowed her to graze, and the two of us shuffled about for a good hour while she found the best grass. It was the very next day that the duty vet came to examine her and came to the only conclusion possible and that was, she should be caste, which meant she was unfit for further Police duty.

I was very sad about Ultra's fate and it was with a deflated gait I walked to my car that evening wondering what I could do, if, in fact, I could do anything. I returned to work the following morning and was told that the horse box was coming for her at 10.30am and she would go down to Imber Court. By the end of the tour of duty the news reached me that Ultra was booked to go to the slaughterhouse in Upminster the following week. "What day?" I asked and I was told. Finally, I knew what I must do.

We were in our final wind-down from the day's tour, getting into our civvies and generally having a gossip in the tearoom until the big hand of the wall clock hit the magic hour and we could go home. The Inspector came into the tearoom and began to make some final adjustments to the duty board.

"Sir?" I began, "I understand that Ultra is due to make her final journey next Thursday."

"Yes"

"Can I go with her please?"

"No,"

I was taken aback. "Why not?"

"I think that it is unwise for you to go, you will be too upset."

"No I won't, why would I be?"

"Because she's your horse."

"No she isn't, I only have one horse and she is grazing in a field in Surrey. Can I go with her please?"

"No you can't. You're a girl, girls get upset about these things."

"That's not a valid reason, why can't I go?"

"Why do you want to?" the Inspector look exasperated.

"Because she has been issued to me, and I want to see the job through."

"You don't have to do that"

"Yes I do, I owe it to her, and I want to see the job through to the end."

"Well you're not going, get over it."

After something of a pregnant pause I hardened my resolve. "You can't stop me."

"Can't I indeed? We'll see about that."

I felt increasingly defiant. "I'm on weekly leave next Thursday."

"Your point being?"

"I don't live far from Imber Court. I can be there before they leave and there is nothing you can do about it."

"Is that a fact? Well you won't be able to go to Imber Court if I post you on duty for the day here at GSY."

"With less than eight days' notice Governor? I don't think so."

"What?"

Can your budget run to double time and day off in lieu?" I asked. "I'll follow the horse box if I have to." Doggedly I stuck to my guns.

He began to exit the tearoom with the parting shot "You're not going, and that's that."

But before disappearing out through the door he turned and added "In my office, NOW."

I followed him down the ramp wondering what can of worms I had opened, I was no stranger to being in trouble, but, do you know what? I came out of his office triumphant. Calling me back in he added, "you do this as a regular tour of duty, none of this 'less than eight days' notice' stuff."

"Yes Sir, thank you Sir."

I can't explain why I wanted to go with her, I just wanted to be with her, she was my responsibility. The guys back in the tearoom seemed impressed with my tenacity. They told me, "there was no way he was going to back down and allow you to go with Ultra, we don't know how you did it."

It was the saddest of journeys though, and I don't think I let the side down given that I was just a girl. Ultra was put on to the lorry with another Police horse which pleased me that she had company. I took some apples with me for her to nibble on the journey, sharing them with the other horse. I was fully prepared to hold her while she was shot but a kindly slaughter man took her from me, "You don't have to go in here with her," he said. "I'll take her." I smiled gratefully, and handed her over, he took the lead rope from me and patting Ultra gently on her neck, he said, "Come on my ol' darlin'."

Returning home, I wished that Gemma was not away with Mandy. Thank goodness I had Sylvester to cuddle.

Chapter Twenty-One: A Rare Horse Indeed

Mandy and Gemma returned from the New Forest having had the most fabulous time together. It felt like a lifetime for me and I wasted no time in taking her out across The Great Park first thing the following morning. I had to ride early because I had arranged to meet some of the old crowd from Imber Court on Smith's Lawn in the afternoon as we were going to watch a polo match and I had to do my bit to contribute to the picnic. The match was informal and friendly and we sat in spacious luxury on the soft grass with the best view of the pitch. At half time spectators ran out on to the pitch to press back the divots of sward that had been kicked up by the ponies. The game, as always, was fast and furious and the most entertaining of all sports.

We retired to The Sun after all the matches had been played and Mandy joined us following her tour of duty at work. She broke the news to me that there was some bad feeling between our Town Green Farm and the training yard next door and we were no longer allowed to use their jumps to train Gemma over. I had been hoping for some tuition from Geoff over the fences next week so it was something of a disappointment. Although we did consider ourselves extraordinarily lucky to have had the opportunity in the first place.

While this was a bit of a blow for us, it was an insignificant interruption compared with the devastation for our farmer. The German Shepherd from next door had jumped the fence and killed one of their Jack Russell terriers and seriously maimed the other terrier. She was a very sorry sight when I saw the damage and I cannot imagine the worry of living next door to an unpredictable dog. I like German Shepherds, having been brought up with them but the imbalance of size between the breeds meant that it was always going to end in tears if they fell out.

Mandy went ahead to Crondell the next day with Gemma and Queenie. Ruth and David and I followed afterwards arriving just in time to see the action. The Dressage earned us 35 points, and the show jumping was clear. The cross country was nice, I thought, although there was a quarry which always worries me. With this particular obstacle there were only two strides at the bottom to rebalance the horse before three steps and another jump. Gemma sailed over it all with ease, then she refused at the coffin. Having started the course under a beautiful blue sky it was now clouding over at a rate of knots and spots of rain were beginning to fall as Mandy came over the finish line. I took Gemma from her and we ran to put her into Queenie before the heavens opened. Ruth took hold of Gemma while I tackled the catches on the ramp as the deluge was already falling on us. I turned the catch frantically to release it. Water was cascading over the top of the lorry roof and now running down my outstretched arm and under my clothes. The ramp was wet and slippery and Gemma took one look at it and said "I aint goin' in there."

"Oh yes you are" I argued and it took no small amount of self-control for me to relax and gently coax her in. She is so sensitive and the urgency of the situation alarmed her and the only way was for me to adopt a nonchalant aspect. Not at all easy when you are getting drenched. We all got drenched.

***

I had continued to see Erika throughout the summer, when time allowed, and I had joined the Egham and District Riding Club. Their Annual Show was the following day on Smith's Lawn and I would have entered some of the jumping classes but as always after a one-day event Gemma had the day off. Ruth and David came with me to enjoy the day and we caught up with Erika there too. It was really nice to be at a horse show without the responsibility of a horse.

Erika kept her ponies over at Chobham, just a mile or two down the A30. I met Joyce who owned the field and she said I would be able to take Gemma there for a holiday when the summer events were all over. I had been with Erika several times to see her ponies so I knew the field well and it looked good. I had read in the club's newsletter that volunteers were needed to help clear away the jumps and show equipment that same evening, it also said anyone with a large vehicle would be made very welcome. So I took Queenie over to Smith's Lawn to help out. I have rarely had such an enthusiastic welcome, in fact I do not know how they would have managed without Queenie providing transport. Having completed the work in record time we all retired to a pub to finish the evening off. It was an evening well spent and I could see that my involvement with Egham and District Riding Club had potential for growth.

Mandy's life was changing too, what with the new boyfriend she had plans to move away at the end of the summer after the one-day event at Longworth. I knew we would have to sell Queenie, I could not afford to buy her out, sadly, and also there were things to be done before we could offer her for sale. I had arranged to have the damage repaired which thankfully was put through the insurance but the MOT was running out. I took her down to Egham to one of these Private Light Goods MOT while you wait centres. They put her on to their ramp and raised her up, or tried to! She was not far off the ground, when of one of the stanchions began to bend. I couldn't see it but the owner of the garage could and there was much panic amongst the employees to get her back down before it all ended in tears. They were not at all happy with me and I was sent away thoroughly chastised. Crickey! It wasn't my fault, how was I supposed to know, I'm just a girl.

I told the worrying tale to Richard that evening over a meal in a nice little restaurant in Windsor. "I don't know why they were so cross" I complained to him, "If they don't have the equipment to do the job how is it my fault?"

"Realistically they were silly to agree to test the truck if they couldn't handle that sort of vehicle" he said reassuringly.

"I don't know what to do now" I said, "Do you know anywhere I can take her?"

"I do" he said thoughtfully. "Can you bring it to our council depot, I might be able to help."

"What! Kensington and Chelsea council depot?"

"Yes, Kensington and Chelsea council depot."

"Ok, I've never driven her in London before, that'll be exciting."

"Oh, you'll be fine, it's this side of London at least."

"When shall I bring her, I'm at work for the next couple of days"

"How does Thursday evening sound, bring it then if you can, 6.30pm OK?"

"OK, I will," I smiled at the realisation that, to me, Queenie was a personality, to Richard she was just a truck. "That would be great, thank you" I continued. My memory senses kicked into action and after a long pause I added "I have driven another lorry into London, years ago. I delivered some hay and horse food to a riding school somewhere round the back of the Albert Hall, or at least I remember driving past the Albert Hall a few times trying to find it."

"What sort of truck was that?" Richard asked.

"A Thames Trader" I said, "It was a tipper as well" I added because at the time it seemed to impress everyone.

"That's practically a vintage model."

"Well, it was round about 1967 or 68 and it was an old lorry then. I remember the stables had no space for storage whatsoever and the bales were stacked against the wall. They piled the bales on their sides because it took less room and they were only at a single depth with the wall. They were all roped up to stop the stack from falling. I was impressed with what they did."

"How come you were doing that?" Richard asked.

"Oh, a previous husband, a previous life."

"How many husbands have you had for Heaven's sake?"

"Only two!" I said, I didn't think this should come as any surprise to him being confident Erika had told him everything about me that she knew. Maybe she didn't say. I was happy to bare my soul but Richard changed the subject.

***

The following Thursday I took Queenie down the Cromwell Road at the appointed time and turned into the Central Depot in Pembrook Road. It was a large building full of various municipal vehicles from dustcarts to mini vans. Richard was there ready to direct me into a bay purpose built for testing vehicles of all kinds and immediately adopted an official pose as he began making his checks. I remained in the driving seat putting lights on when requested, applying my brakes when told to do so. Richard turned his attention to the engine and from behind the open bonnet he called "Sound your horn please Madam."

I leaned out of the driver's window, "the horn doesn't work" I told him.

Richard peered at me round the side of the bonnet, "Sound you horn please Madam."

"But I said..." Richard gave me one of those looks. "OK," and I pressed the horn. There was a rather insignificant click click from the engine.

"I heard that" said Richard, "Did you hear that?"

"Yes I heard that" I replied, and he took out his clip board and ticked the 'audible warning sound' box before continuing his checks. He disappeared into the office to formulate the paperwork before he gave me my certificate plus a receipt, on the bottom of which he had written 'now you really owe me.'

***

I continued with my lessons with Geoff who told me constantly I should 'ride' her, I should not be so lazy, I was not a passenger out for a nice day.

"So have you entered for the event at Waynefleet?" Geoff asked me.

"Yes, it's pretty scary but I feel I must do this."

"You are at an age when you should be giving this up not taking it up."

"Thanks, you say the nicest things" and I shot him a wry smile.

"Listen," he said, "they run instruction days at Waynefleet, for our own officers in the Met. Why don't you ask Mr Walker if you can tag along with your horse, I am sure he might be able to help you?"

"Do you think? That is a very good idea Geoff, thank you, I will ask him."

I had to visit Imber Court within the next week because I had to collect some Crime Prevention stands I kept stored there. I needed them for a horse show in Hyde Park that weekend and I had undertaken to attend with my crime prevention expertise. Mr Walker was not difficult to find and he said I could join them next Monday and Tuesday, but I would have to sign an injury indemnity form. No problem, and I felt quite excited about training with Gemma alongside police horses.

***

I thoroughly enjoyed my weekend on the Crime Prevention stand in Hyde Park. There was a quirky bit of a by-law which stated that no advertising was permitted within the park grounds and of course the many horse boxes which were parked there displayed advertising of all kinds. It was mostly the advertising of sponsors for the various showing and jumping teams, and it was with great amusement we watched officials from the Royal Parks armed with stepladders, rolls of brown paper and Sellotape busying themselves to cover all the lettering on the lorries. The wind in the night was quite fierce plus torrential rain, so by morning most of it had blown away and the covering paper remaining was sodden and looked a mess. This was the topic of the day throughout the showground.

Standing in my foot duty uniform at the front of our stand, I watched, agog, as the pairs of heavy horses pulling harrows filed past us on their way to the main arena to perform their musical display. One pair in particular filled me with delight, an outstanding couple of Suffolks being driven by a lady I recognised. I only knew of her through the pages of the Horse and Hound but had watched her career with great interest from the first days when I vowed I would, one day, own my own Suffolk horse. In one of my moments of boldness I called out to her "Good morning Mrs Clark."

"Good morning" she called automatically in a broad Suffolk accent and looking over to me quizically as she did so.

Not long afterwards a rustic figure of a man, sporting mutton chop side burns and a 'son of the soil' aspect, came to our stand and asked me the question in broad East Anglian dialect. "My Mrs Clark wants to know if she should know you?" said Tom.

I explained that 'no' she didn't, but I knew her and I expressed delight in seeing her here today with her wonderful horses. "Well then you must come and join us for a cup of tea in our lorry if you get the opportunity" he invited me. My understanding colleague, Chris the Crime Prevention Officer from Wembley, said he did not mind one bit if I wanted to nip off for half an hour while it was quiet. I had a really jolly time sitting in their lorry drinking tea and talking about their two Suffolk horses, Richard and Thomas. I came away having made two new friends and I felt very pleased with myself.

September dawned a bright, encouraging month and the last of the British Horse Society One Day Events was at Longworth. Gemma didn't go particularly well but Mandy and I were so well practised in our routine now that the day went like clockwork. Within a few days Mandy and I said goodbye to each other and I felt a vacant cavern in my heart. She said I could keep Queenie until after the Police event at Waynefleet but then we would have to advertise her for sale. I decided to make hay while the sun shone, so to speak, and took Gemma to a cross country day at Heckfield.

The following day was the first of our instruction days and I felt pretty excited as I drove through Weybridge on my way to Imber Court and the Waynefleet Estate.

Everyone was pleased to see me and my Gemma was much admired. Our instructor put across his thoughts extremely well. I had never realised what a knowledgeable man he was. He made everything crystal clear and I began to realise that Gemma's recent problems were probably my problems. We took the various elements of the course in sections and Gemma performed well for me, notwithstanding that she put in a couple of stops. "The bit you have is too harsh," he told me, "you can see she is not happy with it; do you have anything else you can change it for?"

"We have been eventing in a French Snaffle" I told him, "but she gets very strong and I struggle to hold her."

"Rather that, than have her refusing to jump at all" he told me. "I suggest you change it back."

Sitting in bed the following morning and changing the bits over on my bridle I mused how nice it was not to have a husband. I couldn't have done this with a feller in the bed I thought happily to myself as the little brown specks of general grot fell from the bridle onto the top of the duvet.

On the second day Mr Walker came over to see how the instruction was going with everyone. Gemma started off really calmly but as the jumps disappeared behind us she got stronger and stronger. We flew the style and this is where I lost her, she was like trying to hold a steam train. Mr Walker stepped forward to offer advice and I managed to pull her up, the wrong side of the approach to the next fence. "You are going well" he said, "press on." I pressed on and opted for the easy route over the 'E' but she dropped her hocks a bit early and fell, straddled across the large fence. I leapt off and told her to stand still, which thankfully she did. One of the eventing hopefuls was nearby and before I could consider the wisdom of what he did next, he smacked her across the rump several times with a riding crop and she scrambled over leaving the front of her hind legs slightly skinned. We established she was not seriously injured and so I continued to the end of the course and she jumped better for the experience.

I bet Mr Walker was relieved that I had signed the indemnity form.

Chapter Twenty-Two: "Move your car Sir!"

The day I had been waiting for began at 4am, and I had unbelievable butterflies. The Dressage was good for me but I was eliminated in the show jumping which should, by rights, have excluded me from the cross-country. I was overwhelmed with the pointlessness of the whole day now as I had built myself up for this to such an extent. I found Mr Walker in the steward's office and asked if I could ride the cross-country hors concours, he generously said I could though I would not be in the judging either for time faults or refusals, but I could at least ride the course. I will be forever grateful that I was allowed this opportunity and I am happy to report that Gemma gave me a fabulous ride, but I chose my fences.

"SUE, you've missed a fence out!" I heard my friends call after me, but I rode on without having time or wit to explain. I finished in good form but I couldn't help feeling generally disappointed with my abilities, or lack of them. I was just a bit down in the mouth, how could I even think I could do any of this without Mandy?

***

I had kept in touch with Tom, from the event at Hyde Park. He rang and invited me to stay with him and his wife Sandy in Ipswich, and so I stayed with them for a week and enjoyed some fabulous hunting with the Essex and Suffolk Foxhounds as well as going out with them in the little market cart pulled by a rather delightful Welsh cob. They had a Suffolk mare of their own as well and I was just blown away with how beautiful she was. I became more convinced that I wanted one too. Driving through Stoke by Nayland with Tom and Sandy, I spotted a pair of Suffolks ploughing in a field. Tom told me that they were the Clark's hosses and we drove down the track to Valley Farm to see them. We found old Gerry ploughing with a pair of geldings Richard, who I had met at Hyde Park, and Rupert. Gerry was the handy man on Cherry and Roger's farm, "only called a handy man because he lives in a garden shed nearby," Tom explained. He was not a man to care much for his appearance, speaking to us in a series of grunts while a single long dew-drop hung from one nostril. Tom and Sandy seemed to have no problem understanding him, which was remarkable, and they chatted to him warmly.

One of the plough horses, Rupert, had quite a history. In 1978 they had taken him to a pulling contest which he won. He pulled a stone boat that weighed 1ton 2 ¼ cwt, 22 feet in 4 seconds from a standing start. "He would have pulled more" Cherry told me later "but they ran out of weights." I hoped I might get the opportunity to visit them all again, I had so much to learn about these heavy horses.

***

Returning home to the old routine I think I was utterly worn out from a more than hectic summer and I decided to turn Gemma away for the winter. Joyce said I could go to her field in Windlesham, it was in a sheltered spot so with a good rug I considered that Gemma would be OK to live out. I did continue with my lessons with Geoff once a fortnight and I rode Gemma gently when I felt like it. I didn't have the Great Park to ride in but Chobham Common was lovely and I found a good farrier in the village where I had to visit his forge for shoeing. Erika and I saw a bit more of each other now that Gemma was out with her ponies.

Queenie was advertised and sold and slowly we drew a close to the most fantastic summer imaginable and I settled down to try and re-adjust to a new way of living. With Gemma turned away, there was no dressage for me to study for, no eventing to get excited about, there were to be no more pantomimes and no more being permitted to go to the Horse of the Year Show either. In fact, what was there to look forward to? Not much I concluded.

***

Police, Ponies & Husbands in-between

The evening of the 15th of October in 1987 was uneventful enough, I had my supper and I watched the television. Being a weather watcher, I listened with interest to Michael Fish's famous weather report when he gave his reassuring address to the nation. *"Earlier on today, apparently, a woman rang the BBC and said that she had heard there was a hurricane on the way, well if you are watching, don't worry, there isn't"* and he continued to reiterate that it might be a bit windy.

I woke the following morning at my usual 4.30am to prepare for a days early turn in London. On leaving the house to get into my car I noticed the 'For Sale' sign outside next door had fallen over, 'The weatherman was right,' I thought to myself, 'it must have been a bit windy last night'. As I drove through the village of Englefield Green, I couldn't help but notice the amount of debris across the road, in fact it was all over the place. There were branches, waste bins, advertising boards and hoardings, if it wasn't nailed down the stuff had taken on a life of its own. There were no other cars on the road but this was not unusual being so early. I turned east on to the A30 and expected to see a bit of traffic, but there was nothing, it was deserted. Even before descending Egham Hill I could see that there was the most enormous tree right across the road successfully blocking any passage for traffic. Traffic? There was only me. 'Oh well, I'll slip down the back of The Royal Holloway College I thought, and I returned to the lights and turned left. No sooner had I turned left again into the little backwater behind the College when it became apparent that we had a serious problem here. There were trees everywhere, across the road, leaning against other trees, the lovely old brick wall that surrounded the college was smashed in places. I had to reverse back to the junction before I could turn. 'Where to now?' I thought, and headed back down the high street towards Windsor. Again, there was no escape from our village, I couldn't get out and I tried every option I could think of with no success. I returned home.

There was no television and the phone lines were down, but with the help of some fresh batteries I managed to spark some life into an old transistor radio. The news revealed the devastation that had hit the South of England that night and I sat, initially dumbfounded, and considered my options. I had always been a swot at Police Training School and I recalled the guidance that was buried deep within the

Police, Ponies & Husbands in-between

pages of the hallowed 'Instruction Book'. Under the heading 'National Emergency' the advice prepared me for the path ahead and the action that was expected of a serving police officer. It seemed to me that this qualified as such an emergency and I knew exactly what I should do. I dug out my old foot duty uniform and dusted off my push bike from the garden shed, and I set out into the blackness, bound for the local Police Station in Egham where I intended to present myself for duty.

I was in some degree of disarray when I arrived having had to scramble over several trees as well as lifting my bike over as well. I have to say, the good policemen of Egham were rather surprised to see me but did not turn away my offer of a day's work. Egham is part of the Surrey Constabulary, and I was an officer of the Metropolitan Police so goodness knows what administrational juggling went on, if any. I didn't lose a day's pay anyway.

They put me in the reserve room to answer the phone, which became unbelievably busy as the morning began to dawn. Most calls were about animals straying and I did wonder how Gemma had faired, so I rang Erika.

"Oh you just won't believe what's been going on over here" she told me all pith and moment. "I'm just going up to the field now, I've spoken to Joyce and she says our horses are all in the field next door with the polo ponies."

"Can you cope?" I asked, "I've come into Egham to see how I can help, so I'm stuck here till this afternoon."

"Yes, we can cope, I'm meeting Joyce and David at the field, and I'll keep you informed."

I day-dreamed about how many times I had seen polo ponies being exercised around the Great Park, sometimes with just two riders and up to 6 ponies being led. They made a wonderful sight stretching across the width of the road on route to Black Nest Gate.

The Sergeant looked round the door at me, "Is that a private call Miss Blackhall?"

"Sorry Sarge, I've got a horse out at Windlesham" I said "and I just wondered how she was."

"Ok, I'll let you off, our regular telephonist has come in to work now so I am going to send you out to Wentworth."

"What's at Wentworth Sarge?"

"There is a golf tournament on today, and we need extra

manpower for the car parks, most are out of action."

I peered into the front office which was now full of policeman who had come on duty especially for the golf, the air was full of banter and bewilderment, "I can't believe they are still going ahead with this" said one.

"Too much money wrapped up in it" said another.

"The marquee has been blown several hundred yards down the fair-way apparently." A chorus of voices chatted on marvelling at the strength of the night's happenings.

"Oh hello, who are you?" one of them asked me as I appeared in the doorway of the reserve room. I told them who I was, and that I was from the Metropolitan Police Mounted Branch. "You're weird" said he.

'True enough so it is" thought I.

I was posted at the end of the drive to the prestigious 'red' car park, I had been instructed not to allow any vehicles to enter due to the fact that there were several trees down blocking the route through to the parking area.

"What do you mean? I can't go down there?" shouted a red faced driver of an Audi when I broke the news to him. "I have paid for the right to park my car down there and you can't stop me!" he continued in disbelief at my insubordination. Obviously, he had never met a Metropolitan copper before so I gave him a fool proof explanation in double fast dialog.

"It's quite indiscriminate you know Sir ….the wind. It cares not who you are or what you drive. And if you think you and your vehicle can limbo under those fallen trees then you are more stupid than you look. There's no way you will be able to push them out of the way pal, because you don't look that strong either. Now be a good chap and turn your car round and go to the green carpark as I have suggested and don't for one minute think you can get away with abandoning your vehicle here because I will have it forcibly towed away to where you will pay handsomely for its liberation." He gaped back at me in silence. "Is there any part of this conversation which you fail to understand - Sir?" and I held his gaze in defiance.

He turned his Audi round and left with a parting shot, "I play golf with your Chief Constable. You haven't heard the last of this." It was a lame threat because the Chief Constable of Surrey

Police, Ponies & Husbands in-between

Constabulary was nothing to do with me.

Far away on the streets of Kensington and Chelsea, Richard was having a similar experience. He was a very 'hands on' kind of guy and being the Assistant Director of Cleansing and Transport, he felt he had to be out there with the cranes and tree surgeons. The general circus of the street clean-up was going on across London on that fateful morning after the storm.

Richard retold the story to me over supper in a posh Windsor restaurant. We had such a good evening together, exchanging tales of derring-do, and it was lovely to have the chance of seeing him before he went off on his annual three week break to visit his brother Frederick in Hong Kong.

But I digress, so I'll get on with the story he had to tell, it is not my story but it is worth telling.

After several hours of clearing streets, Richard and the team migrated into Beaufort Street off Cheyne Walk, where yet another scene of mayhem greeted them. There were trees everywhere, they were across the road, across cars, across buildings. These were largely residential buildings with smashed windows and smashed roof tops and the first job was to remove all the parked cars, both damaged and unscathed ones. There was a foot duty WPC on duty helping with the vehicle removal, after all, it is only the Police who can insist with such an action. She was a pretty little thing and Richard was quite taken with her; he must have a thing about uniforms! She worked as hard as the men banging on doors and climbing the endless stairs up to flats and apartments requesting removal, which, after all, was for the benefit of the vehicle owners.

Incidentally, this was not 'bed-sit' land, this was way posher, and the residents cut a certain upper-class aura. So as to facilitate the safe removal of the uprooted trees, the road was soon free of all private traffic except one. A blue BMW, parked right underneath a

Police, Ponies & Husbands in-between

London Plane tree boasting gigantic proportions.

The WPC knocked on the apartment on the fifth floor of the building that the tree was leaning on. "Good morning Sir" she greeted the sullen faced young man already cross that his peace had been interrupted. "I understand that you own a blue BMW, registration number A297 BOB Sir?"

"What if I do?" he barked.

"Well, it's parked outside in the street Sir."

"What if it is?"

"Can I ask you to move it please Sir, as you are aware, we have a tree leaning against these buildings and we wish to remove it safely without any damage to your car."

"You can ask but I'm not going to move it" he growled.

"It is for the safety of your own car Sir" the WPC persisted. "We cannot guarantee that the tree will not fall …Sir."

"I couldn't care less" he said, obviously a man not used to being told what to do by a slip of a girl.

"And your justification for this action, or lack of it, is…?"

"I pay good money to the council for my Resident Parking Permit, and I am hanged if I am just going to shift it on your say so."

"If you fail to move your vehicle Sir" bless her she was getting cross, "I cannot be held responsible for the outcome."

"Oh yes you can" he snarled. "You damage my car and you will have to pay."

"I'm sorry Sir" she said smiling her best smile, "We do seem to have got off on the wrong foot, let me rephrase my request" she took a deep breath, "MOVE YOUR CAR - SIR!"

"NO!" He shouted back, and he slammed the door in her face. She was not best pleased with the outcome as she emerged into the street, and she retold the story to the crew.

"I cannot force him" she shrugged, "I could arrest him for obstruction but then I would have to take him into Chelsea nick and you need me here. You'll just have to do the best you can."

So, with a difficult job on their hands, Richard and the rest of the gang set to work. A tree surgeon shinned up to the branches and encased the top of the main trunk with cable and once he had it secured the crane set to work lifting the tree free from the duvet of roof tiles that cushioned its resting place. Slowly, oh so very slowly the weight of the tree was taken by the crane which began to swing

Police, Ponies & Husbands in-between

carefully sideways, away from the apartments, in the hope of laying this great mother of a London Plane along the road with all the other trees so it could be dismembered and taken away. It was going very well, but that was before the top branches snagged on the telephone wires, and this seriously complicated the operation. Then all their worst fears happened in the blink of an eye, a substantial branch broke free and fell to the ground. OK not quite the ground because it landed on the roof of the blue BMW - which should not have been there. The car was trashed.

"YES!!" exclaimed the WPC, jumping in the air with jubilant satisfaction, throwing her fist into the air she shouted, "Got ya."

Sometime later, back in the Kensington and Chelsea council administration office, Percy, the cleansing manager was going through the post. Just because I like name dropping, I have to tell you that Percy Powell, a seasoned skydiver, later set a world record by jumping from 6 miles above the earth's surface in aid of The British Legion at the age of seventy nine.

"Look at this one Richard" he said handing over a letter from a notable insurance company.

The gist of it read; '*We understand from our client, that the Council have wilfully damaged our client's blue BMW, resulting in the car being completely written off. The compensation he is seeking is £..........*'

"I'll enjoy replying to this one" said Richard taking the letter. "I think they should know a thing or two about their client."

"We have a very concise report from that pretty little WPC" Percy reminded Richard, "I'll dig it out for you."

"Good, we'll send that as well."

The moral of the story being, if an officer of the law asks you to move your car, then BLOODY WELL MOVE IT!

Chapter Twenty-Three: The Dignity of the Force

I was delighted when I received a long letter from Richard, who was away on his fifteenth trip to the Far East. It was a nice letter, all about the Motorcycle Grand Prix in Macau, wherever that was. I did not entirely understand why he was there but Erika tried to explain as best she could. Richard's brother Fred lived in Hong Kong in fact he was the Ferrari agent, and he was the one who had introduced Richard to the Grand Prix some years ago, securing a job for him scrutineering the motorcycles. It might have helped if I knew what scrutineering meant, but reading his letter he retold how discontentment had grown among the local racing riders because their bikes had failed on every count as safe to race. Such failings as cobbling their bikes together by tying their exhausts on with string, household cushions being taped to the seat brackets instead of purpose built ones fitted, and brakes having similar Heath Robinson arrangements. They were given an overnight time-out to return early with their bikes in proper order before the racing began the following day. Then, due to the inevitable delays that often happen on race days, the organisers announced the Novice Races would be cancelled to help make up time. Fights between the local Macanese racing boys and the track officials broke out in the pits and it all sounded jolly entertaining. This sojourn that Richard was enjoying was a world away from the action that came to my neck of the woods.

***

Christmas time was fast approaching and the festivities at work were beginning to kick in with the stable party again being in fancy dress. For me, this was a time for living the dream, and I had long fancied myself as having a figure of desirable proportions. My school girl impersonation had been enhanced by extra padding and I felt inclined to follow this theme. 'Boobies,' I thought, 'that's what I need plastic boobies,' and I considered that this was something I could purchase while out on patrol. I was booked that day for riding a spare horse, Dragoon, a simply massive grey about 17 hands high.

Even with the mounting block I struggled to get on board, so getting off was not an option while I was out on the streets. I took him up to the top of the Seven Dials where I knew there was a party shop, selling everything from party poppers to complete gorilla outfits. I waited outside in the street hoping to attract the attention of the shop assistant through the big shop window. Eventually she scuttled out and asked me "Is there anything wrong Officer? Is everything alright?"

"Yes, yes, everything is fine," I said, "I was just wondering how much are the plastic tits in the window." I wanted to go dressed as a nun, obviously.

"Ooo the bust!" she said with no small amount of excitement. "Would you like the ones on display or the delux version with the flashing nipples?"

"Oh! Do I have a choice? How lovely" I replied. "In that case I'll take the delux ones." As she bustled back into the shop I called her back. "Could you do me a great favour, would you mind putting them into a bag for me please?"

"Certainly Officer" she replied and returned with them in a clear plastic bag!!

I think there is something written in the ancient runes that talks about: *'behaviour not within the keeping of the dignity of the force.'*

***

Ruth and David came down to me at Christmas and we enjoyed lots of walks in the Great Park and the usual festive cheer around the dinner table.

"Sylvester! You naughty boy!" exclaimed Ruth from the kitchen as the black and white cat fled past me up the stairs carrying a turkey wing.

"Oh for goodness sake" I said, "where was he?"

"He was sitting on the work surface looking at it" said Ruth, "He only grabbed a bit of left overs when I came in."

"That cat!" I said. "He's a rascal."

"I've been thinking Ruth" I approached the subject with difficulty. I have been thinking about this for some time but I finally ploughed in "Would you, um, you and David if you like, um would you both consider, think about at least, um coming down here, you know, um, move in with me?"

She digested this proposal for a moment. "Oh Mum? Yes I could, what about you Dave?"

"I could do I suppose," he said with just a touch of hesitation, "I'd have to find a job round here but I could come."

"It would be wonderful for me, having you both in the house, I'd love it, but think on it, talk about it together." I could not believe my luck that they were both so amenable to the idea. So they talked it all through between themselves and not long afterwards, they moved in. David got a job with McDonalds and Ruth, who worked for Bupa, transferred to the office in Staines. I was as happy as I could be.

***

With the tail end of this fateful year came the paperwork that was to herald yet another kind of storm. The failure of the Sogat Union to influence the decisions of both Margaret Thatcher and Rupert Murdoch at the beginning of 1987 brought vengeful consequences. Vis: the dreaded form number 163, complaints against police. The numerous allegations of 'Discreditable Conduct' and 'Abuse of Authority' were to be fully investigated by a Chief Superintendent from another police force. There must have been over 20 police officers being asked to answer these charges from several individuals involved in the demonstration, all looking for heads to roll, mine included. The internal post groaned under the pressure from the increase in traffic of various investigation files and complaints forms floating hither and thither through the offices of the Met. The shit had seriously hit the fan and we were all diving for cover to escape the onslaught.

***

Police, Ponies & Husbands in-between

It gave me much to ruminate on as I took my new police horse, Eileen, a bright bay mare of questionable manners, off to Hammersmith to get her shod. This was a regular task for every horse, approximately 5 or 6 weeks in between each visit. It was an 'all day' job going to the farrier as Hammersmith was quite a trek from central London. There was quite a lot of traffic on the way home and Eileen and I slid down the outside lane of vehicles waiting at red traffic lights in Kensington High Street. I spotted a Willis Jeep ahead of me and mused about my days at Woodcock Farm and the military vehicles stored there by Bapty and Co. who supplied armoury to the film industry. Our friend Jim (he who taught me how to use a twelve bore) had got a Willis Jeep at that time and I remembered how much it had been his pride and joy. I drew level with the Jeep and glanced back at the driver to nod my appreciation for him having such an iconic vehicle. He looked at me and for a nano second we held our gaze in disbelief of recognition. It was Jim!! "Cath?" he said "Cathy! What are you doing up there?"

I laughed "I'm just doin' my job."

"Have you got time for a coffee? I'm just round the corner from here."

"Yes, why not" I replied and I followed him to a tiny cobbled mews. The salubrious flats were fronted by ground floor garages alongside a door leading to the dwellings above. "You'll have to bring my coffee down to me I'm afraid, Eileen can't climb stairs" I told him jokingly.

"Will she be OK in my garage?"

"I don't see why not" I replied and popped her inside letting out the girth on her saddle and taking the bit and cheek pieces off her bridle. I trotted upstairs for a right good old catch up. When I came to reconnect with Eileen we found she had knocked all Jim's 'Workshop Manuals' off the shelf and left a suitable deposit for the roses, if he had any. For the rest of the journey back to GSY my head was filled with tales from 'back in the day.' "Eileen," I announced after much thought, "I am going to have to write a book."

"I think you should," she said, ever the supportive police horse.

***

The only blight to my future was the interview to answer allegations

Police, Ponies & Husbands in-between

from the dispute at Wapping. The day at Tintagel was eventful enough with the endless questions which I didn't answer, now all we had to do was wait for the outcome.

In the meantime life continued pretty much as normal. Ruth used the train to go to work, sometimes I dropped her off at Egham station and sometimes I picked her up. Sometimes I cycled down and we walked up Egham Hill together to the accompaniment of the occasional toot of a horn or a wolf whistle from a building site. It wasn't meant for me! It was meant for my beautiful daughter. She hated it but I took a trip down memory lane. David was easy to live with, a pleasure in fact, not shy of putting on the marigolds or pitching in to help with Gemma.

One of the nice things about living in Surrey was the high street shopping in Windsor. I had parked the car in the multi-story and was taking the back entrance through M & S, as I pulled the door towards me a young man was pushing from the other side to exit. It was David!

"David!" I exclaimed, "What are you doing here you are supposed to be at work, in Staines"

"Arh" he offered, which was not much of an explanation.

"Well? Shouldn't you be at work?"

"Um, I left" he mumbled, looking at his feet and shuffling around giving quite a good impersonation of a small boy having been caught bunking off school round the back of the bicycle sheds.

"Come on" I tapped him on the arm reassuringly, "If you are going to bunk off then you can make yourself useful carrying my shopping." We continued to the High Street where I wanted to look at some upholstery material in Cayley's. Erica had very kindly offered to cover my three piece suite for me. I loved the suite but it had got extremely tatty.

When we got home David insisted that he was not going to go back to work at McDonalds. He hated it. "I don't know what I'm going to do with all of this stuff," he told me, laying out his aprons.

"I've got a use for those" I said. We wear blue fatigues at work for cleaning our kit, but everyone else wears an apron over the top to keep the polish off."

There was so much polishing! Saddles, which have wallets attached to the front, a long stick hanging from the rear for wielding at the unruly public. I could hardly reach mine especially if I was trussed up in all that riot gear, so I can honestly say I have never used it. The great expanses of good quality English leather polished up like a mirror. For ceremonial duties we would spend extra time with a little water in the lid of the Parade Gloss and alternately apply this in small circular movements with the index finger. What they used to call 'spit and polish' in military circles, or 'boning-in'. Our head kits in daily usage were also polished each time after riding, the leather was about an inch wide and polished well. There was the addition of a breast plate, which had a white metal Metropolitan crest on the horse's chest.

There were also chains hanging from the bridle to the saddle. Traditionally intended to be a substitute for reins should the leather ones be cut in a crowd control situation. I have never known this to happen but it does make the 'turn-out' look very smart. These chains were kept shiny by placing them inside a long sleeve called a 'shaker bag' with added strips of newspaper, sawdust and metal bits of debris like nuts. This would burnish the surface by swinging it in the air using a circular movement. These were not issue equipment, we all had to make our own and it was quite an art learning the skill to keep the momentum going as you swung the bag around, very similar to a skipping rope, but sideways.

"That's great," said David, "you can have both the aprons." So that's how I got to acquire my very own aprons, good tough twill material in a lovely maroon colour.

"What's that on your apron Miss Blackhall" our Chief Inspector barked at me when he came visiting from Hyde Park.

I was in the tearoom polishing my black top boots. "What do you mean Sir?" I didn't know what he was talking about.

"That" he said pointing to my bosom.

I looked down at my chest, "What?"

"That, that embroidery, there on your apron."

"Oh! Sorry Sir" I stammered, "It's what they call 'the golden arches' you know, Sir, McDonalds."

"Is it indeed, and what, may I ask are you doing wearing a McDonalds apron?"

"Um" I simply couldn't answer that one.

"I'm not suggesting you have come by this by foul means but do you really think it is appropriate to wear this at work?"

"It's the only apron I have Sir."

"Well it's not within the keeping of the dignity of the force."

"No Sir" I said properly humbled, "I'll take it home today, Sir."

"You can wear it here" he added kindly, then, wagging his finger at me he continued "But you have to remove that yellow stitching first"

"Yes Sir."

***

Back in the humdrum of the working day, life was not without the odd adventure. As often happened, when we took our turn at having our weekly leave days, someone else in the stable would ride your horse for you. My colleague, Roly, was weekly leave that day so I was riding his horse Inca, a stocky and somewhat rotund grey gelding, and I set off for theatreland down Shaftesbury Avenue. I stopped on the paved layby outside Queen's Theatre where I stayed idly watching the world go round. I did rather fancy going to see Les Miserables which was showing there but the cheap tickets we were sometimes offered from the Cab Office rarely included prestigious shows like this one.

The Police Force, along with many of the London Hospitals, were regularly given tickets for new shows being launched and for a nominal fee you could secure some tickets on request. The income from these sales helped to cover administration and the swelling of funds for the office tea club, when I say nominal, I really mean nominal. £1.50 or something like that.

As I sat there ruminating, I was approached by two little boys, about thirteen years of age I suppose. They asked me for directions to Soho, and I spent some time concerning myself with why two youngsters should be roaming the streets of London. They were just looking around the sights they told me, and as these were daytime hours, I saw no harm. Anyway, they seemed to give a good account of themselves and so I dug out a pocket map that I kept in one of my wallets.

"Right," I began. "do you see those pedestrian traffic lights up the road, turn right down there, the theatre on the corner is showing 'Lettuce and Lovage' you can't miss it"...... and I leaned down towards the boys so that they could see the map as well as me. Holding it there as still as I could I continued my dialog. Inca stood like a rock, he was a good copper. Because I was leaning over to one side of him for such a length of time, I not only began to feel my back stretching but also the girth around him came under some strain. I felt the saddle begin to slip! Wondering how I could possibly regain my seat without losing my elegant posture, I became aware that the two boys had also noticed this change of position, and they began to try and push me back.

"Oh my goodness," I said by way of explanation, and they in turn puffed and strained in their attempt to lift my great hulk skyward. This really was the most ridiculous situation and I began giggling. The boys began giggling too and in no time at all the three of us were laughing uncontrollably, until I fell, like a stranded whale in the gutter. The two lads helped me to my feet, I was just dying of embarrassment, while tourists took photographs!

"Are you alright Officer?" one said, I nodded a scarlet faced nod.

"Your Police horse is remarkable," said another. "He has just stood there through all of that."

In sheer embarrassment I retorted, rather unfairly, "He's a typical Policeman, dead from the neck up". It got a laugh anyway, even though I wanted the ground to swallow me up and Inca with it. Not within the keeping of the dignity of the force indeed.

I returned to the stables - and said nowt.

***

I asked Ruth if she was interested in having her own horse. "Spring is coming and Gemma will be coming into season," I said to her, "we could put her in foal, if you wanted". Ruth was agreeable, in fact she was quite enthusiastic, and so the hunt for a suitable stallion began.

We travelled all over the area and beyond, looking at Irish Draughts. We needed something with height as Ruth had inherited her lofty aspect from her father. Certainly not from me!

Doing the daily Changing of the Guard at Buckingham Palace did provide me with much thought as I watched the Household Cavalry do their ceremonial thing up the centre of The Mall each day to Horse Guards Parade ground. Back in the tearoom at GSY I asked the boys for advice.

"If you want some proper advice," said Andy. "I suggest you go down to the Royal Mews and speak to the head coachman, Arthur. There isn't anything about horses he doesn't know."

I took Andy's advice and after the guard change the following morning I popped along on Eileen. Arthur was most accommodating, and at his invitation I parked Eileen in one of the lovely old Victorian stalls, synonymous with the Royal Mews, and he showed me round. "Many of our horses are Cleveland Bays." he told me. "They are a good choice for putting some substance on to your Thoroughbred."

"I'm told they can be quite headstrong, would you agree with that?" I asked him.

"All horses can be headstrong" he replied "But if you do look for a Cleveland Bay then I can strongly recommend a stallion called Osberton St David, we have never had a bad horse of his breeding. I don't think he is alive now, but you might find a son or a grandson".

"I will take your advice, thank you" I said.

"Follow me into the office," he said kindly, "I can give you his owner's telephone number and he should be able to point you in the right direction".

I was extremely grateful to him taking such trouble to help me and with this information ringing in my ears I couldn't wait to receive the Stallion issue of the Horse and Hound which was due out the following week. It was an exciting time planning Gemma's next 18 months, and a project for Ruth which was something we could all enjoy, David included.

Before I could get around to making the telephone call my eyes settled on an advert for a Cleveland Bay horse called Thornset Major. His stud fee was within our grasp and when we visited him I fell in love. He was outstanding in my view and by a lucky chance of fate, his father was Osberton St David. "That's our baby" I said to Ruth and David on the way home.

The owner of the stallion, Mo, was tremendous fun and we got on like a house on fire and I had no reservations whatsoever with entrusting Gemma to her care. All we had to do now was set a date and travel her down there. "Do you know anyone who does horse transport?" I asked Chris one evening when he happened round to visit. He got on well with Ruth and David and they liked him enormously. I had lost a lover, but I had gained a brother and a best friend.

"Call yourself a mounted man" he replied in disgust, "Ride her down there, what's the matter with you, it's only round the corner".

"It's all of sixty miles if it's an inch" I protested, "it's crazy"

"Well, what's that to a seasoned trooper like you, ride her, why wouldn't you?"

"I am not riding my horse across country the best part of seventy miles, she's not fit enough. That's an end to it" I said finally, and I repeatedly reminded myself for days afterwards in case I forgot.

Chapter Twenty-Four: Going the distance

While sitting in bed with a cup of tea several days after, Sylvester and I were surrounded by ordnance survey maps and I was thumbing through the British Horse Society booklet of bed and breakfast for horses. I could not help but ruminate over what Chris had said about riding Gemma to West Sussex. If I was going to ride down to West Sussex, and I probably wasn't, but 'IF' I was, I would need to do the trip in two days which would mean I would have to find an overnight stop en route for Gemma and me. My eyes rested on the details of a nice-looking Farm between Peaslake and Ewhurst. 'Mmmmmmmm' I thought, "I wonder?"

I had begun to get Gemma fit for the journey and there had been some local events to take her to without transport. A last-minute weekly leave cancellation because of a football match stopped me from attending a Dressage Test. All the horses at work were kitted up and the blokes were making ready to leave the stables bound for Millwall, when, in an unexpected desire to answer a call of nature, I galloped upstairs to the ladies. The boys from the Diplomatic Protection were on the same floor as the lady's lavatory. The lazy blighters preferred our loo to theirs, for some reason, and I often found it engaged. The emerging officer usually came in for some ribbing and back chat, before disappearing through the door of his department with a flea in his ear. On this occasion, the loo was vacant, thankfully, as I did not have much time. While I sat listening to the merry dancing tinkle I noticed, on the window shelf, there was a Smith and Wesson. I imagined the scenario, one of the DPG officers had used our loo again and couldn't drop his trollies with a shooter in his pocket. Bloody cheek of the man. I rescued the gun and knocked on the high security door for attention.

"I think this is yours" I said handing the piece over. It was received with the accompanying red face and a bit of a stir was caused within. They did find the offender and it was some time before he lived it down.

All this took more time than I had available and when I got to the bottom of the ramp with Eileen, I found to my dismay that my colleagues had left for Millwall without me. Bugger! I was now on automatic and trotted with a purpose down Northumberland Avenue towards the River Thames to try and catch them up. I was half way along the Victoria Embankment towards the City of London when I realised this was not the right way to Millwall. Bugger! Stupid as this may sound my mind went completely blank and parking on the side of the road overlooking the river I stopped and dug out my little map of central London. Instead of going on to Blackfriars Bridge which might have been quicker, I turned round heading back to Waterloo Bridge because this was the way I knew. Once I'd got my brain in gear that is.

I was a very apologetic constable when I arrived at The Den which was humming with activity as fans and opposition were arriving en masse all excited with anticipation for the match to come. "What happened to you?" asked Steve, my ever-patient skipper.

"You won't believe what I found in the ladies loo" I said.

I loved football matches, not the game you understand but the fans. The unison of chanting fascinated me and I found it quite moving.

"We're going to Wembley, we're going to Wembley, you're not, you're not" they sang as the first goal was scored. The stadium hummed with testosterone.

"Let im die, let im die, let im die," they chanted as a player for the opposition lay prostate on the pitch. Then, later on, in disgust prompted by a referee's decision

"Who's the wanker in the black, in the black?"

Wonderful stuff, one brain cell between the lot of them, as was usually illustrated outside in the streets after the match. There were always going to be winners and there were always going to be losers, but it is my opinion football violence was only a problem if the fans were down wind of the urinals.

***

Back in Windlesham I continued to battle with getting Gemma half ready for the journey ahead. Again, I was thwarted and missed out on the Annual Windsor Sponsored Ride round the Great Park because of a demonstration in London, 'Gays against Clause twenty-eight' of all obscure things. Obscure if only because I had no idea what Clause twenty-eight was. This was good on the pocket but made it rather difficult to keep Gemma going. I had the opportunity to go to Ascot Farm where I entered a dressage test, the Working Hunter class and a 2'6" show jumping class, which was the kind of height Gemma and I were happy with. It was not too small for her, and not too big and scary for me.

Ruth made a picnic for us all and David pitched in to help where he could. Richard came along too, and the use of his car meant Ruth and David did not have to walk and we could take extra stuff needed for 'Madam'. It was a jolly family day out and made a big difference to my constitution having a fan club to cheer me on.

We had gone clear and we were in the jump off against the clock. Outside the ring we were waiting to go and take our turn, Gemma was fairly switched off. "C'mon sleepy head" I said to her, "It's our turn now" and I felt pretty chipper as we entered the ring.

She brightened up as if to say "Goodo, more jumping, my favourite, which order then boss?"

"The same order" I said "but with a few missed out". We cleared the first fence and I looked across to the right,

"Is that the next one?" she asked.

"Yes. Go for it, we're against the clock."

"At my own speed" she asked.

"As fast as you like" I told her, and we left the ground.

"Wow" she said, "this is fun" and we sailed over the third.

"You left that a bit late to set yourself up" I criticised.

"Two full strides" she said indignantly.

"Turn here TURN HERE," I urged, pulling hard at her left rein.

"Oh, you mean that one," she sounded surprised.

"Do your best" I said.

"Hold on to some mane if you are frightened" she suggested.

"Cheers Gem, I think I will".

We came an admirable 2nd. I was so chuffed.

Police, Ponies & Husbands in-between

***

The ride to West Sussex began 2 days later. I had previously taken a bag of necessaries for myself to the overnight stop-off point at Coverwood Farm. I took feeds for Gemma, one supper, one breakfast and one lunch, they were providing her hay for the night. I was up early and keen to get going having arranged to meet Joyce en route as she said she would like to ride some of the way with me. It was good to have company so I was really upbeat until that is, I found Gemma in the field with a shoe missing. So much planning had gone into this I couldn't reconcile myself to not going but I knew I had not got far to go and I would pass the forge in Chobham. If Albert was unable to help me then I would have to turn back and think of another plan for another day. Joyce was in the woods waiting for us and we rode together in good spirits. Joyce was a keen long-distance competitor and had much good advice for me to follow. Albert was golden about squeezing me in between existing appointments waiting to be shod. Gemma was delighted too, complete with four shoes had an immediate effect on her wellbeing. I said 'Good-bye' to Joyce and we were on our way at last to find our way through bridle paths unknown and the simplest of maps to guide me.

 I followed Monument Road out of Woking and as I skirted round the periphery of Guildford it began to spot with rain. It got heavier so I unpacked my long mac, with the epaulets taken off, that I had borrowed from work. I was negotiating main roads and I just didn't feel it was that safe to stop anywhere to buy some lunch for myself so we pressed onward, sure that we would find a little store a bit later.

 We crossed over the A3 thanks to a flyover and took a left hand turning down a quieter road to East Clandon. I stopped there to give Gemma her lunch as it was already 2pm and she was showing signs of fatigue. I went hungry, there wasn't even a carrot I could pinch off her. I fitted her feed bag as the heavens opened. I took off my police mac and threw it over her, I had my Barbour jacket on underneath but I got much wetter than I would have liked. Water ran down the back of my neck and I began to wish I had not started this adventure. I let Gemma graze for about half an hour until I could bear it no longer and I wanted my long mac back over the two of us.

We pressed on southward with it raining for about a further hour, but the ride was more pleasant once I hit The North Downs Way which took me into the heart of the Mole Valley. Richard had told me there was the most fascinating clock tower at Abinger Hammer. "On the hour" Richard said "the clockwork farrier 'Jack the Hammer' comes out and strikes the bell for the appropriate number of times before returning inside the clock." As I only had about 15 minutes to wait I decided to dismount and sit under the bus shelter while I waited for the historic event to happen. I was not disappointed, and neither was Gemma.

Gemma was practically all in but she gave me a respectable canter up Holmbury Hill. We reached the Farm at a quarter to five. Anne and Nigel could not have been more welcoming. I settled Gemma in her cosy stable next to the cattle and she seemed to be very happy with arrangements. They let me hang my sopping wet long mac over the Aga to dry out. I had a lovely hot meal with their family and resolved to have an early night as it had been such a long day, which seemed at the time to have begun weeks ago, not just that same morning. In my bedroom I found something that has had a lasting effect on me. I found a little vase of field flowers. They were so lovely and unexpected I resolved to do the same for anyone who might come and stay with me.

Over breakfast they had told me of The Thurlow Arms on the disused railway line that formed part of The Downs Link. They seemed surprised by the map I was using, I suppose, it was a bit inadequate for the journey I was taking. They photocopied some ordnance survey pages for me with a great deal more information and this was to prove invaluable, even in black and white.

We saw an abundance of wildlife during our ride including deer. The route I was following was delightfully picturesque and my horse and I swung along cheerfully. Sure enough, when we arrived at disused Baynard Station The Thurlow Arms proved to be an excellent pub and restaurant serving everything from simple home cooked fayre to frogs' legs and snails. I ordered ravioli in a cream and cheese sauce. If yesterday's lunch had been a disaster then today's lunch more than made up for it. The timing was superb and I listened to the afternoon instalment of The Archers on my Walkman radio. Gemma had her nosebag and they brought out a bucket of water for her. The sun was brilliant and I was filled with confidence about the remainder of the journey. I should not have been so optimistic.

***

I had seen a good number of fallen trees following the storm of the previous October but nothing to slow us down. So I idled for a good hour to let Gemma's lunch go down while I gave her a bit of a brush off as she picked grass. A cuckoo sang from deep within the adjoining woods, it was all quite magical. The landlord had told me that Billingshurst was no further away than about an hour or so, and the afternoon looked good. Once I was on board Gemma again I could see over the wall of the old Baynards Station. I have a fondness for traditional railways and I was delighted to see it had been restored and gave every impression of being a railway station in operation, I could almost hear the train coming along the tracks. I wanted to linger and learn more but time was pressing.

We left the Downs Link at Slinfold, and with it the disused railway which had made for very plain sailing. We experienced our first difficulties at a dairy farm where there was about a mile of cattle fouled muddy fields, the farm yard itself was blocked off and I had to disentangle wired gateways and cattle yards. We crossed the road and entered what I thought was the continuation of the bridleway but it soon became apparent that I was in the garden of what looked like a private house. The resident lady was rather surprised to find a horse and rider in her back garden but her agitation softened once we got talking. I told her where I was heading and she informed me that the bridle path was the next gateway down. "I don't know what it's like though" she said, "I haven't been down there all winter". Not long afterward I wished we hadn't. The gateways were like soup and the gates themselves were dreadful arrangements with no hinges and heavily wired together. My heart bled for the lovely highly polished leather riding boots, more used to ceremonial duties than navigating something more like a military obstacle course. Storm damage lay everywhere and we had to scramble over and under as best we could. How I was ever going to get Gemma delivered without injury was beginning to dawn on me.

We were in a lower gully between fields flanked by trees and heavy undergrowth. There were bluebells everywhere just coming into flower and looking their best but I couldn't spare time to dwell on these delights, we had to press on; time was getting short. As I looked ahead I could see a fallen tree, held aloft by the banks that flanked the bridleway, with quite a decent gap underneath. Getting up close to it, I dismounted and assessed whether Gemma would fit underneath and concluded that if I removed her saddle and she bent her knees a little she just might. I lay my Barbour jacket across her back for protection and asked her to limbo dance, we had barely the width of a lolly stick to spare.

We left the farm behind and there were the remnants of cross-country jumps on the side of the field. "This is a good sign Gems" I said to her, but it was short lived. Not far after going through the tunnel under the railway, we came to a series of fallen trees that were just beyond passing. We stopped and I realised I would have to consult the maps Anne and Nigel had given me. With additional knowledge of the lie of the land we turned back and cut across country to Duncans Farm at a respectable canter until we joined the road which we followed to Coneyhurst. There I came across a public telephone box and rang Mo at Badger's Wood, Richard had been there waiting for me for about one hour, it was now 6pm and still a good trek ahead of us. I missed the path I needed completely and took another by mistake and we found ourselves in a field of pigs. Gemma was not impressed with this one little bit especially when the pig's inquisitive nature had them making their way over towards us. Gemma tossed her head about and spun on the spot, she could see where this was going and could think of better places to be. We were rescued by the farmer's daughter, a chatty girl who escorted us to the nearest road and put us on our way with some clear directions. It was all road work from here on and after the catalogue of blocked pathways at least I knew the way forward would be clear.

Police, Ponies & Husbands in-between

Badger's Wood Stud Farm was but a few hundred yards the other side of the tiny Hamlet of Gay Street. We were four hours late and both Gemma and I arrived to a very warm welcome. We tucked her up in a big warm stable inside an 'American Barn' layout. She had a warm feed, a big haynet and Mo put a night rug on her to keep the chill out after her long two days of slog. Across the barn 'Clive' the Cleveland Bay stallion, whom she had come to visit, looked over his stable door at her with great interest. No doubt he would turn on the sweet talk during the night and they would just get along wonderfully well. I was so pleased to see Richard, and I was full of the adventures that we had experienced.

What a tryer my horse is I reflected on the way home. She had been sure-footed and willing with not a sign of lameness and not so much as a bruise or a cut on her after all we had been though. As Mandy would have said: she was a real star.

Gemma was served on 23rd May and when I went down to see her she looked really well and I could not have been happier with the arrangements. In the meantime, I needed to find somewhere else to keep her, somewhere where she could live in peace with her foal. Thanks to Joyce, I was offered a four-acre plot at Windlesham Park. It was in a lovely secluded location in the grounds of a big country house, a mansion in fact. There was a neighbour, Diane, who had three horses on the plot next to mine so I was sure of some company for her when she came home. It was post and rail fencing and the grass was knee high so I set about finding a contractor to cut it for hay.

Chapter Twenty-Five: Right Royal Occasion

Out of the blue, a gratuity was sent to the police stables from the Royal Mews, in the form of two tickets for Royal Ascot. Nobody else wanted to go so I asked Erika if she wanted to come with me and she jumped at the chance. We caught the train from Staines, all dolled up, and joined the other racegoers off to have a fabulous day out. The train was practically empty when it left Ascot station. Erika had a talent for picking winners, so the day's entertainment had substantial benefits. We mingled and we explored, and we found to our surprise, at one point, that we had wandered unchallenged into the Royal Enclosure. What a view we had and the excitement of the races was quite an experience. We didn't stay there for long but when we tried to get back in again, we were turned away. "I've been thrown out of better places than this Erica muttered."

I felt sure that if the Queen had been present she would have called me over. 'Ooh look, Phileep, there's Sooo, hello Sooo, do come and join us."

***

While Gemma was away Richard asked me if I fancied going on holiday with him. I most certainly did, and we chose Corfu. It was a fabulous week of relaxing, and we hired a car so having transport meant we could see a lot of the island not normally accessible to tourists. We stopped at a tavern for some lunch, but they didn't speak English and sent a child to fetch someone who could interpret. I loved the olive groves and took my sketch book with me which caused something of an attraction with the village children. The weather was hotter than normal and many fires were breaking out in parts of the island. We watched planes scooping water from the sea to drop on to the burning acres.

***

I had spoken frequently to Cherry, my new found friend with the

Suffolk horses. And it was not long before I was heading off to stay with her and her husband for a week at their farm near Ipswich. I could not believe such a place existed - it was wonderful, it was like stepping into a world a hundred years earlier. There was loose hay stacked in an old-fashioned rick, horse-drawn implements parked in all corners of the farm yard, and pigs running loose and a bevy of terriers busy busy after rats. TV companies have made pilgrimages to enjoy the privilege of filming the Suffolk horses at work. Books have been written about them and videos made, and in the background the rhythmical fall of Roger's hammer on the anvil came from the forge. I returned home so fired up with enthusiasm, my mind was made up; I was going to look for a Suffolk Punch. This ambition had nagged away at me for years and now I was resolved to make it happen. Goodness only knows what Gemma was going to think.

***

I was feeling pretty chipper when I returned to work at the usual crack of sparrow fart on the Monday morning. I was sailing past Buckingham Palace when I saw a kerfuffle of white feathers explode in front of one of the cars ahead of me. It slowed the traffic slightly and along with other vehicles I moved into the kerb of the road to avoid the ex-goose, which was lying prostrate in the middle of The Mall. With an air of 'what a shame I was in no position to stop and bag the catch,' I continued to the end of my journey and parked my Escort on Horse Guards Parade ground. I walked with one of my colleagues, Crispin, through the arches into Whitehall. The sentries either side of the arch did one of their smart ceremonial parade ground style clicking heels to attention and presenting arms. Or something like that anyway. I think they do this when they start to seize up after a spell of standing to attention.

"They always salute me as I walk through here," said Crispin, "They must know who I am."

"Oh really?"

"Yes, really."

"Who are you then," I asked him.

And he looked at me aghast. "I'm Crispin," he said.

"They were saluting me," I told him, "not you, anyone can see that."

Police, Ponies & Husbands in-between

"What do you know?" he asked.

"I know there was a goose run over in the Mall," I said. "If I had had the time to stop I would have picked it up."

"What for?"

"There's nothing wrong with a bit of road kill for a slap-up Monday tea," I said.

"You're weird," he told me as we walked under the archway of Great Scotland Yard.

One by one the officers drifted into the tearoom as the kettle came to a jolly boil by the kitchen units in the corner. Steve, our sergeant, attending to the duty board juggling with the available manpower. I disappeared upstairs to our changing room to get into our blue fatigues before pitching in to get the mucking out done. As the yard clock ticked to the ninth hour, the lorry from the Royal Parks reversed into the yard, neatly positioning itself under the hatch through which we would drop all the fouled bedding. We all stood in a row leaning over the balcony watching the truck manoeuvre with no small amount of skill into position by Jock the driver. It was then that I saw what was on the back of the truck. It was a large white goose.

Without hesitation I ran down the coconut matting covered ramp shouting to the others. "Don't throw any muck down, DON'T THROW ANY MUCK DOWN." And grabbing the mounting block I dragged it to the side of the truck and I climbed in. I hauled the goose out and carried it triumphantly back up the ramp to the stables.

"What are you going to do with that?" they asked, almost in unison.

"I'm going to eat it." I said as if no explanation should be necessary.

"A dead goose?"

"Are you mad?"

"You don't know how long it's been dead."

"I saw it run over in the Mall," I told the doubters.

"She did," said Crispin. "She told me about it on the way in."

"Hasn't it got to hang for a few days?" said a knowledgeable fellow in blue.

"Nah!" I scoffed. "It'll be just great, I had been wondering what we were going to have for supper."

Crispin and the others wandered back to their daily tasks shaking their heads. "You're weird," they said.

Suffice it to say the goose was plucked and drawn ready for the oven before I left for home at 3pm. "Yummy, yummy," said Ruth and Dave when they saw what I had brought home with me.

***

I had been in the habit lately of going down to The Embankment as part of my patrol, where I had become friendly with a bag lady who sat on the pavement. I saw her, without fail, every time I rode past. There were a number of dossers hanging around in that area and quietly tolerated provided they were not causing any trouble. These were more enlightened times than the days of Queen Victoria when the government's answer to the homeless was to simply make it illegal in the belief that the problem would go away. The problem did not go away.

Maggie was probably younger than me, but looked a decade older. The dependence on alcohol had made her overweight and her life on the streets had played havoc with her complexion which was reddened and pitted. It looked dry and painful and she cannot have been happy with her lot.

Just along from where we were talking a coach full of tourists pulled up against the kerb and the passengers began to disembark on to the pavement. It did not take much observation to tell you that they were mostly adults with learning difficulties. For a few moments the conversation between Maggie and me fell silent and then she said to me: "Hey Sue, why don't you go and speak to those folks so that they can stroke your horse. I can talk to you anytime, but you will make their day if you do that." I smiled and nodded to her with an air of wonderment, much as I had admired Maggie's ability to converse and be interesting, I had never given her the credit of compassion.

"That's a good idea," I told her. "You take care, Maggie. I'll be along this way in a day or two." I took Eileen up to the coach and they welcomed me with open arms, asking questions and fussing Eileen's soft muzzle. I stayed with them until they went on their way towards Parliament Square and I turned towards the boundary with City of London. Maggie gave me the thumbs up and a big smile as I rode past her.

On another occasion she has not feeling very well at all. When I had finished work I parked the car near the arches by Waterloo Bridge and picked my way through the many homeless who were there semi-sleeping in the gloom. I had to ask if anyone knew her because vision was difficult and I was directed politely enough to a pile of rags under which Maggie was nursing her misery. Speaking gently, I handed over a packet of Paracetamol, which she took from me graciously. I'm not sure she knew who I was without the horse. I tell you this, not because I want to brag about how kind I was being, Lordy the cost was less than fifty pence, but I do marvel at how brave I was in those days.

In later years, and in another life when I was wearing a different hat, I returned to see if I could find her. I had just come from BBC Broadcasting House were a presentation was made each year for the most innovative design or creation to further the welfare of the blind and visually impared. It was called The David Scott Blackhall Award and generated by The Patient's Aid Association. This year the guest had been Princess Anne and I was presented to her along with my sisters and mother, an unbelievably wonderful moment.

Maggie was still there on the pavement where I had last seen her, she had not changed. I sat down beside her, something I could not have done when on a horse, and asked if she remembered me. "I used to ride a police horse," I told her.

"Sue, yes I remember you," her face brightened. She told me that the Greater London Council had given her a flat. "It weren't much of a place, but they did give it me," She pulled the collar of her tattered coat tighter round her neck and shoulders as the chill of the evening was starting to bite. "I was lonely there, I was on my own, I would rather be here with the people I know." She nodded towards a bearded man in rags who claimed to be her boyfriend. I didn't speak to him much, his Scottish accent was so broad I struggled to understand him.

Some years later one of the television companies made a documentary about her and her reasons for being on the streets. On the train going home I reflected on the events of the day, I had curtsied to royalty and I had sat on the pavement with the destitute.

Maggie was not the only homeless person I exchanged words with during my working day. There was Eric who used to follow the guard change most mornings. I didn't know his name, I just called him Eric. It was quite amusing the way he enjoyed the ceremony, marching alongside the regiment Parumping to the beat of the band. "Par par parump arump arump di tump de dump de doo parump arump par par……." He swung his arms back and forth in turn and held his head up high, his shoulders bouncing in time with the music and his tattered jeans striding forward, the only soldier in step.

***

I was early turn a week or two later and the skipper was pondering the duty panel. "I've got a little job for you," he said. "You'll have to start work early, is 4am OK with you?"

"What doing?" I asked.

"The Royal Mews want an escort for one of their coaches. You will need to be turned out well but this is not ceremonial stuff."

"What's that all about then?"

"They are taking it out for a road test, I think it has been recently renovated. That's on Wednesday, OK?"

"OK."

I arrived in good time at The Royal Mews on the sergeant's horse 'Lydia'. It was a fine spectacle watching the horses being harnessed up to the Irish State Coach on her maiden trip before we set off out into the relatively deserted streets. The crew inside the coach were very attentive listening for any creaking or weaknesses, often hanging out of the

Police, Ponies & Husbands in-between

windows looking for problems or assessing where adjustments could be made. It was a wonderful job to do that morning and I felt very privileged to escort one of the state coaches on such an important journey round Hyde Park. It had been built originally in 1851 but in 1911 a fire almost destroyed it and it lay in derelict storage until its restoration, completed in 1989. She was a seriously beautiful coach and I felt proud to have been a part of her return to service.

As mounted officers we were quite used to going to the Royal Mews because during the summer months there was a veritable catalogue of ceremonial events. In preparation for these some of our senior foot duty officers had to learn to ride, such dizzy ranks from the Commissioner down would attend weekly to hone their skills, whether they wanted to or not. And some of them, I am sure, didn't. These lessons were taken on our own police horses in the indoor school at the Royal Mews and those which were suitable for the job were selected and entered on the duty board.

I had a new horse issued to me, another pretty little grey called Debbie. Eileen had gone up to West Hampstead to be issued to a new probationer. Debbie was one of those selected for the Senior Officers' rides and once a week I took her down to the Royal Mews along with six or seven other horses and their riders. We would then wait patiently while the lesson was in progress, trying not to giggle, because it was often quite amusing for us to watch these poor high-ranking fellows, so powerful in their own comfort zone, trying to master a skill that showed them to be a touch inadequate. It was not unknown for the Queen to look in and view the progress. That was one of those 'best behaviour' moments.

The weeks that engulfed the annual Trooping of the Colour was known by us as the 'Silly Season'. Saddles were burnished to perfection and horses were scrubbed witless. Some of my colleagues had special head kits gleaned from sweet talking our saddler or illicit purchases from retiring officers and these they kept squirreled away especially for ceremonial duties. You could almost see your face in the shine on the leather and it was a cardinal sin for a tourist to handle the bridle parts while engaging an officer in conversation out on the streets. Most of the tourists did, and you could see the pain on the face of the rider having so lovingly prepared their kit for such an occasion, only to have it sullied by a plethora of grubby little mitts.

Chapter Twenty-Six: Accidents Waiting to Happen

Erika's pony, Beau, had come to share Gemma's grazing at Windlesham Park and by New Year my field was looking worse for wear. By the February both Gemma and Beau looked decidedly unhappy with their lot so Erika found a small yard with stables and a sheltered field that we could take the horses to. I kept Windlesham Park on as the rent was so reasonable I could afford to rest it for the winter.

Erika rang me at home one morning. "It's Gemma," she said. "She's walking as though she has wet knickers on and her tail is held quite high." I scuttled straight round to the yard to see her and assess my thoughts; and she was indeed walking very strangely with her hind legs apart. I rang the vet who came the following morning. I was on late turn so conveniently available to dance attendance on her. Erika met us at the yard. She was a good friend who would always find time to be there if I needed her.

"I think I know what has happened here," began Frank as he disentangled himself from the stethoscope and re-appeared from under Gemma's armpit.

"The fact is that the foal is quite mature and it has moved up into the birth canal and cannot get back down."

"Goodness."

"You obviously feed hay and bucket feed."

"Twice a day," I said.

"Well, her gut feels fairly solid and this is making it harder for the foal to move," Frank continued to explain.

"She needs bran mashes," said Erika.

"Indeed she does, or grass, that's good, too, if you can find any this time of year," he said. "But in the meantime I will give her an injection of Equipalazone, and give you some sachets to complete the course over the next few days."

"She doesn't seem to be in pain" I said, knowing this was a commonly used pain killer.

"Is that what they call Bute?" Erika asked.

"Yes, it is the same thing, but I am not prescribing this for pain. Bute has an unusual side effect in that it prevents the release of the hormone which tells an animal to give birth."

"Goodness me."

"Anyway, it's very useful for us in this instance."

"I don't have any bran," I said, "and there's no time now to get some before I am due at work this afternoon".

"I don't have any either," said Erika.

"I could borrow some from work though," I said. "We have some there and I am sure the skipper won't mind, I'll only be borrowing."

"You need to get her gut good and squidgy as quickly as possible, you want it nice and soft otherwise the foal will stay where it is and that won't be good. It is too early for this foal to be born. I'll come back to see her in a couple of days." And with that Frank left us to ponder the problem in hand.

"He's very nice," I said to Erika as we waved him goodbye.

"Yes, he is," she agreed. "I could fiddle in his knickers anytime."

"You'll have to fight me for him," I argued.

I had a bit of time to spare before heading off to work so I walked Gemma along the verges to see what grass we could find, and then I was off to work for late turn just a little more than worried about her.

My sergeant was such a lovely man, "Yes, OK," he said pensively, "if you promise, I mean really promise, to return the same amount you take before the week is out."

"Yes, I promise Sarge. Thank you very much, Sarge."

"Let us all know how she gets on," he added caringly.

11pm that evening I was offering Gemma a bran mash. She refused to eat it. "What's this muck?" she said with the look of a nasty smell under her nose.

"It's a bran mash, it's lovely."

"Yuck". She said.

'Hummmf, what a mardy mare she is' and I left it with her to eat during the night. She didn't.

The following day I added some molasses to a fresh mash and offered it to her. She waggled her mobile muzzle about across the surface of the mash and gingerly tried some.

"Ooo, that's not bad," she said, tucking in.

"Phew, at long last."

"You'll eat anything when you're hungry," she mumbled with her mouth full.

"Well, get used to it. It's all you're getting for the next few days," I told her in no uncertain way. I bought a bag of bran and she was on little else for the next month while we watched her like hawks. I returned the borrowed bran with interest, thanking Steve profusely.

***

Meanwhile the nation was rocked with horror on 15th April when 96 people were crushed to death during a football match at Hillsborough Stadium. The government decreed all stadiums should be fitted with seating thereafter and major adjustments were made to further public safety while they were watching the beautiful game.

Because I worked full-time with quite a demanding job I was very aware I could not necessarily be able to handle an emergency, if there was one, when Gemma's time came to give birth. I asked Mo if she could return to Badger's Wood to foal down and Mo readily agreed that she could. No worries then. No worries until there was a disturbing local outbreak of Rhinopneumonitis, or Equine Herpes to you and me. It featured in the national press and the Mounted Branch were alerted to the dangers of interaction with civilian horses. There had been two horses found dead in Windsor and we all held our breath. Mo had been advised by her vet not to have any incoming horses from within 15 miles of us. But good ol' Mo, she was happy with Gemma still going to her because she did not think we were a risk due to our isolation. Phew! That was a big relief because I don't know what I would have done if she could not have gone.

As it happened we got her down to West Sussex just 4 days before the foal was born.

***

"It's a boy," Mo told Ruth on the phone Sunday night. "He's beautiful, not a bit of white on him anywhere, a real Cleveland." We were all excited and immediately began to think of a name for him.

"It was a bit dark last night" Mo told Ruth on the phone when she rang again on Monday morning. "It's not a boy it's a girl." Ruth rang me straight away while I was at work and told me the news and if you could see my face you would notice some egg. Much jollification followed in the tearoom thereafter and all the boys pitched in to think of a name for her.

"Koh-i-Noor", Ruth decided. "I'm going to call her Koh-i-Noor, and Koko for short."

"She is the jewel in the crown," David added.

***

All football matches had come to a standstill while the main stadiums round the country were being refurbished and seating was being installed in the standing areas, where fans had previously been expected to do exactly that – stand. There was something of a panic because Liverpool and Everton were waiting to play the Cup Final and there was much to do in getting the Wembley stadium ready in good time. In just under five weeks following the Hillsborough disaster, the game went ahead but it had been a close call. I won't say that the seating was still being installed on 20th May but certainly workmen had not yet vacated the stadium and the match was delayed by two and a half hours or thereabouts. Round to the right of the old stadium if you were to look at the front where the twin towers had been in the old days, there was an area known as the 'Pinch Point.' As the name suggests it was a wide and spacious walkway from the car parks and the generous expanse at the front of the building, narrowing to just a handful of turnstiles. The space was hemmed in by boundary walls and the stadium itself.

It was a screaming hot day. We wished we could be in shirt sleeve order, but because of the nature of the duty, full uniform was the order of the day. In fact, we were all wearing our riot helmets as we did at most football matches now. We were used to trouble. It's what we did, but the challenge for this day was to keep the fans in good order and prevent overcrowding. Everyone was aware of this in the wake of that dreadful disaster and the waiting around was tolerated by all in quite a civilised manner. But the turnstiles were not turning and irritations did begin to manifest themselves as the people at the back began to wonder what was happening at the front, which was a big fat nothing for quite some time.

Our inspector had a brilliant idea. He told us to turn our horses' side-on to the expected flow of the crowd and stand nose to tail with each other. There was a pair of horses nearest the turnstiles holding back a section of the crowd and then twenty feet or so further back there was a line of three horses doing the same job. I was one of those. Even further back still there was a line of about five horses and further back there was a great deal more space and mounted officers were patrolling.

I chatted happily enough to those around me, and believe me, it was tight. There were people packed around us dodging about just a little to avoid the nodding of our horses' heads as we baked in the small box of concrete.

"Officer," one chap asked. "Do we know what's happening yet?"

"No, mate" I replied. "Nothing has come through for a while now."

"Can't you find out," he said.

I tapped my personal radio to illustrate the silence. "They'll let us know as soon as we can start moving."

"We're baking here," they told me as if I didn't know.

"We are too," I said.

We exchanged some pleasantries about the horses and some bright spark came out with some jokes, adding to the banter, it was all relatively good humoured. Then I saw what I thought was some fellow pushing against the others around him.

"Oi," I pointed at him on impulse. "Stop shoving."

"I wasn't shoving," he replied.

"I saw you," and I leaned down towards him to further my point.

"No, you didn't. You couldn't ave, cos I wasn't."

"Don't argue with me, I did see you." And I began to stab the air towards him with my index finger.

"Well, I wasn't shoving anyone, so you can just back off." And he came towards me stabbing the air in my direction with his index finger. The rest of the crowd fell silent.

"Back off? I'll tell who's gonna back off." I told him as I leaned closer to his face, "have you forgotten what happened a month ago?"

"No, I 'aven't." And he came even closer to my face.

"Well we all 'av' to co-operate here, and that includes you, shmuko." Our noses were practically touching.

"Don't you talk to me like that," he growled "and my name is not Shmuko."

"I'll talk to you how I bloody well like, and I'll 'ave less of your lip while we're on the subject," I snarled in retaliation.

He said nothing, and I said nothing, and we eyeballed each other with venom and I found myself wondering where I could take the situation from here. I did realise at the time that I was in part responsible. I should have been more patient but it was so hot. We continued to glare into each other's eyes, so I did the only thing I could possibly do in the circumstances . . .

. . . I kissed him.

The silence was broken and the rest of the crowd laughed heartily. He beamed the most delightful smile at me. I had made a friend, and as the crowd shuffled gradually around, he kept catching my eye and nudging his mate while pointing at me and giving me a little wave. I gave him little waves back and I like to think that he is somewhere in the country dining out on the same story. In the fullness of time everyone filed into the stadium to watch the game and from outside in the Pinch Point we joined in the minute's silence before kick-off. We listened to Gerry Marsden and the fans of both Liverpool and Everton singing 'You'll Never Walk Alone'. It brought tears to my eyes.

***

When Koko was sturdy enough Mo brought her home to Windlesham Park. Gemma was on the case without delay instructing her baby by showing her the perimeter around the field. She began by cantering and trotting right round the fence line, then she turned and cantered directly across the middle of the field to the opposite fence where she skidded to a halt and blocked Koko's path. She then trotted to the fence line across the top of the field and did the same thing through the middle of the field to the opposite fence, again coming to an abrupt halt in front of Koko. Then, and only then, did she put her head down to graze, getting on with the important aspect of being a mother.

"I've never seen that before," said Mo.

"Neither have I" said Diane, from next door.

"Your horse is a thinker," said Joyce, as if we didn't already know.

***

While on my travels around the countryside, I saw a man with a pair of shire horses in a field. Having this underlying passion for heavy horses I stopped the car and got out to watch what he was up to. One of the horses was wearing a harness and he was hitching it to a set of chain harrows. Obviously, I considered there may be something I could learn and I lent on the gate and watched him with great interest. It did not end well. As soon as the horse began to take the weight of the harrows in the collar and move forward the resulting jangle of the links took the horse by surprise and he lurched forward. The man tried to hold him, and couldn't, tripping, he fell and was dragged a few feet before letting go of the plough lines. Now there was nothing to stop the horse as it careered around the edge of the field at break neck speed with the harrows chasing it. As it followed the line of the fence the harrows were forced outward and the centrifugal force took hold. They hit a fence post, and another and another, and several more cracking, one or two with the force of the centrifugal. The other horse trotted up and down and round and round in a "what's got into him" kind of a way.

The man picked himself up and dusted off his knees as the Shire came around for a second time. He raised his arms and called "Whoa, whoooooaaa there, Triumph! Whoa!" Being unfit and tired, Triumph came eventually to a standstill and the man took hold of his bridle. I leapt the gate to go and help. "God, that was scary," I said to him. "Are you alright?"

"Here," he replied handing me the reins, now broken. "Can you hold him for a minute and I'll try and get him unhitched?" I took the reins not being entirely sure I could hang on to him if he decided to go again. The man unhooked the harrows and hung the plough chains up on to the horse's harness. Triumph jiggled about a bit as the chains rattled. "I had better remove these altogether," he said almost to himself and he lowered the chains in turn on to the floor and Triumph immediately became a different, and more relaxed horse.

"That'll get the field harrowed," I said grinning.

He nodded. "You could say that. The name's Phil by the way," and he held out his hand which I shook enthusiastically.

"Sue," I said by way of explaining my name rather than my intention of court proceedings.

"My wife's a Sue," he said. "She is usually here to give me a hand."

"You have done this before then?"

"Oh yes, but it makes a difference if there are two of you and this is the first time Triumph has been in the harrows."

"You don't say." I said not a bit surprised about that.

"He's usually so quiet," Phil said puzzled.

"If I can help anytime, just ask," I explained, "I am fond of heavy horses, my ambition is to buy a Suffolk."

"Those bloody things; what do you want one of them for?" He looked shocked.

"I like them," I said.

"You can't beat a flashy Shire hoss, in my view." He insisted.

"I couldn't be doing with all that hair," I laughed.

"Each to their own," he shook his head smiling at the banter, we chatted on before eventually parting company and I felt pleased with myself that I had come across a fellow enthusiast.

I had the pleasurable delight shortly after this of mingling with those wonderful heavy horses. I was once again allowed a posting at the annual horse show in Hyde Park. It was always enjoyable but this year the weather was not with us. Saturday brought us torrential rain and thoroughly soaked Cherry and Tom whom I had met the year before. I volunteered to take their show jackets home with me to dry out overnight, they stank and the house filled with the smell of wet heavy horse.

Chapter Twenty-Seven: Who the Hell is Cathy?

It was during this hectic time of spit and polish when Koko went down with a virus. I noticed a quietness about her when I returned home after a tour of duty on the second rehearsal for the Trooping of the Colour. She was just over a month old and I knew from experience this was a dangerous time for foals. "She's quieter today," said Ruth, content in the knowledge her little horse was settling down at last. She had proved to be something of a handful. I didn't want to alarm Ruth or overreact so I decided to see how she was in the morning. She was still quiet and Gemma's udder told me that there was an excess of milk. It did not look good.

Richard came to help and offer support, and Erika came with her thermometer. I had already called the vet and he was due that afternoon. Koko had a temperature of 104. It was a very hot day with many flies. Frank the vet, the pretty one, administered an injection of penicillin but the drop in her temperature was short lived. Ruth and David and I returned later that evening and I stripped some of Gemma's excess milk to ease her swollen udder. There was about a half pint, which I took home and put in the fridge, just in case. Thankfully, the evening was warm and pleasant.

I was early turn the following day but the skipper allowed me to go in a bit later so long as I was there in time to do the Changing of the Guard. The vet was coming again at 8am and Ruth, David and I were with her fussing and worrying at 7am shortly to be joined by Erika who was yet again proving to be the good friend that she always was. The vet did not give much hope for Koko's chances. This was not what I wanted to hear but I looked back to the days when Gemma was fighting the same kind of infection and she had been so much worse than this and yet she pulled through. While I was at work Erika covered for me with Koko's care, in fact she was remarkable, staying in the field all day turning her and feeding her. By Thursday she was out of the woods.

You know everything is going to be okay when the vet has a smile on his face. He had a lovely smile too, did Frank. We all did, and that night we all slept the sleep of the eternally contented.

Police, Ponies & Husbands in-between

I have always thought that an ideal companion for a mare and foal is another mare and foal. The opportunity for this came when Phil and Sue, they of the Shire Horses, happened to say they were looking for some nice grazing for their Shire mare Kate and her pure-bred colt foal Angus. I jumped at the chance of having them come to stay with us; Angus would be so good for Koko and the company would help them both develop in play and social skills. Everyone but everyone fell in love with Angus. He was the munchiest of foals and Kate was a very sweet mare.

One of the things I had been concentrating on over the winter was studying to further my 'horse husbandry' knowledge. I had a private British Horse Society tutor who came to the house every week and I found the subjects we covered a sheer fascination. I learned so much and enjoyed the journey. I took my British Horse Society Stage 3 Theory Exam and I passed! I took the Riding Exam shortly afterwards and didn't.

***

My riding skills were not in question when they were put to the test again and I was part of a mounted serial posted to Roundwood Park for the annual Irish Festival. The park was beautifully laid out with gardens of horticultural delights and large landscaped areas for picnickers and ball games and general sunny days out, for the populous of Harlesden and Wembley. Our sergeant was in charge of the motley crew from different stables. Only Doug and I were the family members from GSY and the tour of duty ahead of us looked set to be something of an overkill in man power. All concerned were out for a lovely time in the sun-soaked park and the spirits were buoyant.

We languished by the horsebox, we patrolled spasmodically when boredom set in and we looked forward to the time when we could all go home, although, as it happens, that was not going to happen until almost midnight. The gathered crowds made merry with their Gaelic dancing and the sound of their jolly Irish jigs filling the air with bonhomie.

I spoke to some of my old 'B' relief colleagues from Willesden Green. They asked after Hugh and I had to tell them we had parted company. They were surprised, "We thought you two were solid" they said.

"So did I," I nodded agreement..

Then as the sun began to drop into the herbaceous borders, the drinking in the beer tents began to reach fever pitch. I was no stranger to the feisty Irish with a pint or two swilling around their guts. It was with great amusement I remembered my foot duty service at Willesden Green, and the state of many a drunk staggering home from 'The Dog,' out of his brains with overindulgence and ready to take on the world. Then the following morning the same man would be placid and polite in front of the magistrate and asking the arresting officer with sincerity: "Was I any trouble last night, Officer?"

Fights began to break out and the odd scuffle did not alarm us but when the Chief Superintendent forcibly closed the beer tent the aggression was turned upon us and we took a somewhat different view. The foot duty officers were taking a pasting and were unprepared with no riot gear, dressed only in regular foot duty uniform. We were not dressed for a riot either but we were on horses. We wasted no time in getting stuck in and began to clear the park. "Go and fight somewhere else," we told them.

"Bugger off," they said, or words to that effect. Horses pushed sideways bearing down on those prepared to stand their ground. German Shepherds strained at their leashes snarling the ever-serious threat that one false move and the dog could be set free. They snapped at heels and they barked the bark only a German Shepherd can. The crowd was leery, they were uncouth, and they were the Irish at their worst. I grabbed a chappie's collar who was refusing to move, and dragged him kicking and screaming to the edge of the park where I deposited him in the gutter.

"I suppose a fuck's out of the question then," he said looking up at me from the tarmac.

"Oh, get a life," I muttered, letting out a lung full of air.

What was so lovely about the aftermath of that particular day were the letters of appreciation from the governors of 'Q' District. An inspector wrote a personal handwritten 'thank you' to all of us on horses, and presumably to those with dogs too: "We didn't envisage disorder on that scale. Foot duty colleagues spoke highly of both Dog Section and Mounted Branch. "…your presence saved our day."

An official form 728 came through the internal post from two separate chief superintendents talking of: "Thanks to the courage and professionalism of the Mounted Branch and the Dog Section ……. the injuries sustained by foot duty would have been far greater …… restoring order would have taken longer ……. Mounted Branch responded magnificently."

But best of all was the 728 signed by four individual foot duty police constables, all from 'N' District, who gave us their "heartfelt admiration" saying we had "true professional behaviour, bravery and sheer guts under the continual barrage," concluding with, "well done from all of us."

It was on occasions such as this that I was glad I did what I did.

***

It was also good having Ruth and David in the house. Apart from the company it meant I was able to go away occasionally without having to worry about the horses. This year, my father's charity for blind climbers, the Milton Mountaineers were heading up to Scotland again to climb Ben Nevis for the second time. My two sisters came too along with George our leader and I had continued the habit of writing some verses to perform at the traditional ceilidh on the last evening. I usually wrote them during the weekend so as to incorporate some of the exciting things that might have happened.

Exciting things such as the sad discovery the commemorative plaque we had put at the entrance to the hotel, had been stolen during the winter months of closure.

Other little incidents such as when we had a couple of miles to walk along the road back to the hotel one of our number flagged a passing bus and won for himself a free lift. This was no mean feat for John, a man who was both totally blind and deaf.

Here follows an example of my scribblings

The annual trip of the Milton Mountaineers
Has unrivalled delights with the company and beer
But the bonus we find, when we go with George Male
Is the pleasure of travelling by British Rail.

Police, Ponies & Husbands in-between

Mid industrial strife we got on the Royal Scot
Without worries of whether we'd get there or not
But we had to ring Glasgow to tell them of our fate
When this fast intercity was three hours late.

We've stayed at The Milton now three times in all
And the last time we put a nice plaque on the wall
As we drove in this year our hearts simply sank
It was stolen by thieves and the wall is now blank.

We returned from the climb, we were tired and wan,
And we coped with the slog as best as we can,
Some hailed a taxi without any fuss
But John travelled free on a one decker bus.

John, my Milton Mountaineer friend with the vision and hearing impairment worked for the Royal National Institute for the Blind as a braille transcriber. Not long after our trip I was out and about on Debbie in the company of one of my collegues. We were heading in the direction of the RNIB offices and I told her all about John and suggested we go and visit him. My collegue held the horses for me while I jumped off. I asked at the reception if he could be fetched from his office. When they brought him down into the street John was just so thrilled I had called by especially. He had never met a horse before, let alone a police horse.

One of the other places I took Debbie to was the Kings Road in Chelsea. My sergeant, Steve, was with me on Lydia and I happened to remark that I knew someone who lived in one of the side roads, Bywater Street. I asked him if he minded if we called in on Peggy, Jim's mother from back in the days of Woodcock Farm. She had always been very kind to me and Steve didn't mind a bit. I jumped off Debbie and handing the reins to him, I knocked on the door. She did not recognise me at first but was quite overwhelmed that I had called by. "Cathy, you look so different. It was such a long time ago, I am so pleased to see you."

"Cathy?" Steve asked, "why Cathy?" he persisted as we rode back down to The King's Road.

"Oh it is a long story, Sarge," I said brushing the embarrassment aside. "I'll tell you all about it one of the days."

***

The distant days at Woodcock Farm seemed a lifetime away, but suddenly I was back there. "I don't like that name, Susan," my husband accused me, as if I had chosen it. "Have you got any other names?" I told him I had been christened Catherine Susan Scott, it was a family tradition to be brought up by the second name. "Well, you have a new family now so you can forget about all those ideas. I'll call you Cathy, I like that, it's a good name, yes Cathy, that will do nicely."

It wasn't often I was addressed by the name I was known by back in the Woodcock Farm days, let alone hearing it when I was at work. But one of these other occasions was during the London to Brighton Run for Veteran Cars. I was patrolling on Debbie in the company of Dougy on Devon and we were weaving our way through the magnificent vehicles assembled in Hyde Park. The veteran engines were ticking over gently with a musical popping and spluttering, all of them playing a different tune. Devon and Debbie were both a bit on their toes with all this unusual noise and I remarked to Doug that these cars had been frightening horses since their day of manufacture. I was just saying how nothing had changed when I heard a voice calling to me, a voice I knew extremely well. "Hello, Cath," the voice said.

"John?" I questioned, turning to see the father of my children. "How are you?" He was with his friend, another John. "Hello, John," I added, "You're a face from the past, nice to see you here." We engaged in some polite conversation before going our separate ways. I turned to Doug and explained with a 'tut.' "That's my ex-husband."

I must have had a look of distaste on my face because he replied; "Don't give me that old baloney, Sue, or should I call you Cath? You must have loved him once."

"I suppose, I did," I said wistfully.

***

The annual breed show for the Cleveland Bay Society was at Ascot and I really wanted to be part of that, showing off Gemma and Ruth's lovely Koko. We needed transport and I found a one-man operation with a dinky Lambourne horse box. He arrived on the appointed day to find Gemma polished and Koko looking her usual magnificent self, all fluffy mane and bottle brush tail. She was not proving an easy foal to handle. We had already had some issues with her being manger proud: that is, lashing out with her hind legs every time anyone went near her while she was eating. She got instant discipline and we soon cured the problem, but she was far from compliant when it came to doing as she was told.

Gemma walked up the ramp like the old soldier that she was and Koko didn't. No! She really didn't, not hell or high water could persuade her this was a good idea. Chris had looked by and he pitched in with wise Mounted Branch advice but little good did it do us, because she wouldn't go in. Erika was keen to add her three pennyworth, to no avail. Ruth was at a loss and David even more so, we coaxed and we caressed, we pushed and we pulled, all of us together shoving and shunting and gasping and straining, meanwhile the owner of the little lorry fussed about like a mother hen because he did not want his precious box damaged by a nasty little foal. Gemma stood bemused by the entire goings on, munching her hay with half an eye on her baby putting up such a fight.

In the end there seemed no other way forward but to go to Ascot and ask for help. It wasn't far away after all and I knew there would be disappointment if they were one entry less on the day. We had elected to go the day before and stable them in the posh racehorse boxes, which is just as well, really, as, we wouldn't have got there at all. I returned with lovely man who happened to be a farrier with the muscle power to simply pick Koko up and deposit her next to her mother inside the lorry. Job done, and we all set off for the racecourse. The little lorry knew a different route going all round the Wrekin to get there so I had to wait for quite some time before they caught up with me.

We dropped the ramp and Gemma came down but Koko didn't. No! She really didn't. In fact, she lay down. My kind farrier friend came to help but we still couldn't get her up, she just lay there. "Do you have any water?" he asked me. This was no time for giving in to thirst I thought quietly to myself and I fetched a bottle of Evian I had amongst my baggage. "I could open my flies" he said, "I've done that before but this is more gentlemanly." And with that he promptly tipped a little drop into Koko's ear. She got up pretty quickly then and shot down the ramp like a bullet. "Needs must," he said over his shoulder as he left to go about his affairs.

Richard joined us the following day with a video camera that he had bought. It was seriously state of the art at the time and about the size of a small tea chest but we had endless fun with it. Gemma won her class, and so did Koko.

***

I thought that it might be a jolly idea to have friends round as Ruth had a birthday fast approaching. I rang my old friends from 'back in the day'. They all came, Lynette, Sheila, Ronni, Roger, Erika and Jim. We were all together again and picking up the conversation just as if we had seen each other a week ago. Of course they still all called me Cathy, apart from Erika, who embraced my name change back to Susan.

"Do you mind?" asked Sheila.

"Certainly not," I replied, "It makes me feel sixteen again". And I did feel sixteen again, the years just melted away.

Richard came too, as it seemed we were now walking out together, to use an old-fashioned expression.

Ruth had been just a toddler when they had last seen her. "For goodness sake", she said when some of the buffet fell on to her lap. "Last time these people saw me I was chucking food all over myself. They must think that nothing has changed," she laughed.

Chapter Twenty-Eight: A Gift Horse in the Mouth

My visits to Suffolk were becoming a necessity if I was to find the draught horse of my dreams. As the summer drew to a close I pilgimaged East especially to see for myself the annual event known as the Suffolk Spectacular. This was no ordinary show. There were no entry opportunities as such, although there was a braiding competition, an obstacle drive through traffic cones with big lumbering brewery drays. There was an inspection of the horses' feet. The Suffolk Horse Society was very particular about the status of their horses' feet. There was a gymkhana with young riders bouncing bareback on lovely chestnut animals. There was a big parade too, a long magnificent row of gleaming golden coats, spectacular harnesses and proud upstanding stallions perfectly behaved rubbing shoulders with the mares and foals. Sons of the soil sporting mutton chop sideburns handling their giants with quiet firmness as wives and girlfriends danced attendance either with their own Suffolk or helping with someone else's. A witty and informative commentary kept us all abreast of the happenings in the main ring from Cherry's husband Roger.

"The perfect Suffolk," he began, "should have the face of an angel and the arse of a farmer's daughter."

I told Cherry what I was thinking, 'I really want one!'

"There is a college course I am helping to run, on how to handle and drive the heavy horse." Cherry told me.

"Are you tutoring a course?" I said all ears and interest. "Where?"

"Otley College"

"Really?"

"Yes, really,"

So I returned to Suffolk shortly afterwards to learn about farm horses. It was for a whole week, and I stayed with Cherry and Roger and lived and breathed the old ways. We had four horses to practise our driving skills on, Samba and Noble, were two of Cherry and Roger's own Percherons from Weylands. Orchid and Punch were Suffolks from Hollesley Bay, the young offenders prison. It is a little known fact that the prison unit has always been a strong supporter of rare breeds of farm animals. Giving young men the chance to work with these lovely horses was a great contribution to their rehabilitation. I had the most delicious time while looking out for a Suffolk foal that might be for sale. I re-joined the Suffolk Horse Society and searched through their list of breeders.

***

I brought Gemma back into work after we had weaned Koko and as we had not enjoyed the Great Park for quite some time; it was a rare treat to get out there. With Joyce's influence I thought it might be good fun to enter some long-distance events. This was fairly new sport for the British Horse Society and our first goal was to qualify for The Bronze Buckle, which was a mere thirty mile ride over open country. January 1990 brought some more hefty storms and it was through these draughty days I stepped up Gemma's fitness programme. Ruth and David enjoyed the commitment looking after Koko and shared all the responsibilities necessary for her care. She was fast growing into a very nice youngster.

Gemma was a minx. Somehow a kid's football had got into the water trough in the field and she would not leave it alone. In the end she stuck her foot into the water to give it a bit of a stir and caught it on the sharp edge of the ball cock housing. She sliced through her coronary band, 'cuticle' to you and me, and the damage was irreparable.

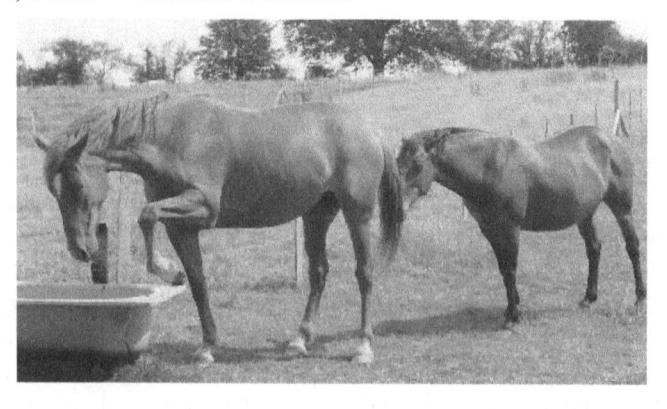

It didn't look like much at the time but it interfered with the growth of horn that covered the hoof. It took a couple of months to manifest itself but it looked like there would always be a crack down the front of her foot. I asked Cherry's advice when I next spoke to her on the phone and she suggested I ask my farrier to put double toe clips on the front shoes and feed extra biotin. This is a vitamin, sworn by many, to solve all your foot problems. I had great faith in Cherry's knowledge. She was, after all a registered farrier herself. There was no harm in getting the information confirmed though and the next time I took my horse to be shod I ran the problem past the police farrier at Hammersmith. He agreed this was excellent advice.

Phil and Sue, they of the Shire horse Kate and her foal Angus, came to supper one evening. They were a fun couple and I did get on so well with them. Knowing that I felt hampered by having no horse transport, they offered me an old horse box without wanting anything in return. The lorry was currently storing some furniture in their back yard and Phil made no secret of the fact it was going to cost a bob or two to make it road worthy. But if I was interested then the horse box was there for the taking. A complete exhaust system was one of the obvious requirements. Driving it to the garage for renovation was a musical journey, if nothing else. The lorry was a BMC FG with a threepenny-bit cab, often called a suicide door because the first sign passing traffic saw of someone alighting from the vehicle was the person. There was no early warning of an open door because it was hidden by the body of the truck. I decided to call it 'Miles,' because he had done a few.

"You've gone and got what?!" Richard was horrified "I worked on those twenty years ago," he said. "They were a load of rubbish then and I don't suppose they have improved with age." Oh well, this was my one chance of transport for Gemma and you just have to make the best of it. It was going to be a long haul, though, and it did not look like I would have it roadworthy for at least a couple of months.

***

I wasn't the only one in our house making plans. A big fat envelope landed with a slap onto the hallway mat. Ruth picked it up rather sheepishly and disappeared upstairs to her bedroom. "What have you got there?" I asked her when she finally resurfaced.

"Um, this is going to surprise you, Mum."

"What is?"

"I've joined the Territorial Army."

"Have you?"

"I have, The Royal Signals."

"Oh . . . Good for you, Ruth" I said, though I must confess it came as a shock. I hadn't got Ruth labelled as military material. I had always referred to Phillip affectionately as 'my little soldier.'

"So I'm your little soldier now, aren't I?" she announced.

"Yes, indeed you are."

***

The question of finding a suitable Suffolk horse to breed from had not gone away. I scoured the pages of the Heavy Horse World and I made plans to visit horse shows where there were classes for Suffolk foals. Unfortunately, these were mostly in Suffolk. Then Cherry rang out of the blue, "I've found a Suffolk yearling for you," she announced.

"Really?"

"Really." And Cherry continued to tell me all about her. Ruby of Virginia House was still on her mother. "But as least she has not been spoilt, Sue. I've broken in hell an all osses for folks and the worst ones are those who have been messed about with."

"Messed about?"

"Yes, people have tried to break 'em themselves and failed, often spoilin' a good 'oss in the process."

"That's bad news" I said.

"That's when they send em to me to sort out. I could tell you some tales."

"I bet you could."

"But your Ruby, she'll be a blank canvas and that is the best sort."

"Leave it with me, Cherry." I told her, "I'll be over as soon as I can get a couple of days off, probably next week."

"Good Lord," Ruth laughed as I put the phone down, "do you two actually need to use a phone? I heard every word."

I dropped everything and headed off to East Anglia as soon as work would allow. I could not believe that at last I had found my very own Suffolk Punch and I wasted no time in getting her vetted. She passed and I completed the deal.

I kept her at Town Green Farm for the first couple of weeks; Gemma was not impressed. Their stables were right angles to each other and Gemma could see right into Ruby's but not the other way

Police, Ponies & Husbands in-between

around. Gemma stomped around her stable, huffing and puffing and pawing the floor, chucking her bedding in all directions. As soon as I went into her stable to ask her what the problem was, she became immediately pacified. "Oh, what are you playing at?" she said to me nuzzling her head into my chest with such determination, and what appeared to me could only be genuine affection.

"It's my new horse, it's Ruby, she's a sister for you." I couldn't understand why she was being so possessive.

"You're my sister," she said. "I don't need another one." I gave her a healthy pat and went to exit the stable. She manoeuvred herself between me and the door shouldering into me. "You're not going anywhere."

"Oh Gemma, what am I going to do with you?" I whispered into her nose and gave her a goodly hug.

***

Much to the surprise of everyone, Richard was made redundant that summer. Kensington and Chelsea Council put their street cleaning operation out to private tender, along with so many other local authorities throughout the country. He formed a company with Percy and financial wiz, Janet, and together they put in a bid for the contract but the good councillors of Kensington and Chelsea saw fit to award the whole circus to an outsider.

Richard was promptly offered a job as production manager to a family firm manufacturing dustcarts. 'Refuse Collection Vehicles' Richard would insist on calling them. Kensington and Chelsea council had been long standing customers of Jack Allen's and the marriage had been a happy one. Richard had never asked to be wined and dined and no fat brown envelopes had mysteriously landed on his desk. Janet was also offered a position as the Assistant Company Secretary. The line was cast to hook Percy on to the team as well but he found greener grass elsewhere. So the two of them headed north to Birmingham without a backward glance and I said 'goodbye' to Richard wishing him a happy life.

There is no doubt, I did ruminate on this, had I let a good man go!?

***

The horses were now back at Windlesham Park and my own sparkly horsebox now on the road, I felt good to go. Gemma and I were back enjoying some more adventures together and the first event I set my sights on was a long-distance ride near Redditch and, what do you know? It was not far from where Richard was now living in his new house. This was not entirely a coincidence.

We all set out for Bridge Farm in good spirits to a Bronze Buckle qualifier, Gemma in the back of Miles and me, Ruth and David in the front. We were well on our way when cruising down the hill coming out of Newbold-on-Stour near Stratford-on-Avon, for reasons I could not explain, Miles's engine began to splutter and stalled. I drifted into a convenient lay-by half way down the hill out of the village. We needed help and in these pre mobile phone days there was nothing else for it but to leave Ruth to look after Gemma, while David and I walked back to the village to find a phone. I rang Richard but there was no answer, neither could I get hold of the event secretary. We returned to the lorry feeling so forlorn in the lay-by. Gemma was happy enough munching on her hay net and luckily I had brought plenty with me. After a bit of a discussion David and I again set out, this time down the hill to a rather grand entrance leading to The Ettingham Park Hotel where they were extraordinarily helpful. There was still no answer from Richard or the event secretary, so I tried a private transport firm with the help of Yellow Pages. They were in no position to help, so as a long shot I asked Directory Enquiries for the number of Bridge Farm where the event was being held. Finally we had one big fat stroke of luck.

Sam the Man came like the cavalry bringing with him a CF Bedford in case Miles failed to start. The problem was I had allowed the engine to idle as we sailed down the hill and the petrol had evaporated in the pipe before it could get to the engine, the valve had stuck shut and the engine could not suck any more fuel through. What a star Sam was, he primed it by hand and started the engine on jump leads as our battery was now as flat as flat with all that engine turning. All he asked for was his petrol money.

Richard was at the farm to greet us as we arrived and I was keen to relate to him our tale. We settled Gemma down for the night before returning with him to his new house. The summer evening was balmy and we were relieved at long last to be sitting in the garden sipping Pimms and soaking up the ambiance that Kidderminster could offer.

We had an early start in the morning getting Gemma ready for her big day. The qualifier was twenty miles and the rules stated that I could not complete this course in less than 2 hours 40 minutes. This is to prevent riders pushing their horses too hard. I knew from timing Gemma round Windsor Great Park that she was capable of at least 8 miles an hour. She had the most amazing trot. She could really cover the ground with every stride and I spent several miles standing up in the stirrups to rest her back and mine. By clutching a fist full of mane and leaning over her centre of gravity at the withers, I could steady my balance and stay there for quite some time. In a snaffle bit she simply flew. With no stopping, I had done the first 10 miles to Cruise Hill in just an hour, which was way too fast; I would have to steady up more if I was to qualify for the Bronze Buckle. Ruth, David and Richard busied about sponging her down but Richard was in motor racing mode keen for me not to dally.

The second ten miles, however, there was a bit more dallying than I anticipated. It's all very well drinking all that juice to keep yourself hydrated but this brings with it the problems of answering calls of nature. Actually, two calls of nature and Gemma was well practiced in the drill. Keen as mustard when I was on her but as soon as I dismounted, she stood like an old donkey waiting patiently for me to attend to my ablutions. Finding an uninhabited spot was more of a challenge, thank goodness for the cover of well-grown bracken. I wasn't a bit worried about the time we would take; I knew what she could do. In fact, I still had to hide in the bushes a mile short of the finish line to kill the time I had clocked up. We crossed the line in two hours fifty-nine minutes, which was very respectable, and because I had given her a rest not long before the finish line, her heart rate was very impressive. Forty-four per minute for a horse which had just travelled twenty miles.

Richard had packed a lovely picnic for us all, which we ate in the horsebox as it was beginning to drizzle. I was well satisfied with the all-round perfect timing and the journey home was, by comparison, uneventful; all I had to remember was to keep the engine revving and not to let it idle. I had not seen the last of this particular problem; in fact, I would go on to say that Miles pretty much broke down every time I took him out. But now, I knew what to do and with another long-distance ride not ten days away, I was on 'Easy Street.'

Joyce was also competing at this event, riding the distance on her lovely grey, 'Tina,' and we agreed to meet there and ride together. I was on my own this time with Gemma and Miles and Diane, who was next to me at Windlesham Park, crewed for the two of us. Not surprisingly I had to stop for fuel on the way and Miles refused to start. It was so silly of me; I should have known the engine would be hot and the petrol pump couldn't cope. Richard was adamant that the petrol pump was in good working order but it still evaporated in the pipe if it stalled or if you stopped for some reason. "They were a load of crap twenty years ago and they are still a load of crap" said Richard for the umpteenth time.

I removed the hood from the engine, which sat rather inconveniently right in the middle of the cab. I unscrewed the fuel pipe from the carburettor and I began to suck the end of it. URGH!!! You really dread the petrol coming through and having to taste it but there is nothing else for it, that's what you have to do. It doesn't always work first time because you have to get you thumb over the end to stop the fuel retracting back and then you have to screw it in keeping the vacuum intact for the same reasons. Finally, I got going.

We were running very close to my veterinary inspection time, which, if I missed it, I would not be able to compete. Gemma really was the most patient of horses, not being one bit phased by the experience. As we pulled on to the field Sue, Diane and Joyce waved me into the space they had saved for me next to their trailer and Gemma came down the ramp and straight into the veterinary ring bang on her time. You just don't cut it any finer than that. Gemma's pulse rate checked in at forty and given that she had just walked off the lorry it was only two points less than her rate when she finished the twenty-five-mile ride. Joyce and I both got grade two rosettes so we went home pretty chirper.

***

The other bit of news that made me feel pretty chipper was that the Director of Public Prosecutions finally decided that the last of the complaints from the Wapping dispute would not result in criminal proceedings nor would there be any disciplinary proceedings taken against me or the other officers. Oh, happy days.

Chapter Twenty-Nine: Jewel in the Crown

Steve, my sergeant said to me one early turn as he studied the duty board, "Would you like to be on duty for the London Van Horse Parade in Regents Park?"

"I love you Sargent Rouse and I want to have your babies." I replied by way of saying I wanted to go.

"You're welcome to them," he continued without hesitation, "You'll find them squabbling in front of the television."

It was a fabulous duty to be given. There were five of us altogether, including Roly and of course the sergeant himself. Obviously, there is no point in having power, if you can't abuse it. We were there to see to it that every turnout paraded in good order and behaved themselves. We were each given a commemorative horse brass as a memento of the day. There were beautiful drays pulled by huge Shires to tiny Shetland ponies and little donkeys pulling dinky little carts, and there was everything in between. There were lots of faces famous in the heavy horse world, Richard Gifford had a flatbed dray on parade and his wife, Angela, gave us a very respectable commentary. I saw black and white gypsy cobs flashing their snowy-feathered legs as they drew their costermonger wagons smartly behind them. There were skewbald vanners pulling a butcher's wagon or a baker's van with their drivers smartly turned out in straw hats and stripey aprons. All the carts and wagons were lovingly painted and presented in tip top order. Everyone looked so proud to be doing what they did, and my goodness me, didn't they do it well.

Juggling work and horses and family kept me out of mischief for much of the time but I just had to find a couple of days free to return to Kidderminster to see Richard. When I came home I was so excited and keen to give Ruth and David the news, which they received favourably. The next job was to go and visit Erica and I could not wait.

"Richard has asked me to marry him," I blurted out with great excitement.

"And...?" she asked

"Well, I said yes, of course! Do I look like someone who has just said no?"

"I did wonder why you were grinning like a Cheshire cat," she said doing the Cheshire cat impersonation back at me.

"He has told me to go and choose an engagement ring so I had better get myself into Ratners."

"RATNERS!!!" exclaimed Erica "Bloody Ratners! You are not going to Ratners! I'll tell you where WE are going to go!" The following day Erika took me to the High Street in Maidenhead. The shop in question was one of those where there is a security door and customers are allowed in one at a time and only when they have passed muster. We made ourselves comfortable and had a variety of the most beautiful gems paraded in front of us. As soon as I saw it, I knew this was my dream ring. It was a rectangle ruby with diamond shoulders with four tiny emeralds on each corner. It was delightful and they promised to put it by for me until I could bring Richard down south.

As it happened, he was due to go, with his boss, to Paignton where the company was exhibiting their refuse collection vehicles at the Annual Show run by the Institute of Waste Management. I liked to call it the 'Dustcart Convention.' Richard asked me if I would like to accompany him for the week and I wasted no time in getting some annual leave booked. There were several companies under the umbrella of Jack Allen Holdings and their different trade stands were impressive with various paint jobs on the vehicles and matching livery for the sales teams. There was a stand for their company of Waste Hoists, dashing in black and yellow strips. There was a stand for Municipal Vehicle Hire emblazoned in bright red and maroon, and then of course, there was the Refuse Collection Vehicle Manufacture itself in bright green and white. They were the nearest competitor to Dennis who only occasionally beat them past the finishing post in the sales race. This was the branch of the organisation where Richard was employed as the Production Manager, the whole show stretched along the Paignton sea front where rolled up trousers and knotted handkerchiefs would normally be the dominant attire along with the 'kiss-me-quick' hats.

These days were different from anything I had previous experience of. Richard's boss was an imposing character, king-pin of operations and the man in charge, no question. I felt like a timid little mouse in his presence. During the heat of the day, he took his entourage of followers to the ice cream van for refreshment. I was an object of interest to many, being Richard's bride-to-be, plus being a policewoman always invited interest. "What'cha gonna have?" John asked me as we walked, "Chocolate or nut?"

"Oooh, nut sounds very nice, thank you," I replied, being on my best behaviour.

"I didn't say nut," he corrected. "It's me Brummy accent, do you want chocolate or not".

"Chocolate would be lovely, please," I wanted the ground to open up. "Thank you," I said feebly.

***

Police, Ponies & Husbands in-between

The return back to Surrey was all planned out with a quick skip into Maidenhead where I was keen for Richard to see the ring I had chosen. We were cutting it all very fine and at 5.25pm we hurried down the High Street to the jeweller's shop that Erika and I had visited not a couple of weeks before. As we approached the shop, I could see the roller shutter slowly clattering its way from the top of the doorway. Richard was breathing a sigh of relief. I, on the other hand, was stepping smartly forward bending down to see if I could catch the eye of the operator. I did, and he recognised me, the roller shutter stopped in its tracks and began juddering its way back up to the top.

The front door was opened wide and we entered and my beautiful ring was presented to Richard for his inspection. The deal was struck and he gently slid the ring on to my finger symbolising the commitment we were both making. These certainly were exciting times, and of all the places in the world, I never thought that I would be going to live in Kidderminster.

Many years ago, before I married Hugh, I had a boyfriend, also a policeman. He had come to collect me from North Wales because I had had an accident on my motorbike the week earlier. Passing through Shrewsbury, he seemed convinced we should follow the signpost pointing towards a place called Kidderminster, as that was the way he had come, not to mention via Bristol. He did get a bit lost! The trip had been a catalogue of disasters thus far and this was the last straw so I kicked off big time with what I thought of Kidderminster, which incidentally, up until that moment I had never heard of.

"Bloody Kidderminster! Who in their right mind would ever want to go to Kidderminster? I would have to be dragged kicking and screaming before I go within a mile of the place. It's so far away even the burglars don't go there. It's only worth knowing so that you can stay well away. You would not catch me dead in Kidderminster, I have no intention of going there, ever. So, in answer to your question, no! We do not have to follow the sign; we keep straight on. Look ahead of you and do not stray from the A5, on pain of death you stay on this road, or you'll never hear the end of it. If that is OK with the police?"

And now I find myself planning to go and live in Kidderminster. It is a funny old world.

***

One of the things I was keen to do with Ruby was to take her to her first show. This was in Alton, Hampshire and Erika came with me. Phil and Sue parked next to us with their Shire horses and not surprisingly I found we were the only Suffolk there. These bigger horses stood way higher than little Ruby but I was not daunted and success was sweet when we came a respectable second place. I think that because Shire judges are not familiar with having a Suffolk in their lines they quite often don't know where to place them. Being in fear of being seen to put a good horse down the line I came to learn that often it can work in your favour and you are placed higher than where you should be. Ruby wore her second rosette with pride and I trousered the prize money. She was a pleasure to show, a sweet little horse in every respect.

***

My friend Linda from work had been coming over to help me with Gemma. She had done some dressage with her and I had asked her if she would like to take her round Waynfleet, the Mounted Police one day event in Esher, Surrey. She was delighted to be asked and offered to crew for me on the Bronze Buckle ride which was in September, just 11 days before Waynefleet. Linda and I travelled separately to Salisbury Plain so she had her car to get around the meeting points to help me with Gemma's needs on route. We stayed at the Old Mill Hotel on the River Nadder. It was lovely there and a short walk around the millpond took us to the same view of Salisbury Cathedral that John Constable had seen on the day as he set up his massive canvas to paint the famous scene.

Gemma was stabled at the racecourse not far away and because we had Lin's car we could travel easily to and from the hotel. We rose early to go and feed her and muck out her stable before returning to the hotel for a cracking good breakfast and checking out. Thirty miles was no distance for a seasoned campaigner like me, nor for Gemma in fact. Following a relaxed night she ran up sound for the vet and had an unusually low pulse for her at thirty eight. I met one of the Egham and District Riding Club members, who had been on the last long distance ride with me. To the surprise of both of us we were starting at the same time, another member was just five minutes in front of us so it was a very chummy affair.

The National Championships were being held on the same day, which was a hundred miles for a Golden Horseshoe; they were a pretty feisty bunch getting ready for what was also a race ride. We watched in awe as they galloped off at a cracking speed, each with their own start time. For the first few miles, until our route diverted, we were constantly being called upon to move over and let a racer through. "Stand aside!" we would hear the shout from behind, or "Out of the way!" and "Horse coming through"' They hurtled past us on wiry little Arabs types mostly, sweaty and swift, we were glad to see the back of them. Lin had little time to spare between map reading and driving from point to point to meet us but we finished in the required time with a pulse rate of 50. The highest so far but quite acceptable, so we got our Bronze Buckle, and I was very happy as I drove home with Miles. He behaved well although I did keep the choke out all the way home. 'What else do you hang your handbag on?' I hear you ask!

Drunk with the 'long distance' bug I rode out for four and a half hours a few days later starting with the farrier in Chobham and riding on to the saddlers near Wisley. The event at Waynefleet followed a week later and Lin had entered in the military class as she was a leader for the Air Cadets.

Richard came down from the Midlands with his video camera. It was very exciting to watch them go round the course which I was so very familiar with. We managed to film a surprising number of cross-country fences but we had to run. Gemma refused three times altogether at two fences where we had expected problems. The dreaded 'Fairy Ring' then the Trakehner which is a rail over a ditch. The ditch can be frightening for the horse, and so a good test for their bravery. This particular fence had a ditch hidden by long grass, and caught a lot of the horses out, not just us. Lin was dumped on the ground for her trouble but then naughty Gemma refused a second time at the same fence.

"After the second fence she was going on so strongly I thought I would take the quick route through the Fairy Ring." Lin told me afterwards. "That's why she refused, I suppose, the first element is not very inviting, it was a big ask."

"I thought she was descending the steps very steadily," I offered.

"She was, that's why she took me so much by surprise when she put in a stop and I sailed over her head."

"Then she refused a second time! What a naughty girl," I said.

"I know, I'm sorry I had to smack her." Lin rode her very sympathetically and it was a joy to watch them together, quite like those lovely old days when Mandy occupied her stirrups.

So, no prizes but it was a very enjoyable day. The new Commissioner came visiting the horse lines and he stopped to talk with us for quite some time. It was just so lovely having Richard there to watch Gemma doing what she does and meeting many of the people I worked with. We followed Lin to the beer tent where she wanted to catch up with her Air Cadet friends. Many of my old class mates from the days at Imber Court were there making merry. "Watch out, Beadle's about," said HP his eyes fixed suspiciously on the video camera, as we walked through the marquee entrance. Chris took one look at us, and pulling up his collar he mingled with the crowd as far away as he could get. I dragged Richard behind me to seek him out.

"Are you ignoring me?" I asked him in my usual forthright manner. Chris looked embarrassed. "Chris! This is Richard, my fiancé. Richard! This is Chris, my ex-boyfriend." If that doesn't break the ice then nothing will I thought. But Richard had no issues and engaged Chris in conversation naturally enough.

We drank, we chatted and later on the phone Chris said to me. "OK, you were right. He is a nice man; you can go ahead and marry him if you want to."

***

Life was changing, and we all had to adapt to the passage of time. My journeys to Kidderminster increased as often as I could manage and my days at home were peppered with handling and long reining Ruby, much to Gemma's disgust. I rode Gemma lightly and I looked around for where I could move both horses to when I finally took them to the Midlands. I found Castle Farm, registered with the British Horse Society, and not two miles from where Richard lived but I did feel that I needed a job to go to.

I noticed in the pages of The Horse and Hound there was a vacancy at The British Horse Society head office in Kenilworth for their Chief Welfare Officer and I duly applied for the job. I still consider that I had done extraordinarily well to get to the final two applicants but I was not offered the job.

I put in an application to transfer to the West Midlands Police, knowing that if they accepted me then I would be back shaking door handles for a living, but it was all I knew.

***

Faced with another winter on the way and a lively youngster to look after, Ruth reluctantly decided to sell Koko. We advertised her widely and found a lovely lady, in Maidstone, Kent. It was that time of year again for the Grande Prix in Macau and Richard was off to the Far East. Excitement of excitements, I was going with him! Although it did mean I was not going to be about to help Ruth if Koko was sold, and also, I was not around to help with the transport. Phil and Sue said they could pitch in if help was needed. In fact, they were needed and they transported Koko to her new home while I was away. Ruth and David went for the ride but it was a very sad day for Ruth, even though we all knew this was the right decision.

Chapter Thirty: Sunlit Uplands

Another big adventure lay ahead of me going east with Richard, for three whole weeks. I was glued to the window as we flew into Kai Tac Airport in Hong Kong, navigating between the high-rise blocks of condominiums; so close that you could see what people were having for supper and the colour of their smalls pegged out to dry on the balconies.

Richard's brother Fred met us and took us back to Hong Kong Island on the famous Star Ferry. We stood in a rather unimpressive little compound while passengers coming to Kowloon vacated their seats. Then a barrier slid across to the side and we filed through. How the 'Morning Star' failed to hit anything, I was left to wonder. It nosed its way through the flotilla of little boats and big boats that littered the waters between the mainland and Hong Kong island. It was utter marine madness. There were fishing vessels, tiny boats just bobbing up and down with the swell, big liners and military visitors. I was spellbound with the activity of it all. And busy! Oh, my good Lord, Hong Kong was something else again. Stepping into Fred's swanky limo we joined the traffic queue and shuffled half way up the peak to Pearl Gardens where his Fijian wife, Joan, waited to greet us. After such a long flight and very slightly jet-lagged we slept fitfully.

"It's Rip Van Winkle." Fred greeted Richard the following morning. "Mr Winkle I presume," he continued in good spirits. Greeting each other warmly, the family was far flung so meetings were cherished. I was to learn that they also had a sister, Susan who lived in Labrador, Canada. There was so much to learn about the Merrills.

The next stop was Macau for the Motorcycle and Formula Three Grand Prix and Richard, Fred and I took the hour's journey on the Hydrofoil. I discovered what scrutineering meant and Fred was coming with us because he was a driver in one of the safety cars. Filomino met us at the jetfoil. He was there every year to collect Richard and take him to the Sintra Hotel. Richard had known Filomino from when he had been a schoolboy coming to the pits to see the big boys doing their thing. He was a useful ally, being local

Police, Ponies & Husbands in-between

and fluent in English, Portuguese and Cantonese and invaluable showing the guys where to get their money changed, where the best restaurants were, the best market stalls, the best casinos and the best brothels. BROTHELS!! Whatever next?!

***

I have no experience whatsoever of motor racing, but Richard suggested that I get up early with him on the race days and hide myself behind the Armco at one of the most exciting spots on the whole course. Once I was in, I was in. Smuggled by Ian on to the racetrack at the back of The Lisboa, which was a hotel, a casino and a brothel all in one. I was able to watch the racing at Statue Corner with Filomino and the rest of the gang from New Zealand. I watched Mika Häkkinen cream his vehicle against the Armco down the Lisboa Straight. I watched Michael Rutter handle the big two-wheeled beast round Statue Corner, along with Ron Haslam, and Robert Dunlop, the list of known race riders and drivers went on. Statue Corner was a death trap, four lanes down the straight, reducing into two on a right-hand bend. It was no place for feeble driving and the first lap usually harvested the worst of the pile-ups.

We had taken out some rather grotesque facemasks to have some fun with while we were away. There was one of Margaret Thatcher and one of Mikhail Gorbachev. The guys had endless fun entertaining spectators in the stands between races. They made a lively team acting out all manner of themes to an appreciative crowd. Very often a cheer of enthusiasm would rise from the spectators for no apparent reason. The stand was facing the Lisboa across the other side of the track and it was apparent, from the pointing and clapping, and the gaze of all eyes, that one of the working girls had come to the window to entertain them.

Fred was in high spirits with his safety car waiting to spring into action when needed. And action there was. If there was a massive crash on that corner, which was frequent, rather than fly the dreaded red flag, vehicles had to be removed before the racers came around the course on the next lap. As the race progressed competitors began to string out so there was rarely a proper break when a racing vehicle, bike or car was not coming down the Lisboa Straight to wipe out those doing the rescue.

The organisers did not like stopping a race as there was always a tight schedule to keep to. If cranes and lifting gear were required then the red flag was no option, but often the boys were able to bounce a car to one side in which case a yellow flag was used to warn drivers there was a hazard on the track. The good people in the stands yelled warning cries if they saw anything approaching, but it was important to give the rescuers as much time as posible to do the job. Sometimes there was an injured driver or rider and removal was literally a matter of life or death. There was barely a moment that was not heart stopping in its excitement. I was itching to get out there and help but I was kept sternly out of the way. It was probably just as well.

At the end of the first race day we all re-grouped in what they called 'The Garden Bar'. It was sandwiched along a central reservation outside the main entrance of The Lisboa and adjacent to the statue. This was the same statue that stood at the end of the escape lane and why Statue Corner was given the name. It was an interesting monument featuring a Portuguese warrior mounted on a rearing horse keeping in submission the Chinese dragon. Also nearby was the only bridge at the time across the ocean to Taipa, it was over one and a half miles long.

Just before we had left to go to the far East, I had received a letter from The West Midlands Police offering me an interview and general fitness test on 14th December. This was just a few days after we were due to return home. I was aware I might not be as fit, being on holiday, and Ian suggested I run to the middle of the bridge as a good fitness exercise. Richard thought I should too, Dammit! "I'll come with you," Ian said, seeing that Richard wasn't offering. So, we got to our feet and we ran, believe me it was a long way and in the Far Eastern heat I confess I flagged. But I did it; I really did it and running across such an expanse of ocean was amazing, with main land China over on the right and nothing but sea to the horizon on the left.

When we got back to the Garden Bar, Richard's brother Fred had turned up to drink with us. The facemasks were doing the rounds and everyone had a go trying them on for size. Terry, another police officer from Hong Kong, (I was in good company!) decided to take a drag of his cigarette while the mask was on. There was nothing remarkable about this until he exhaled the smoke, which then filled the mask and he was obliged to pull it off his face coughing and choking and turning a most entertaining colour. We all laughed like a row of buckets as the evening drew on to suppertime and further entertainment was sought elsewhere.

After Macau we flew to Bangkok to stay with a friend of both Erika and Richard.

Armed with yards of Chinese silk I had bought from the Hong Kong markets I was able to get some truly wonderful clothes made, along with some more that I had made in Thai silk. We returned back to old blighty, tanned, and rested, and in love. Plus, I had an impressive wardrobe.

***

I attended the interview with the West Midlands Police and it proved to be a day of toil and worry. I did the best I could in the interview and I thought I had excelled in the fitness programme. I cannot remember how far it was that I had to run but I stayed the distance longer than some of the other, much younger, hopefuls and finished with a sprint. Not that I had ever been much of a runner. It took them just four days to decide that they didn't want me, but in hindsight I think they did me a massive favour.

***

Christmas was just round the corner and I was keen to stick with my tradition of displaying plastic tits, which had become ever more outrageous as the years unfolded, this time I wanted to be a bit different. As it would be the last Christmas at GSY, I reasoned that I didn't need to spend perfectly good money on falsies when I had a perfectly decent pair of brown-nosed puppies already installed. All I had to do was find some way of covering the chapel hat pegs and I was good to go. It was my way, I think, of saying this was me, whether you like what you see or not.

I looked to Hawaii for inspiration and found some stick-on fig leaves to cover my nipples. Together with a garland of paper flowers I cut a dash in a floral skirt covered in grass effect raffia. "Why aloha."

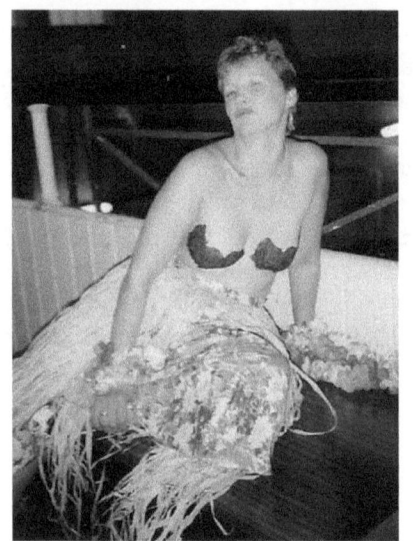

Ruth was also dressing up, enjoying her time in the TA but it meant changes for her and David. She met a fellow squaddie, John, and took up a friendship with him. David also had met someone new and so they decided to part. Well, sort of part, David moved into the spare bedroom and was immediately demoted from 'common law son-in-law' to 'lodger'. I couldn't help feeling sorry about this, I liked David enormously, he was a good egg.

Chris came over to see us and during the course of the evening he told me he had taken my friend, Lin, out for a meal. And, what's more, he thought he would like to take her out again. She worked at Great Scotland Yard with me and I enjoyed her company both at work and her input with Gemma. I told him it didn't mean we could not still be friends, I wanted him to be happy.

He thought I should know, seeing as we worked together and he didn't want to be the cause of any friction. I was genuinely pleased for him, and her.

Later in conversation with my Suffolk friend, Cherry, on the phone, I was rattling on happily about everything and nothing. Such as Chris's new girlfriend, my new fiancé, Ruth's new bloke, etc etc. "I don't know" she marvelled at our way of life, "You city folks, you swap about like 'pigs on the medder.'"

***

Daily life is often peppered with the mundane, I was in 'Scissor Happy' hairdressers, letting Trudy perform her magic on my bubble cut perm. The owner of the enterprise was attending to a customer sitting at the mirror next to me and having inspected her roots he turned and engaged me in conversation. "How is life in the fast lane?" he asked.

Police, Ponies & Husbands in-between

"I have a new horsebox and I've named it after you Miles." I said.

"Really," He was a slim and nubile young thing that most red-blooded women like me would find difficult not to admire. "Is that a lorry or trailer?"

"It a lorry, not a very big one, that's why I've called it Miles because I now have a small box - like you." He coloured up beautifully and Trudy collapsed laughing. I am so naughty.

"By the way," Trudy said, "I'm going on holiday with a mate in three weeks' time, and I asked Ruth if she wanted to come with us, we're going to Lanzarote".

"Ruth didn't tell me?"

"No," said Trudy. "Apparently her new boyfriend won't let her go."

"You leave Ruth to me." I was horrified. "If I can get her on the flight can she still go with you?"

"Yes, of course, she can," Trudy said.

When I got home, I asked Ruth what this was all about. "He doesn't think I should go," she said and broke into a weepy moment.

"Do you want to go?"

"Yes, of course I do, it would be wonderful."

"Well, I think you should go," I said.

"Oh, Mum, no, I can't, I don't know what to do."

"You leave John to me," I told her. And without hesitation I returned to Egham and got the flight details from Trudy. Then I was straight round to the Travel Agent and booked the flight. "You're going," I said to Ruth as I presented her with the tickets. John was not happy but she was under orders from me. So she went to Lanzarote with Trudy and her friend and had, by all accounts, a wonderful girly time. She returned home to a far mellower John.

John could be good fun. He was a 'jack-the-lad' kind of a guy and we got on well. We shared a passion for dogs, particularly German Shepherds which I had grown up with, in the days of white sticks and guide-dog harnesses. John's face always lit up whenever we talked about dogs.

***

Richard managed to convince me that I should sell Miles, the horsebox. He was a pig to drive, with his crash gear-box, and I was getting utterly hacked off with this constant breaking down. His plate was due for renewal and a full year would help with selling him. This is similar to an MOT for larger vehicles but there were only a few Ministry of Transport approved testing centres. I knew of a mechanic who specialised in trucks over by Fair Oakes Aerodrome near Ottershaw. The simplest solution to my problem of getting the lorry there was to put Gemma in the back all saddled up and ready to go and then I drove Miles to the workshop. I think that they were quite surprised when I got a horse out of the back and rode away into the sunset. A few days later I did the trip in reverse riding Gemma to the workshop and loading her up before returning home. It was a pleasant ride across country and a little different from our usual 'same old – same old' run around the block. I advertised him widely and only got one offer. It was a straight swap for a two-horse Rice trailer. I concluded that with Richard's chunky 4x4 this could work well for us and anyway, it looked like being the only offer we were going to get. I said 'goodbye' to Miles after just a year of ownership. Richard was cock-a-hoop.

EPILOGUE

Phillip was now at Sheffield University and would not be able to come to the registry office wedding that we were planning. We were looking forward to having a Church Blessing later in the Summer and I was thrilled that Phillip would be there to give me away.

"So, when to do you think you will be leaving us Sue?" Erika had popped round for a catch up.

Ruth was sitting on the sofa, the newly covered sofa thanks to Erika's expertise. She was usefully employed folding a basket of socks for me.

"You're not getting cold feet are you?" Erika asked.

"No way," I protested "I'm starting to put roots down, I have found somewhere for Gemma and Ruby to live. It's nice."

"Is it a big yard?"

"I suppose so but quite homely, they are into show jumping." I picked up a sock that had fallen on the floor and handed it back to Ruth who had the next pair laid out across her knee neatly lined up together with the heels matched in position. Erika absently watched this procedure while we chatted.

"How many horses are there?"

"I'm not sure, fifteen or twenty"

"That's not too bad." And seeing Ruth laying out the next pair of socks in the same way, Erika removed them from her lap, scrunched the two into a ball, very quickly done, and tossed them into the basket. She gave Ruth a bit of an encouraging look and continued, "What's the riding like?"

"It's on a main road but you can get out through the back, there's Kinver Edge not far and that's fantastic apparently." My attention was taken by Ruth retrieving the ball of socks out of the basket and un-scrunching them to lay them neatly across her knee like all the others had been. She folded them in two and placed them in the basket giving Erika an encouraging look. Erika raised her eyes to the ceiling, and so did Ruth, with not a word being passed between them.

"Is it better riding than round here?"

"No, I don't think so, Rik." I shook my head. "Crumbs, the riding round here is out of this world. I've been very lucky."

"Didn't you say you were planning to have them at home," Rik continued.

"We asked the water board for permission to build a stable and they put a condition on the project that all manure must be removed from sight"

"What's the problem with that, you could throw a tarpaulin over it" Erika said, ever the practical.

"I think, it was supposed to be spelled S-I-T-E." I laughed. Anyway, the Environment Agency stepped in and put their foot down." Sylvester wandered in and jumped on to Ruth's knee.

Erika gave the cat an affectionate stroke. "Is he going with you?"

"Oh yes," I said firmly. "I couldn't leave Sylvester behind, although the house is on a main road which is a bit of a worry."

"It is set back from the road quite a bit though isn't it?" Erika asked.

"Mmmm, yes, about a hundred yards, although that's no distance for a cat."

"It's a sponsored bloody walk for Sylvester," Ruth piped up.

***

So, the time had come for me to finish with my days as a Police

Officer. It was a big step into the unknown for me. I had served for fifteen years but Richard was, as Erika had told me, a gentle man and I was ever the optimist. Damn it! I'd been married twice before how much of an optimist do I have to get!

I threw a little party at GSY and they presented me with a pair of Champagne flutes with the Metropolitan Police crest engraved on them. "So I would like to present you with this small token for your services…." began Inspector Walker as he handed me the carefully wrapped package . . . and dropped it! Hitting the floor there was the unmistakable crash of broken glass coming from inside the box. My face must have been a picture because they all collapsed laughing raucously. It was a dummy box, of course it was a dummy box, and they then presented me with a pristine pair of flutes, still cherished. It's true, I was going to miss all the banter and high jinks. So I sang to them, which probably helped them to be thankful I was leaving. Here is a brief sample of my own words to the tune of Ivan Skavinsky Skavar.

My joining The Branch was an interesting start
To a chequered career I'm afraid
So, hear my confessions before I depart
And I'll list the mistakes I have made.

I turned my attentions to our magazine
With writing I'm always at home
But my sense of humour's not everyone's scene
And I should have left cartoons alone.

I once met two Russians while doing the guard
Who were here for political ends
To persuade them to visit GY wasn't hard
So they came – and brought thirty-five friends.

To celebrate Christmas there is at GY
A fancy-dress party for dudes
Never stuck for a costume, and I'll tell you why:
Cos I always wear big plastic boobs

I know there are more misdemeanours than this
And I thank you for putting me right
But I'll have to stop now and I'll blow you a kiss
Or I'll be here till seven tonight.

***

The horses and I moved to Kidderminster late in 1991, and shortly afterwards Sylvester came with me in the car, protesting all the way.

Richard tasked me with the job of going down to the local Registry Office and booking a suitable day. It had to be a Saturday because of his work and as we were intending to have a big blessing ceremony in the summer, we could do our celebrating then. When I went into the reception the registrar told me that one of the Saturday slots fell on 29th February and there were no other bookings fixed for that day. I couldn't imagine why, this was just the kind of quirky date I would never forget. Or at least, I could forget all about it for three years on the trot. We had a wonderful day with close family and friends launching a new life together for Richard and me on the sun lit uplands of North Worcestershire. I don't think endings can get much happier than that.